CONSUMPTION, RITUAL, ART, AND SOCIETY

NEW APPROACHES IN ARCHAEOLOGY

VOLUME 2

GENERAL EDITOR

Paul S. Johnson, *University of Nottingham*

EDITORIAL BOARD

Marianne Hem Eriksen, *University of Leicester*

Lara Fabian, *Albert-Ludwigs-Universität Freiburg*

Linda Gosner, *University of Michigan*

Christopher Loveluck, *University of Nottingham*

Cheryl A. Makarewicz, *University of Kiel*

Dimitrij Mlekuž, *University of Ljubljana*

Consumption, Ritual, Art, and Society

Interpretive Approaches and Recent Discoveries
of Food and Drink in Etruria

Edited by

LISA PIERACCINI and LAUREL TAYLOR

BREPOLS

© 2023, Brepols Publishers n.v., Turnhout, Belgium.

All rights reserved. No part of this publication may be reproduced,
stored in a retrieval system, or transmitted, in any form or by
any means, electronic, mechanical, photocopying, recording,
or otherwise without the prior permission of the publisher.

D/2023/0095/27
ISBN: 978-2-503-60215-8
e-ISBN: 978-2-503-60216-5

DOI: 10.1484/M.NAA-EB.5.131309

Printed in the EU on acid-free paper.

Table of Contents

List of Illustrations   7

Lisa Pieraccini and Laurel Taylor
Introduction   11

Andrea Zifferero
1. Archaeology of the Grapevine and Wine Production in Etruria   17

Sarah Whitcher Kansa
2. Butchery, Meat Distribution, and Ritual Dining
in Etruscan Poggio Civitate (Murlo)   41

Laurel Taylor
3. Beyond the Banquet, Beyond the Tomb:
Typologies of Feasting in Etruscan Visual and Material Culture   57

Lisa C. Pieraccini
4. Dining with the Dead: Visual Meals, Memory,
and Symbolic Consumption in Etruscan Tomb Painting   77

Daniele F. Maras
5. Fish and Rituals: Working Notes on Religious Practices
Involving Fish in Ancient Etruria   91

Alexandra A. Carpino
6. Death — by Consumption — Interrupted:
The Iconography of Vilia (Hesione) on Etruscan Bronze Mirrors   113

Index   127

List of Illustrations

1. Archaeology of the Grapevine and Wine Production in Etruria — *Andrea Zifferero*

Figure 1.1. Drawing of a banquet scene with wine vessels (highlighted in red) on an architectural slab from Poggio Civitate (Murlo, Siena). 18

Figure 1.2. The circulation of the term *vinum*, compared to the spread from east to west of the cultivated vine (*Vitis vinifera* ssp. *sativa*). 18

Figure 1.3. Reconstruction of the Etruscan *arbustum*, with vines clinging to the live support, during the pruning carried out using a long-handled billhook (= long pruning). 20

Figure 1.4. *Lambruscaia* with wild vines clinging to the live tutor near the Etruscan site of Ghiaccio Forte (Scansano, Grosseto), at the borders of the territory of Vulci. 21

Figure 1.5. The fruit of a wild vine clinging to a black alder, showing hanging bunches composed of small and sparse grapes as recorded at Dorgali (Nuoro, Sardinia). 21

Figure 1.6. Map showing the spread of the wild vine, compared to the historical areas of para-domestication and domestication centres. 22

Figure 1.7. The Etruscan centre of Ghiaccio Forte in the Albegna River valley (Scansano, Grosseto). 22

Figure 1.8. The westward voyage from the Black Sea of the *Marzemino* variety, as reconstructed by Attilio Scienza. 26

Figure 1.9. Schematic reconstruction of the delta of the Po River in antiquity: the situation during the Etruscan period is highlighted in light blue. 27

Figure 1.10. Hypothetical reconstruction of the Etruscan site of Spina in the sixth and fifth centuries BCE. 27

Figure 1.11. The Etruscan sites in Val Padana in sixth and fifth centuries BCE. 29

Figure 1.12. Hierarchy of the Etruscan settlement system in Val Padana in the fifth century BCE. 30

Figure 1.13. Surviving elements of Etruscan viticulture in the modern Italian landscape: example of the *piantata* as practised in Emilia. 31

Figure 1.14. Surviving elements of Etruscan viticulture in the modern Italian landscape: graphical reconstruction of the *piantata* as practised in Emilia. 31

Figure 1.15. Surviving elements of Etruscan viticulture in the modern Italian landscape: the *piantata aversana* before winter pruning, in the area of Casal di Principe (Caserta). 32

Figure 1.16. Surviving elements of Etruscan viticulture in the modern Italian landscape: centuries-old vineyard supported by field maple trees near Figline Valdarno. 32

Figure 1.17. Details of the leaf and bunch of *Lambrusco di Sorbara* vine variety, typical of the areas of Modena and Reggio nell'Emilia. 32

2. Butchery, Meat Distribution, and Ritual Dining at Etruscan Poggio Civitate (Murlo) — *Sarah Whitcher Kansa*

Figure 2.1. Map of Tuscany showing the location of Poggio Civitate and other major Etruscan settlements. Kansa and Tuck 2021.   43

Figure 2.2. Plan of Poggio Civitate's Intermediate Phase. Kansa and Tuck 2021.   44

Figure 2.3. An example of a split vertebra from Poggio Civitate, showing division of the carcass into left and right sides as one stage of the butchery process.   48

Figure 2.4. Heat map of Poggio Civitate, showing the occurrence of sheep/goat left-sided ulnae and right-sided ulnae in the OC1/Residence and OC2/Workshop.   50

Figure 2.5. Heat map of Poggio Civitate, showing the occurrence of pig left-sided ulnae and right-sided ulnae in the OC1/Residence and OC2/Workshop.   50

Table 2.1. Relative occurrence and number of individual specimens by taxon in the OC1/Residence and the OC2/Workshop, compared to all specimens identified across the remainder of the faunal assemblage.   46

Table 2.2. Count of elements from the primary domestic taxa that could be identified to left or right side from the OC1/Residence.   49

Table 2.3. Chi-square tests on left and right ulnae for sheep/goat and pigs in the OC1/Residence and the OC2/Workshop at Poggio Civitate.   51

3. Beyond the Banquet, Beyond the Tomb: Typologies of Feasting in Etruscan Visual and Material Culture — *Laurel Taylor*

Figure 3.1. A banquet scene on the back wall of the Tomb of the Triclinium (early fifth BCE), Tarquinia.   60

Figure 3.2. Tomb of Hunting and Fishing, Tarquinia, *c.* 510 BCE.   60

Figure 3.3. Detail showing egg, Tomb of the Lionesses, Tarquinia, *c.* 520 BCE.   60

Figure 3.4. Banquet frieze, Poggio Civitate, *c.* 575–550 BCE.   62

Figure 3.5. Umbro-Etruscan terracotta food votive set from Todi, third century BCE.   63

Figure 3.6. Vessels, Banquet frieze, Poggio Civitate, *c.* 575–550 BCE.   64

Figure 3.7. Banquet plaque from the 'Veii-Rome-Velletri' series.   65

Figure 3.8. Detail of banquet plaque, Type C, Acquarossa, mid-sixth century BCE.   66

Figure 3.9. Plan of La Corona, Guatemala, Classic Maya 750–900 CE.   68

Figure 3.10. Archaic Building Complex, Poggio Civitate.   68

Figure 3.11. Acquarossa Reconstruction Zone F, Archaic period.   69

4. Dining with the Dead: Visual Meals, Memory, and Symbolic Consumption in Etruscan Tomb Painting — *Lisa C. Pieraccini*

Figure 4.1.   Detail of Larth Velcha and his wife on the back wall of the Tomb of the Shields (mid-fourth century BCE), Tarquinia.   80

Figure 4.2.   A modern reconstruction of a banquet scene on the back wall of the Tomb of the Triclinium, Tarquinia.   81

Figure 4.3.   Detail of the entry wall of the Golini Tomb I (mid-fourth century BCE) Orvieto. An ox head looks up at its hanging torso on a butcher's block.   83

Figure 4.4.   Detail of the left side of the Golini Tomb I depicting the preparation of a banquet (mid-fourth century BCE) Orvieto.   83

Figure 4.5.   Back wall of the Tomb of the Leopards — the man on right side holds out an egg (early fifth century BCE, Tarquinia).   84

Figure 4.6.   Back wall of the Tomb of the Chariots — the man on the left holds out an egg (fifth century BCE), Tarquinia.   84

Figure 4.7.   Photograph of a Caeretan brazier with eggs left roasting on coals from the Maroi Tomb III (sixth century BCE), Cerveteri.   85

5. Fish and Rituals: Working Notes on Religious Practices Involving Fish in Ancient Etruria — *Daniele F. Maras*

Figure 5.1.   Gravisca, sanctuary. East Greek oil flask in the shape of a seashell, *c.* 580 BCE.   94

Figure 5.2.   Pyrgi, South Area. Terracotta *mesomphalos phiale* containing a mussel and a limpet offered at the votive feature *Kappa*, beginning of the fifth century BCE.   94

Figure 5.3.   Perugia, Colle Arsiccio. Two small bronze eels, third century BCE.   95

Figure 5.4.   Detail of side B of two Etruscan red-figured *stamnoi* of the Funnel Group dating from the second half of the fourth century BCE.   95

Figure 5.5.   Populonia, S. Cerbone necropolis, sector C, tomb 4. Drawing of the neo-Punic inscription on a black-varnished fish-plate of the mid-third century BCE.   97

Figure 5.6.   Tarquinia, Tomb of the Inscriptions (*c.* 520 BCE). Watercolour drawing on tracing paper by Carlo Ruspi (1835), depicting the painting on the back wall at the right of the entrance.   103

Figure 5.7.   Quinto Fiorentino, Tomb *della Montagnola*. Drawing of inscriptions and graffiti on the stone slab that closed the right chamber.   104

Figure 5.8.   Veii, sanctuary of Portonaccio. Drawing of a terracotta painted plaque depicting a scene of ichthyomancy dating from *c.* 470 BCE.   104

6. Death — by Consumption — Interrupted: The Iconography of Vilia (Hesione) on Etruscan Bronze Mirrors — *Alexandra A. Carpino*

Figure 6.1. *Uni breastfeeding Hercle in the presence of Aplu (?), Turan (?), Hebe and Tinia*, Florence, Museo Archeologico Nazionale. Late fourth century BCE. 114

Figure 6.2. *Metvia, Heasun, Menrva and Rescial*, London, British Museum. Mid-fourth century BCE. 115

Figure 6.3. *Heiasun being disgorged from the dragon guarding the Golden Fleece*, Berlin, Antikenmuseum. Mid-fifth century BCE. 116

Figure 6.4. *Lamtu, Hercle, Vilia and Echpa*, Switzerland, Collection of George Ortiz. Last quarter of the fourth century BCE. 118

Figure 6.5. *Echpa, Polyxena, and two young men*, Lyon, Musée des Beaux Arts. Early third century BCE. 119

Figure 6.6. *Lamtu, Aplu, Vilia and Hercle*, Rome, Museo Nazionale Etrusco di Villa Giulia. Late fourth century BCE. 119

Figure 6.7. *Vilia, Hercle and a Lasa (?)*, once Paris, Oppermann Collection. Early third century BCE. 120

Figure 6.8. *Hercle and Vilia*, Perugia, Museo Archeologico Nazionale. Second half of the fourth century BCE. 121

Figure 6.9. *Hercle and Vilia*, Perugia, Museo Archeologico Nazionale. Mid-to-late fourth century BCE. 121

LISA PIERACCINI AND LAUREL TAYLOR

Introduction

Tell me what you eat and I will tell you who you are. Brillat-Savarin

The phrase, 'you are what you eat', refers to the impact of food on the body physically, but food also impacts us culturally. As noted by nineteenth-century French lawyer and gastronome Jean Anthelme Brillat-Savarin in his treatise, *The Physiology of Taste*, there is a complex relationship between food, consumption, and identity.[1] Food is central to our individual and collective identity — it exerts an agency within small (family) and large (community) groups. Not only are we what we eat, we are also *how* we eat, with whom we eat, where we eat, and, in some cases, why we eat. The production and consumption of food can express multiple dimensions of identity and negotiate belonging to or exclusion from cultural groups. It can bind us through religious praxis, express wealth, manifest cultural identity, reveal differentiation in age or gender, and define status. As such, food — and drink — have powerful agency in creating and sustaining social and cultural norms and customs. Food can be used as a lens through which to investigate the past; its agency is multifaceted and complex and the twenty-first century has seen more publications dedicated to foodways, feasting rituals, food history, and food culture than ever before.[2] With respect to the Etruscans, whose food culture marks a quintessential aspect of their society, examining the materiality, consumption,

display, and ritual of food, allows for a deeper assessment of Etruscan society.

Archaeological approaches to food and drink in Etruria have moved beyond discussions of diet and subsistence to using food as a paradigm for understanding constructions of status, power, and ritual. While Etruscan food culture has been mined for its potential to illuminate patterns of consumption, production, and human interaction, new approaches to food and drink aim to highlight and connect broader social and cultural meaning. For the Etruscans, food was a transformative material and a powerful symbol. Etruscan food habits and customs were culturally expressive behaviours that defined the collective self and marked core values of society. Thankfully, as we begin to decolonize our approaches to the study of the ancient world, non-'traditional' fields of inquiry have emerged. In Etruria, foodways and the social archaeology of the production, consumption, display, performance, and ritualization of food tell us much about vital aspects of Etruscan culture vis-à-vis agriculture, viticulture, art, rituals, banqueting, and funerary meals (just to name a few).

The papers in this volume explore the intersections between food, drink, consumption, and ritual within Etruscan society in complex and innovative ways. Through a purposeful cross-disciplinary approach, the volume emphasizes the ways in which Etruscan foodways form a vital component of Etruscan culture more broadly. Etruria provides an exceptional opportunity for examining the subject of eating and drinking, precisely because Etruscan material culture, both religious (funerary) and secular, celebrated food. The volume sheds

---

1 Brillat-Savarin 2002 (originally published 1825).

2 See, among others, Hastorf 2017; Broekaert, Nadeau, and Wilkins 2016; Draycott and Stamatopoulou 2016; Smith 2015; Wilkins and Nadeau 2015; Hayden 2014; Hamilakis 1998; Hamilakis and Sherratt 2012; Hayden and Villeneuve 2011; Cianferoni 2005; Menotti 2005; Bray 2003; Dietler and Hayden 2001; and Dietler 1996.

Consumption, Ritual, Art and Society: Interpretive Approaches and Recent Discoveries of Food and Drink in Etruria, ed. by Lisa Pieraccini and Laurel Taylor, NAA, 2 (Turnhout, 2023), pp. 11–15 · BREPOLS ❧ PUBLISHERS · 10.1484/M.NAA-EB.5.132802

light on how cross-disciplinary fields such as archaeobotany, art history, viticultural, funerary, ritual, and material cultural studies are used in the field of Etruscans studies in productive and forward-thinking ways. Collectively, the papers illuminate how food and drink function as important agents, specifically within Etruscan visual programmes, rituals, and funerary practices. While each paper addresses different areas of research, the topics overlap in fascinating and mutually informative ways and share a common methodological principle — placing food, its ritual consumption, display, and use within the broader cultural framework of Etruria.

The complex role of food is best mapped through diverse evidentiary categories and the papers in this volume collectively use multiple lines of inquiry and approaches to explore the subject. From diverse perspectives, each considers food and drink within visual and material culture as well as from a variety of contexts — domestic, urban, religious, and funerary. A. Zifferero considers new methods of analysis for understanding the early production of wine in Etruria in the first chapter 'Production and Consumption of Wine in Etruria: Methods of Analysis and Research Perspectives'. In this wide-ranging essay on the earliest examples of wine making and consumption, Zifferero provides a timely and critical, integrative look at wine production combining scientific research with archaeological and textual data. Recent analyses have sought to correct the long-held misconception that wine use and cultivation in Italy occurred during historic periods as a result of Greek colonization of the Italian Peninsula (generally speaking, the assumption that Greeks are responsible for all ancient technological advances falls into the postcolonial view of the Mediterranean). Seeking to bridge the gap between prehistory and history, Zifferero examines the long-term phenomena of wine production through cultivation and trade networks, going back as far as the Bronze Age. He considers archaeological and textual evidence

hand in hand with advances in molecular biology. By combining these approaches, Zifferero explores the 'stratifications of cultivations' to illuminate the stages of domestication and to establish a historical framework for the appearance of vine varieties and their spread throughout Italy. Of particular note are two innovative projects — VINUM and ArcheoVino — which have made it possible for archaeologists, botanists, and molecular biologists to work in collaborative and integrative ways. Zifferero's contribution offers a complex picture of the role of Etruscan sites in the cultivation and consumption of wine as well as the expansion of the wine trade outside of Etruria.

S. Kansa showcases new ways of understanding settlements and communities through the lens of food preparation and consumption in 'Butchery, Meat Distribution, and Ritual Dining at Etruscan Poggio Civitate (Murlo)'. Using zooarchaeological evidence collected at this important site over the many decades of excavation, Kansa illuminates how such evidence can enhance and deepen our knowledge of both elite and non-elite peoples from a single site. By examining thousands of fragments of animal bones, Kansa notes a clear distinction and distribution of specific bones in elite (habitation) and industrial (workshop) areas of Poggio Civitate. How and why are certain parts of animals distributed to collective groups within a single site? What does this distribution tell us about the agency of meat as a marker of social stratifications? Kansa utilizes the most recent data at Poggio Civitate to uncover fascinating patterns of meat allocations at a single site and one that occupies a very important place within Etruscan studies. Her chapter not only looks at meat as food, but the by-products of meat and the upcycling of the bones.

In 'Beyond the Banquet, beyond the Tomb: Typologies of Feasting in Etruscan Visual and Material Culture', L. Taylor investigates the practice of banqueting in early Etruscan culture and its representation in Etruscan media to better understand how its visual construction reflects social implications. It has long been recognized that the 'banquet' is one of the most common motifs across time and space appearing in multiple contexts and across diverse categories of artefacts. Commensal events signal social, cultural, religious, and political identity and it is therefore no surprise that the motif occupies an important place within Etruscan iconography, particularly during the Archaic period, appearing in tombs, on plaques, mirrors, reliefs, and ceramic vessels. Yet, as Taylor points out, the standard visual formula of these scenes (figures reclining on dining couches, surrounded by the accoutrements of feasting) has historically led scholars to elide 'banqueting' scenes from funerary contexts with those from non-funerary contexts. She proposes, instead, that a closer scrutiny of scenes from these diverse contexts reveals significant differences in critical details and symbolic value revealing a more nuanced reading of consumption iconography during the Archaic period. While banquet scenes from mortuary contexts frequently present vessels for serving and consuming wine they rarely depict food items or food-associated vessels during this period. Conversely, feasting scenes from non-funerary contexts during this same period, such as the terracotta plaques from Poggio Civitate, not only depict distinct and diverse food items, they also show drinking vessels of legible types, particularly imports that have correlates in the archaeological record. Such types signal exclusionary feasting in these scenes and, Taylor argues, express a form of diacritical feasting, a performative behaviour meant to display status through differentiated foods or vessels. As Taylor demonstrates, the symbolic language of these scenes can help us better understand ritual feasting within the specific architectural contexts of which the plaques were discovered.

Food, life, and death share a precarious relationship, especially when painted on the walls of a tomb. L. Pieraccini's chapter on 'Dining with the Dead: Visual Meals and Symbolic Consumption in Etruscan Tomb Painting', explores the visual culture of food and drink with respect to the agency of visual programmes as prompts, negotiators and mediators within the highly ritualized and decorated space of a tomb. Pieraccini addresses a series of questions including: How and why did Etruscan tomb paintings visually 'feed' the dead? How are painted scenes of banqueting active memory triggers for the family depositing a loved one in a tomb? Because painted tombs express an elite funerary ideology (as only the elite could afford to build and paint such tombs), this form of painted message boarding underscores the social, funerary, and artistic palatability of food imagery. The tombs highlight how feasting (as painted on tomb walls) and funerals (food rituals conducted by small groups in the tomb at the time of deposition) coexisted and functioned in tandem to ease/celebrate/mediate and negotiate death. Pieraccini looks at the archaeological evidence of food found in tombs alongside the identifiable food items depicted on wall paintings revealing the intersectionality of funerary food culture in Etruria. Her chapter demystifies the visual gastropolitics and the symbolic consumption of funerary meals through critical compositional analysis of tomb painting and food remains from Etruscan tombs.

D. Maras's contribution, 'Fish Rituals: Working Notes on Religious Practice Involving Fish in Etruria', seeks to understand how the Etruscans, a people famous in antiquity for their proximity to and relationship with the sea, not only consumed fish, but also utilized fish in sacrificial offerings in ritual practice. Maras considers a range of archaeological and visual evidence that confirms the importance of this maritime relationship and underscores how fish were a significant food item and economic resource for the Etruscans. In addition to the well-known imagery of fish and fishing from the painted tombs at Tarquinia (such as the famous Tomb of Hunting and

Fishing), Maras demonstrates that, from a very early period in Etruscan art, ceramics featuring maritime themes confirm a special affinity for the sea and sea creatures. Building upon this, Maras explores how the consumption of fish may have related to its use within Etruscan ritual contexts. Surveying the archaeological remains of fish sacrifices in important sanctuaries such as Pyrgi and Gravisca (both located in close proximity to the coast) as well as in funerary contexts, his paper uses this evidence vis-à-vis other evidentiary categories — images of fish sacrifices and later textual evidence — to illuminate the existence of possible ideological patterns and economic reasons for fish rituals.

In her paper, 'Death — by Consumption — Interrupted: The Iconography of Vilia (Hesione) on Etruscan Bronze Mirrors', A. Carpino investigates symbolic concepts related to food and drink which appear in the narratives engraved on Etruscan bronze mirrors. Such artefacts symbolized the status and prosperity of their owners and served as important forms of visual communication within the domestic sphere. Their iconography includes both natural behaviours with allegorical overtones as well as fantastic acts stemming from mythic origins. In the former category, mirrors showing either Hercle suckling milk from Uni's breast or Menrva withdrawing an immortality elixir from her protégé, Tydeus, emphasize distinctively Etruscan characteristics, ones wherein a drinkable substance emphasizes ritual rather than physical sustenance. The idea that certain liquids functioned as powerful transformative agents, especially when dispensed by powerful goddesses, can also be seen in imagery connected to Heasun/Heiasun, a heroic monster-slayer whose representations in mirror iconography straddle both types of consumption imagery. Among the scenes that illustrate departures from accepted ideas about food and drink are those that either highlight or allude to the motif of the so-called 'consumed human'. In addition to male figures such as

Heasun (swallowed and then regurgitated by the dragon) or Ataiun (devoured by his dogs after being turned into a stag), four mirrors from the later fourth century BCE centre on Vilia (Hesione), the only female sacrificial victim which engravers included in their repertoire. Carpino's analysis of the Trojan princess's story reveals that while the most terrifying aspects of the myth — especially the idea of Vilia as 'food' — were downplayed in favour of a 'happily ever after' ending, the theme of consumption remained an agent of transformation, this time intricately tied to female social expectations in aristocratic Etruscan society.

Together, these contributions not only expand the growing discourse of food and drink with respect to consumption, visuality, rituals, butchery, and symbolism, but they connect important aspects of Etruscan food culture in dynamic and innovative ways. Food can no longer be ignored in the archaeological and visual record. The fact that food was not a subject of intense study until recent times, speaks to modern preoccupations with narrowly focused approaches to the 'classical' ancient world. Aspects such as animal husbandry, food culture, wine production and consumption, not to mention the varied food rituals of the Etruscans, are now subjects of academic investigation. Furthermore, it is these very aspects of ancient culture (not to mention modern culture), where studies dedicated to food inform us of fundamental customs, values, and practices of daily life in ancient Etruria. Now more than ever before, advances in scientific approaches to food open new doors to understanding the past through vinology, zooarchaeology, and paleoethnobotany, just to name a few. Moreover, as visual studies of Etruscan art become more advanced and move beyond taxonomic descriptions, a deeper understanding of Etruscan culture emerges. All of these approaches combine in this volume in ways that highlight the fascinating study of food and drink in ancient Etruria.

Works Cited

Bray, Tamara (ed.). 2003. *The Archaeology and Politics of Food and Feasting in Early States and Empires* (Boston: Springer)

Brillat-Savarin, Anthelme. 2002 (reprint). *The Physiology of Taste, or, Meditations on Transcendental Gastronomy* (New York: Dover)

Broekaert, Wim, Robin Nadeau, and John Wilkins (eds). 2016. *Food, Identity and Cross-Cultural Exchange in the Ancient World* (Brussels: Latomus)

Cianferoni, Giuseppina C. (ed.). 2005. *Cibi e sapori nel mondo antico* (Florence: National Archaeological Museum)

Dietler, Michael. 1996. 'Feast and Commensal Politics in the Political Economy: Food, Power and Status in Prehistoric Europe', in *Food and the Status Quest: An Interdisciplinary Perspective*, ed. by Polly Wiesner and Wulf Schiefenhovel (Providence: Berghahn), pp. 87–126

Dietler, Michael, and Brian Hayden (eds). 2001. *Feasts: Archaeological and Ethnographic Perspectives on Food, Politics, and Power* (Washington, DC: Smithsonian Institution)

Draycott, Catherine, and Maria Stamatopoulou (eds). 2016. *Dining and Death: Interdisciplinary Perspectives on the 'Funerary Banquet' in Ancient Art, Burial and Belief* (Peeters: Leuven)

Hamilakis, Yannis. 1998. 'Eating the Dead: Mortuary Feasting and the Politics of Memory in the Aegean Bronze Age Societies', in *Cemetery and Society in the Aegean Bronze Age Societies*, ed. by Keith Branigan (Sheffield: Sheffield Academic Press), pp. 115–32

Hamilakis, Yannis, and Susan Sherratt. 2012. 'Feasting and the Consuming Body in Bronze Age Crete and Early Iron Age Cyprus', in *Parallel Lives: Ancient Island Societies in Crete and Cyprus*, ed. by Gerald Cadogan, Maria Iakovou, Katerina Kopaka, and James Whitley (London: British School at Athens), pp. 187–207

Hastorf, Christine A. 2017. *The Social Archaeology of Food: Thinking about Eating from Prehistory to the Present* (Cambridge: Cambridge University Press)

Hayden, Brian. 2009. 'Funerals as Feasts: Why Are They So Important?', *Cambridge Archaeology Journal*, 19: 29–52

——. 2014. *The Power of Feasts: From Prehistory to the Present* (Cambridge: Cambridge University Press)

Hayden, Brian, and Suzanne Villeneuve. 2011. 'A Century of Feasting Studies', *Annual Review of Anthropology*, 40: 433–49

Menotti, Elena Maria. 2005. *Cibo: vita e cultura* (Mantua: Tre Lune)

Smith, Monica L. 2015. 'Feasts and their Failures', *The Journal of Archaeological Method and Theory*, 22: 1215–37

Wilkins, John, and Robin Nadeau (eds). 2015. *A Companion to Food in the Ancient World* (Chichester: Wiley Blackwell)

ANDREA ZIFFERERO

1. Archaeology of the Grapevine and Wine Production in Etruria

The Consumption of Wine in Etruria

In Etruscan studies, research on wine has primarily focused on the way it was consumed. During the eighth–seventh centuries BCE, funerary contexts in Etruria show a remarkable concentration of luxury goods, evidenced in particular by the banquet service sets used by the elite. Targeted and systematic analysis has focused on the role and function of the shape of vases meant to contain, add water (and other substances), draw and pour, filter, and finally consume wine. This practice adhered to precise ceremonial rites and rules codified early on by consumption rituals (Bartoloni and others 2012, with references; Micozzi 2016; Cerchiai and Cuozzo 2016). Excavations of habitation areas, as opposed to funerary ones, have also revealed evidence regarding other ceremonial rites centred around wine consumption. Among the most famous examples are the wine service set discovered inside a house at Ficana, dated to the mid-seventh century BCE, and the set found at Satricum. Other non-commensal examples of wine rituals outside the funerary realm include collective libations celebrating the dedication or rebuilding of a hut as evidenced by the nearly one hundred ceramic goblets (*kyathoi*), placed in a post hole of the so-called Casa del Re at Populonia sometime between the late eighth century and the early seventh century BCE (Rathje 1983; Beijer 1991; Acconcia and Bartoloni 2007).

Etruscan and Latin communities adapted specific cultural models of social drinking characteristic of areas from the Near East to the Phoenician-Cypriot world (which eventually led to the practice of banqueting and the symposium in Greece). The consumption of wine in Etruria, from the late eighth century BCE onward, however, assumed a role which transcended mere sustenance among elite groups (Cristofani 1991; Murray and Tecuşan 1995, 164–235; Rathje 2013; Acconcia and Piergrossi 2021). The controlled consumption of wine was a key instrument in binding together communities during important social events. Such practices were often a form of acculturation and can be clearly distinguished in the archaeological record. In the Greek world, wine was mixed with water and enriched by other components such as honey, barley flour, and grated cheese, producing a beverage in some ways similar to an energy drink known as *kykeon* (Villing 2021). Yet in other cases, wine was consumed in ways reflective of the Phoenician *marzeah*, a custom of eastern origin, in which the wine was enriched with spices that had been finely ground using special pestles and then strained (Bartoloni 2003, 195–215; Ciacci 2005; on furnishings in pre-Roman Abruzzi, cf. now Acconcia 2014; on the transmission of the Phoenician *marzeah* in Etruria, see Botto 2013 and 2016; Bellelli and Botto 2018, with references; first attempts to

Andrea Zifferero Dipartimento di Scienze Storiche e dei Beni Culturali, Università degli Studi di Siena (andrea.zifferero@unisi.it)

Figure 1.1. Drawing of a banquet scene with wine vessels (highlighted in red) on an architectural slab from Poggio Civitate (Murlo, Siena). Ciacci 2005.

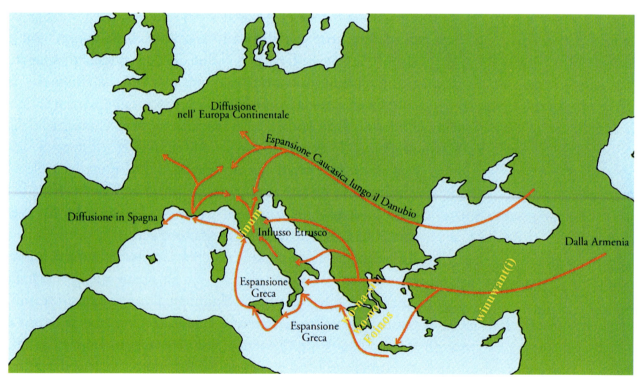

Figure 1.2. The circulation of the term *vinum*, compared to the spread from east to west of the cultivated vine (*Vitis vinifera* ssp. *sativa*). Ciacci 2005.

detect Phoenician wine in Moricca and others 2021) (Fig. 1.1). Ceramic evidence dated to the eighth–seventh centuries BCE reveals the introduction of morphologically specific vessels associated with new consumption behaviours, a phenomenon that suggests the Etruscans were experimenting and adopting new customs.[1]

In recent years, scholars of Mediterranean Protohistory have also carefully studied the use of wine in funerary rituals in the Final Bronze Age and Early Iron Age. The results have helped fill the gap separating Prehistory and History, but the existence of this gap has meant that long-term phenomena, such as the consumption and trade of wine, have not yet received a balanced assessment.[2] However, recent analyses have upended the long-held misconception that the introduction of vine growing and the consumption of wine in Italy was a result of Greek colonization in historical times and the phenomenon is now correctly assigned to the Bronze Age (in particular to the late Middle Bronze Age and especially to the Recent Bronze Age). This was a period during which the Mediterranean had become a hub of contact and cultural exchange and the term *vinum* was eventually assimilated by many communities to identify the same

fermented beverage (Fig. 1.2).[3] In Etruscan areas, archaeobotany and residue analyses have played a key role in demonstrating how Early Bronze Age farmers produced wine both from wild and cultivated vines.[4] More intensive contacts between indigenous Italic people and Mycenaean seafarers occurred later in the Recent Bronze Age, a fact also confirmed by the wide geographical distribution of vascular shapes meant for wine drinking.[5]

Despite all these recent advances, it remains difficult to establish the origins of wine based strictly on archaeobotanical data and chemical analysis and to understand how these processes intersected with the formation of proto-urban communities in ancient Etruria.[6] The Late Iron Age (and most of the eighth century BCE) wit-

---

1 From at least the Iron Age, this entire area partook in new forms of wine consumption: an interesting case in point is the adoption of a Sardinian *askoid*-shaped pottery vase, of which local imitations also exist, within the funerary tradition of Vetulonia. The chemical and gas-chromatographic exams of the organic residues present on the inner surfaces of the jugs indicate they were used especially for wine (Delpino 2002; Botto 2013, 112–13; 2016, 89–90). Studies have also established the existence of a prevailing binary code which dictated the deposition of each shape and was based on numerical factors directly proportional to the rank of the deceased (Bartoloni and others 2012, with references; Micozzi 2016; Coen and others 2018).

2 Regarding this research approach, see Delpino 2012, with references; for a critique addressing the problems with this approach cf. Guidi 2016, with references; on the relationship between vase shapes and wine consumption in Etruscan Protohistory, see also Torelli 2000.

3 On the beginning of viticulture in the Italian Peninsula, cf. Forni 2012; an overview regarding the formation of the term *vinum* and its spread is in Ciacci 2005, including a bibliography. It might be useful to point out that this term indicates the product of grape fermentation exclusively. Gaetano Forni believes the oldest type of prehistoric wine, produced by fermenting non-grape fruit, e.g. rowan (*Sorbus aucuparia*), had a different name, i.e. *temetum*. The term *temetum*, a Latin noun, has been assigned different meanings but might refer to the product of a para-domestication phase. This stage would call for the protection of spontaneously growing plants deemed capable of producing fruits, with a view to subjecting these to fermentation. This phase would predate actual vine domestication: Forni 2012, 108–09, with references.

4 Mariotti Lippi and others 2012; Pecci 2012.

5 For an overview see: Forni 2012 and on the Tuscan area Aranguren and others 2012; on the contacts between local communities in southern Italy and Aegean sea-farers, see Bettelli 2002; the introduction of new vase shapes linked to wine consumption in the last phases of Protohistory is again confirmed in Torelli 2000 and Colivicchi 2004. Also of note is the recent discovery of a semi-globular vessel of Aegean manufacture containing traces of herb enriched-wine from the island of Vivara (Gulf of Naples). Dated to the seventeenth century BCE, it confirms the production/circulation of wine (possibly of eastern origin) in the southern Tyrrhenian area at a very early date: Pepe 2016.

6 For a subdivision of viticulture in the Etruscan and Latin

Figure 1.3. Reconstruction of the Etruscan *arbustum*, with vines clinging to the live support, during the pruning carried out using a long-handled billhook (= long pruning). Drawing courtesy of Andrea Sgherri.

nessed the expansion of cities and the cultivation of new territorial land as people and luxury goods began to circulate at an increasing pace. Contacts with Phoenician-Punic merchants provided the primary stimulus for these movements and for the reception of valuable goods and consumption models mediated by Greek colonization. Wine, in particular, was considered an ideal gift among aristocrats (Cristofani 1991; McGovern 2013).

The importance of this period in the history of wine consumption and viticulture is reflected in the Roman textual record in which sources remember King Numa's introduction of precise rules for pruning grapevines along tree trunks. These rules aligned Roman viticulture with that of Etruria where the practice of growing the vine along live trees (the *arbustum*) was by then flourishing (Fig. 1.3).[7] While some planting innovations in Roman viticulture may have been adopted later, during the reign of Tarquinius Priscus (see Braconi 2012), abundant evidence confirms that Numa's reign was characterized by administrative and religious reforms related to agriculture in general and to the growing of cereals and grapevines in particular (Ciacci and Zifferero 2007).

The period between the eighth and seventh centuries BCE was undoubtedly foundational to viticulture in Etruria, setting the enduring base for the great vine growing and wine production of southern Etruria in the Archaic period, particularly at Cerveteri and Vulci. It is also in this period when Greek wines, Phoenician-Punic wines, and wines from the east arrived in central Tyrrhenian Italy, as an increasing number of transport amphorae have shown.[8] This paper examines this critical period within viticultural history using a synergistic model of combining humanities and scientific analyses. Genetic

---

areas, see Ciacci and Zifferero 2007, accepted in Forni 2012, 108–14.

7 See Gras 1985, 367–90; Ciacci and Zifferero 2007; Viglietti 2011, 191–201. On the technical aspects of cultivating the Etruscan *arbustum* and the Roman *vinea*, cf. Braconi 2012.

8 For traces of viticulture in Magna Graecia and Sicily see Boissinot 2009; on new vascular productions linked to the consumption of wine in Etruscan areas, see Neri 2010 and ten Kortenaar 2011; on the arrival of the first Greek wines in the western Mediterranean, cf. Docter 2000; for the Etruscan area Rizzo 1990, is still relevant, adding Rizzo 2015; the first wine-growing efforts in southern Italy are now addressed by Brun 2011 and Sourisseau 2011, see also van der Mersch 1996. On the beginnings of viticulture at Cerveteri and at Vulci see Zifferero 2005a; 2017a.

aspects introduced by molecular biology are assessed vis-à-vis archaeology's strategic role in elucidating the phenomena of formation and varietal circulation of vine subspecies (grape varieties) in antiquity. The goal is to highlight the usefulness of an in-depth study of the chronology and geographical extension of possible centres for germplasm accumulation in central Tyrrhenian Italy, supplied by grape varieties from the southern peninsula's Greek colonies.

From the Wild Vine to Current Grape Varieties: The Long Road to Domestication

The ancient Italian grapevine belongs to a species called *Vitis vinifera* L.: the cultivated varieties (called *cultivars* or simply grape varieties) fall within the subspecies *sativa*, to distinguish them from the wild vine (*Vitis vinifera* subspecies *sylvestris*). In nature, the species grows in humid plains or well-watered hilly areas, particularly riverine banks and canals. As the species needs large amounts of light, they usually thrive on the edge of woods, in clearings, and along hedges. Like all members of the *Vitaceae* family, the vine can grow creepers along the trunks of trees chosen as tutors and finally reach the treetop at considerable heights to produce fruit (Figs 1.4–1.5).

The grapevine reproduces either through generative propagation (through the pips of the main plant) or through vegetative propagation in which vine branches grow roots and become autonomous plants if separated from the original plant.[9] Humans and grapevines have interacted

---

9 Vines born from the pip seeds are always genetically different from the original plant. On the contrary, vegetative propagation transmits the original plant's same genetic code (Failla 2007, 2–21; Castiglione d'Orcia 2011, 167–81). The vine's leaf-shape, the shape of the tip of the bud, and the bunch, which in wild varieties carries few, small-sized grapes are all characteristics which indicate its polymorph nature. The domestic

Figure 1.4. *Lambruscaia* with wild vines clinging to the live tutor near the Etruscan site of Ghiaccio Forte (Scansano, Grosseto), at the borders of the territory of Vulci. Photo by the author.

Figure 1.5. The fruit of a wild vine clinging to a black alder, showing hanging bunches composed of small and sparse grapes as recorded at Dorgali (Nuoro, Sardinia). Courtesy of Attilio Scienza.

22　ANDREA ZIFFERERO

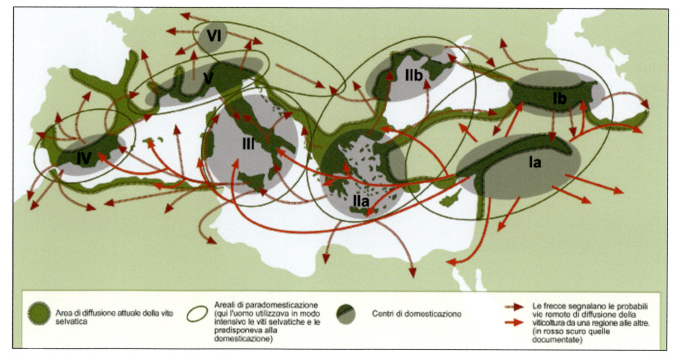

Figure 1.6. Map showing the spread of the wild vine, compared to the historical areas of para-domestication and domestication centres. Forni 2012.

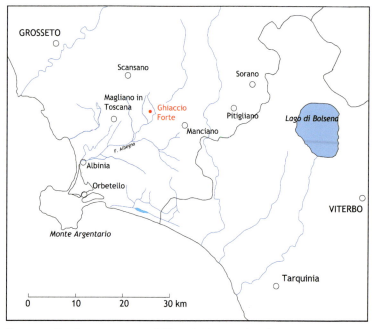

Figure 1.7. The Etruscan centre of Ghiaccio Forte in the Albegna River valley (Scansano, Grosseto). Courtesy of Marco Firmati.

for millennia, first during the processes of domestication of ever-increasing complexity, and then in the diversification stage during which subspecies (grape varieties) evolved through plant selection based on recognizable and desirable features (i.e. the size and development of bunches, greater or lesser sugar concentration, etc.).

From the sixth or seventh millennium BCE, the vine was slowly but progressively domesticated, following human migrations from the Near East and the Caucasus towards the western Mediterranean, in tandem with the progressive development of cities and with the exchange of goods and technology.[10] Our knowledge surrounding these processes has improved dramatically, due

character of the cultivated varieties is enshrined in the plants' sexuality. Those planted in vineyards all carry hermaphrodite flowers, capable of self-fertilizing to produce fruit. Wild vines are instead dioecious; individuals carry uni-sexual flowers, which determine the plant sex (Failla 2007, 2–21).

10　On vine domestication most recently Failla 2014 and Forni 2012, with references to the author's previous publications; for a different point of view on viticulture

to an ever-increasing number of archaeobotanical discoveries mostly of grape seeds, but occasionally of vine-branch fragments and parts of the vine trunk or roots. Uniting the archaeobotanical to the archaeo-metrical approach has often led to brilliant results most notably with residue analysis on ceramic vessels helping to identify the *primary domestication centre* in the vast region now part of Syria, Anatolia, and Mesopotamia. The area's climate and cultural make-up naturally supported vineyards and wine production. It was during the Bronze Age when intensive cultivation techniques from the east reached Greece making it a *secondary domestication centre*. During the Late Bronze Age and Iron Age, seafarers and Aegean merchants exchanged knowledge and techniques with southern Italy and Sicily. And still later, vine cultivation followed the pace of the various Greek colonization phases (making this region the *tertiary domestication centre*). Ultimately, Etruscan, Greek, Punic, and Roman vine cultivation reached northern Italy, southern France, and Spain making these the *centres of the fourth, fifth, and sixth level of domestication* (Forni 2012, 102–07; for Magna Graecia: Forni 1999) (Fig. 1.6).

During the last twenty years, biochemical and molecular analyses (e.g., DNA polymorphism) have played a vital role in identifying the geographical and historical origin of grape varieties and wild varieties.[11] The resulting maps reflect with great accuracy the relationships between vine varieties and describe a real sort of pedigree. One result is that we now know that cultivars with different local names, considered typical of different geographical areas, often share the same genetic identity (Scienza 2004; 2010; Failla 2014).

---

from the chronological and geographical perspective, see: McGovern 2004.

11 Historically, grape varieties have been classified based on the shape of leaves and grape bunches, the general shape of vine branches, and on *tomentum* characteristics of the leaves.

Human migration as well as trade ensured that vine varieties spread and, consequently, tended to concentrate in specific areas within domestication centres, what molecular biologist call *varietal accumulation centres*. These are the places where new varieties appeared thanks to human selective pressure, environmental circumstances, and/or the frequency of gene mutation (Scienza and Failla 1996, 230–345; Scienza 2004, 132–43; 2007). Predictably, germplasm accumulation centres are usually located near a port or an emporium, along popular travel routes, such as Alpine valleys, while at other times they are simply at an urban marketplace (a point of redistribution for agricultural products). The presence of germplasm accumulation in a certain area contributed to the formation of an *area of secondary domestication* within the main domestication centre, an event that leads to further hybridization processes between vine varieties.

In recent years, botanists, molecular biologists, and archaeologists have joined forces to concentrate on the most relevant type of hybridization — the one fusing foreign grapevine varieties with local populations of wild vines. The introduction of genes from different species or varieties, as occurs in the case of multiple cross-breeding events, is known as *introgression*. Introgression, according to new research, repeatedly occurred between vine varieties and local populations of wild vines during the period in which the vine was spreading from east to west. This phenomenon was also foundational to the development of secondary domestication areas in many regions of Italy (*Castiglione d'Orcia* 2011; Forni 2012, 102–12). Indeed, DNA sequencing has demonstrated that various local vine varieties, previously considered native to a geographical location, are actually the result of an (ancient) varietal circulation started often in areas different from those where varieties are today. They created the base for new forms of local hybridization with the wild vine, sometimes dating back to very early times, leading researchers to wonder about the real meaning of the term 'autochthonous' (for the definition of this term and on related issues cf. Scienza 2007; Scienza and Failla 2016).

Varietal Circulation of the Vine: New Paths for Archaeological Research

Two innovative research projects — the VINUM Project and ArcheoVino Project — have focused on elucidating such hybridizations in the history of Italian viticulture. Archaeologists from the University of Siena joined botanists and molecular biologists from the Universities of Siena and Milan to establish the timeline for the arrival and transfer of non-local vine varieties in Italy. Specifically, these projects sought to identify the accumulation centres and the secondary domestication centres, and correlate these with wine production centres mentioned in ancient sources and with those attested by archaeological data (Ciacci and others 2012).

The initial assumption for this research was simple. In some areas, populations of the wild vine can be found growing around archaeological sites (areas of low anthropic impact and high levels of conservation of the surrounding vegetation). As such, the plants' genetic code might be assumed to retain traces of ancient forms of domestication, or introgression with non-local vine varieties (Ciacci and Zifferero 2005). Researchers analysed the polymorphism of the DNA of wild vine varieties near Etruscan and Roman sites in central and southern Tuscany and northern Lazio. The resulting genetic mapping of the vine growing around archaeological sites bears marked differences if compared to those of population samples of the same subspecies, taken from areas unaffected by anthropic presence. This genetic variability has been attributed to ancient domestication, which shows up in the plants' germplasm.

To test these assumptions, the ArcheoVino Project was carried out in the valley of the Albegna

River, around Ghiaccio Forte, an Etruscan site with an archaic and Hellenistic phase near Scansano (Grosseto). Systematic analysis and sampling along the Albegna River and the Sanguinaio stream, proved a strong genetic resemblance between the local wild vine population and vine varieties of *Sangiovese*, *Canaiolo nero*, and *Ciliegiolo* (Vignani and others 2012; Zifferero 2016, 23–30; Scali and others 2018). The results gleaned from ArcheoVino in this region are particularly relevant for several reasons. First, the Ghiaccio Forte site is situated historically at the margins of the agricultural lands belonging to Vulci, to the north-west of the town. Second, Vulci's wine production between the end of the seventh and the sixth centuries BCE is known to have been outstanding and kilns which produced wine amphorae (type Py 3) to transport this valued wine have recently been linked to large numbers of amphorae in southern France and along the Mediterranean coast of Spain (cf. *Scansano* 2011; Ciacci and others 2012, 375–630 with references; Zifferero 2017a; Rojo Muñoz 2021) (Fig. 1.7). In other words, wine produced at Vulci was then moving into Celtic and Iberian areas. Finally, the Albegna Valley should be considered an area of secondary domestication and a germplasm accumulation centre (originating in the Greek colonies of southern Italy). The scale and specialization of wine production at Vulci likely contributed to the Ghiaccio Forte area assuming the typical characteristics of a varietal accumulation centre, a result settling and residing in open sites (i.e. farms) during the Etruscan period.

The research suggests that the Albegna Valley may have acted as an incubator for the *Sangiovese* and *Ciliegiolo* varieties of grape (if not others as well). According to both botanists and molecular biologists, the origin of these varieties can be traced back to the eastern coast of Sicily and the Ionian and Tyrrhenian coasts of Calabria where genetic similarity to various vine varieties there suggests ancient selection by Magna Graecia's winegrowers.[12] *Sangiovese*'s genetic pedigree securely links it to Calabria and Sicily and the viticulture of Magna Graecia. Vine varieties, however, from the Tyrrhenian area such as *Mammolo* and *Garganega* participated in their genetic diversification. According to Attilio Scienza, *Sangiovese* is a first-degree relative of *Foglia Tonda*, of the *Morellini* growing in Casentino and Valdarno, and of the *Brunellone*. This proves that *Sangiovese* had a first important cultivation area centred in Tuscany and Corsica (Scienza 2013; Scienza and Imazio 2018, 159–81). Scienza places this transmission at some point at the beginning of the modern era. However, *Sangiovese* and probably also *Ciliegiolo* varieties could have easily made the journey north in antiquity. If we consider the diversified picture of pre-Roman viticulture in the Tyrrhenian area, we would not be too far off the mark considering both Cerveteri and Vulci's agricultural areas as two potential reception hubs for the two varieties, or diversification hubs at the very least. These two metropolises had massively developed their wine production, possibly achieving a very high quality, and engaging in long-distance trading in the western Mediterranean (Firmati and others 2015; Zifferero 2016). The area retained its marked wine-growing features after the Roman conquest of Vulci and its territory. A major reorganization followed the foundation of the *colonia maritima* at Cosa in 273 BCE. Large kilns for producing transport amphorae were built including structures excavated at Albinia (Orbetello,

Grosseto), where furnaces were active between the middle of the second century BCE and the end of the first century CE (*Ravenna* 2007). All in all, archaeological analysis's potential contribution to viticulture's history can help reveal the stages and progress of the domestication process. This can happen only when we thoroughly understand the overall historical environment in which this phenomenon occurred.

Of course, it is relatively simple to recognize and frame the archaeological data of a site or a region within varietal circulation processes. But the experience gleaned from projects linked to the wild vine has highlighted the need to create new and flexible instruments of historical interpretation for the vine's domestication. Among these, the best is the one which aims to determine the *layering of viticultural contributions*, also defined as *stratification of cultivations*, an investigative process that requires the contributions of both archaeologists and scientists.

Within any geographical space, introgression between wild vines and foreign vine varieties leads to new vine varieties. These are always the result of distinct and progressive stages of cultivation and, over a given chronological spectrum, leave a specific legacy recognizable through autochthonous vine varieties, relic vine varieties, or vine varieties of clearly foreign origin. By looking at the vines' relationship to archaeological sites within a locale (urban centres, minor centres, villas or farms, fortified sites, religious shrines, *mansiones*, and marketplaces, ports, and *emporia*), and the chronology of these sites, it is theoretically possible to reconstruct the stratification of cultivations introduced, selected, and/or enabled introgression of foreign vine varieties in local wild varieties. Analysing and sequencing ancient DNA (i.e. the surviving germplasm) in archaeobotanical finds can reveal vine varieties' genetic identification or at least genetic similarities of these varieties to modern ones (Zifferero 2016, with references). Working in tandem with the botanist and molecular biologist, the archaeologist

---

12 Vouillamoz and others 2007; Di Vecchi Staraz and others 2007; Vouillamoz and others 2008; Scienza 2013; Scienza and Failla 2016; Scienza and Imazio 2018, 159–81; of note also is the presence of the wine variety *Ansonica* in the valley of the Albegna, which grows on the islands of the Tuscan Archipelago having been transferred from the Greek islands (Euboea and Cyclades) by Euboean seafarers who visited Vulci and the harbours under its control, according to the hypothesis in Ciacci and Zifferero 2007; on the ancient circulation of germplasm originated in Greece, see now De Lorenzis and others 2019.

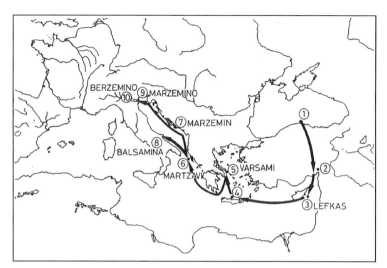

Figure 1.8. The westward voyage from the Black Sea of the *Marzemino* variety, as reconstructed by Attilio Scienza. Scienza and Failla 1996.

can insert the relevant chronological details and establish the geography of accumulation centres as compared to domestication and introduction and/or selection of new cultivars.[13]

A vine's varietal circulation processes can also be interrogated through another pathway, namely that of mythography. Myths often encode the oldest of these layers, or stratifications, through stories that refer to trading contacts, cultural contributions, or migration events (Scienza and Failla 1996, 212–30; Scienza 2004, 101–07; 2006a, 17–50). It was during the Bronze Age

that contacts between the Aegean world and the coasts of southern Italy became a determinant factor in the naming of the region overlooking the Ionian Sea. Greeks of historical times would eventually call this land in southern Italy Oinotria, a name that refers to a growing technique in which a vine grows along a pole of deadwood (*oinotron*). The method, a typical Greek cultivation method, was evidently introduced from outside into local communities who had practised proto-historical viticulture, encouraging wild vines to climb along live, supporting elements. Ionian Calabria's vine populations still express a high level of biodiversity to this day.[14] In the *Odyssey*, the episode involving Ulysses offering Polyphemus the wine of Thracian Ismarus is generally taken to refer to a Greek contribution and may date back to the first contacts between proto-historical communities settled in southern Italy with Aegean seafarers. In the Cyclops's land, vines were not cultivated: they grew wild, producing large bunches, swollen by rainfall (*Odyssey*, IX. 105–11) (Giulierini 1999; Scienza 2004, 129–32; on Homeric geography in general, cf. Braccesi 2010).

A particularly interesting use of mythography with genetic analysis is provided by an investigation of the black grape vine variety *Marzemino*. The expression of an ample family of varietals, *Marzemino* is attested in the regions overlooking the northern Adriatic and has an ancient origin confirmed by congruency between archaeological and biochemical data on one hand and by ancient historiography on the other. According to Scienza, the appearance of *Marzemino* in the area of the northern Adriatic is subordinate to the diffusion of the myths of Diomedes and

---

13 The difficulties in setting a historical framework for the discoveries made in the botanical field and molecular biology lie in the impossibility of precisely establishing the relations between vine varieties that can be reconstructed by sequencing their DNA. In most cases, this results in detailed relationship diagrams, but these fluctuate within excessively wide chronological ranges. The vine variety *Marzemino* provides a remarkable case (cf. *infra*). Its origins were at first explained as a transfer from the Black Sea to the Adriatic coast, the result of Greek colonization. However, they were later linked to the Venetian Republic's commercial activity spanning from the Middle Ages to modern times: Scienza and Imazio 2018, 21–135. About the use of genetic data outside a correct chronological and archaeological grid, see Del Lungo 2016, 37–46.

14 Forni 1999; on the identification of proto-historical cultures of Ionian Calabria with the Enotrians cf. Guzzo 2006; Bianco and Preite 2014; on the exceptional biodiversity of vine varieties in the area around Locri and their relations with the wild vine see Sculli 2004 and now Del Lungo 2016.

Antenor and testifies to the connection with Greek colonization in the Adriatic. Traditionally, Antenor is the founder-hero (οἰκιστής) of the city of Padua and is linked to the foundation of Este. However, the myth arrived in the lands of the Veneti via the Phocaean seafarers. Diomedes' saga could be linked to the Corinthian expansion along the same Adriatic route, via the hub on the island of Corcyra (Corfu) (Fig. 1.8).[15]

By following the diffusion of myths, it is possible to reconstruct the journey of *Marzemino*, from the south shore of the Black Sea via Cyprus, where this variety was present under the name of *Lefkas*. The variety reached insular Greece via the Euboean seafarers. It acquired a new name: *Varsami* or *Marzavi mavro*, to assume the name of *Martzavì* or *Vartzamì* in Corfu, corresponding to its modern name. From Corfu, its diffusion proceeded along both shores of the Adriatic as far as the delta of the Po River. The expansion of *Marzemino* in antiquity reached the Veneto and Friuli-Venezia Giulia and later, in historic times, stretched as far as Lombardy and Trentino. It served to rebuild and define accumulation centres of germplasm of foreign origin in the area between Verona and Vicenza. This partly depended on the proximity to the harbours of Spina and Adria in the delta of the Po, respectively controlled by the Etruscans and the Veneti (Figs 1.9–1.10).[16]

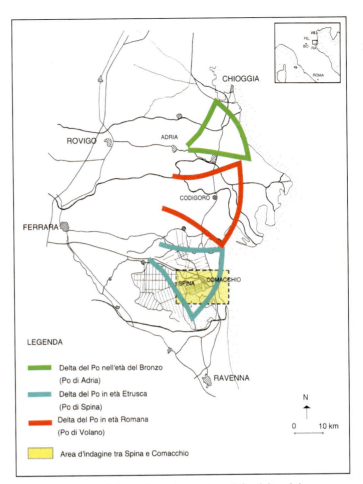

Figure 1.9. Schematic reconstruction of the delta of the Po River in antiquity: the situation during the Etruscan period is highlighted in light blue. Berti 2007.

Figure 1.10. Hypothetical reconstruction of the Etruscan site of Spina in the sixth and fifth centuries BCE. Berti 2007.

---

15 Scienza and Failla 1996, 210–30; Scienza and others 2000; on mythography of the origins of Venetian centres, cf. latest Ruta Serafini 2002, with references; for a new framework of this vine variety see *supra*, n. 9.

16 Scienza and Failla 1996, 221–30; on the accumulation centres between Verona and Vicenza cf. Scienza 2006b, 72–103 and 186–98; on the role of the harbours of Spina and Adria in pre-Roman wine distribution see Cattaneo and De Marinis 1996.

The Vine in Etruscan Val Padana: The Domestication of the Wild Vine and the Origin of the Family of Lambrusco

By examining the chronological succession of phases, we can determine the contributions of viticulture from domestication processes. In Pliny (*Nat.* XIV. 39), we find the first essential reference to the cultivation of the vine in the Po Valley in general and in Modena in particular. Pliny mentions a variety he calls *Perusinia*. It is characterized by black grapes, capable of producing a wine which lightens in colour after four years' aging. The name of the vine variety, based on Roman custom, reveals its origin, referring to the Etruscan city of Perugia. Various authors have recognized that this is a direct link to founding myths of Etruscan cities in the Po Valley — and Felsina in particular. Tradition has it that the Perugian hero Ocnus originally founded Felsina and then Mantua. Ocnus was believed to be the brother or son of Aulestes, founder and king of Perugia (Malnati 1988a; Sassatelli and Macellari 2002; Macellari 2014; cf. also Zifferero 2017b). The mythographic tradition may refer to communities' migration from Etruria itself, which probably occurred in two phases. A first migration may date to the Iron Age, as Villanovan Etruscan culture spread over the Apennine passes. The second migration wave occurred in the mid-Archaic period, during the final years of the seventh century and the whole of the sixth century BCE (L. Malnati in *Atlante* 2003, 33–38; *Bazzano* 2010, with references) (Fig. 1.11). The transfer of people, technical knowledge, and goods from the central areas of northern Etruria through the valleys of the Rivers Reno, Panaro, and Secchia, indicate the complexity of the settlement process and the territorial organization of Padanian Etruria. The process continued until the beginning of the fourth century BCE, when the Celts descended into the area.[17]

In the ample corridor running south of the Po River, the archaeological framework points to settlement dynamics including cohabitation forms between Etruscans, Ligurians, and Umbrians, but within a context of robust Etruscan expansion. This same route was characterized in Roman times by the presence of the Via Aemilia. Since prehistoric times its course had been marked by intersecting road networks, transversal to the rivers and torrential streams descending from the Apennines. These watercourses ensure well-watered plains. The terrain there is specially adapted to agricultural production in general and vine growing in particular.[18] Undoubtedly the Etruscan communities are the ones which have left the most substantial mark on the landscape. Felsina emerged as a proto-urban centre at the beginning of the eighth century BCE. However, many attestations of late Bronze and early Iron Age sites in the plain around Modena indicate that here the proto-urban centre had not yet reached even an intermediate level. This outcome only occurred in Roman times. In a well-known passage, Livy (*Ann.*, XXI. 25–26), refers to a — possibly Etruscan — walled city, which existed before the Roman colony of Mutina was established there. Archaeologists have found traces of an articulated network of open sites, active between the sixth and fifth centuries BCE. The majority of these sites seem to gravitate in the area of the hills and high plains between the Secchia and Panaro Rivers. We only have data from archaeological surveys, but if confirmed, this would indicate the presence of a large-scale centre nearby (Malnati

---

17 For settlement systems in the area of Modena and

on Felsina's westward expansion, cf. Malnati 1988a; D. Locatelli in *Atlante* 2009; Locatelli 2011; Sassatelli 2010; Neri 2012, 9–15.

18 For the hydrogeological setup and agricultural suitability of the lower plain of the River Po, see Ferrari and Gambi 2000; concerning forms of agricultural production in the Etruscan period and the importance of road networks matching the future route of the Via Aemilia, cf. L. Malnati in *Atlante* 2003, 33–38; Sassatelli 2010; Neri 2012, 139–44.

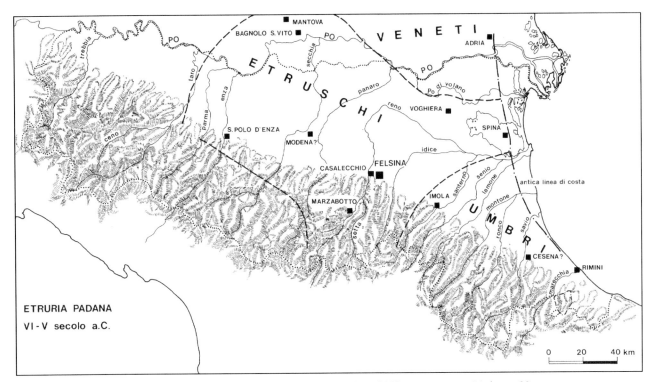

Figure 1.11. The Etruscan sites in Val Padana in sixth and fifth centuries BCE. *Modena* 1988.

1988a; 1988b, 307–09; *Bazzano* 2010; D. Locatelli in *Atlante* 2009, 59–75). The settlement process documented in the countryside surrounding southern Etruria's cities, i.e. Veio, Cerveteri, and Vulci, can act as a useful comparison: the open sites must be interpreted as farms. They indicate a subdivision of arable lands which must have referred to the urban centre and minor dependent centres. Markets and produce redistribution would take place in these smaller conurbations (Fig. 1.12).[19] There is no evidence pointing to Mutina's activity during the Etruscan period, nor any concerning its ability to promote the surrounding countryside. Therefore, we may surmise that Felsina's control over agricultural lands might reach as far as the Secchia Valley. Of the two *cippi* or inscribed stone markers found at Rubiera, the most recent dates to the first quarter of the sixth century BCE. It seems to refer to the exercise of the post of *zilath*. This magistracy is typical of a territorial state and confirms Felsina's role (cf. L. Malnati in *Atlante* 2003, 33–38; Sassatelli 2010).

All in all, we are facing a complex territorial organization which we still can't completely define. However, we should emphasize that archaeological research has revealed drainage systems and channelling networks for surface water. The abundance of water is due to the rivers and sources supplied by phreatic or resurfacing watercourses, typical of the plains of Emilia. In the area around Modena, the regular pattern of water collector channels seems to have inspired the largest of the settlements researched so far. The regular subdivision, the orientation of drainage ditches according to cardinal points, are all clues which indicate a remarkable planning capacity and the presence of a sizeable workforce. These would not be available to single family residents

---

19 For a general view of the phenomenon see: Rendeli 1993; on the organization of the agricultural lands controlled by Cerveteri, among those better known as open sites, see Enei 2001.

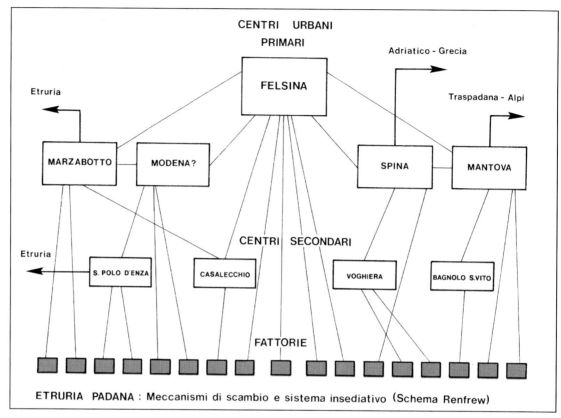

Figure 1.12. Hierarchy of the Etruscan settlement system in Val Padana in the fifth century BCE. *Modena* 1988.

in open sites.[20] Rational solutions regarding control, drainage, and water supply can be linked to intensive colonial settlement policies. These are the results of Etruscan expansion in historical times into areas around the Po Valley. The most tangible relic today of the Etruscan landscape, which probably has changed little over time is the so-called *piantata*. The *piantata* can be explained as an offshoot of the earlier *arbustum italicum*, which consists in growing a single vine along a supporting live tree, usually an elm and/or field maple. The vine was cultivated according to the technique known as long pruning. It evolved into the so-called *piantata* or *alberata*, which consists in planting the supporting trees in regular lines to form the vineyard's regular rows (Figs 1.13–1.14).[21]

Local traditions mean the *piantata* has assumed different forms. Variations depend on the overall shape of the planting, and the ways in which the land is cultivated. Modena is only a short distance

---

20 On water drainage in the region of Emilia see: Ortalli 1995; for the organization of the countryside in the area of Modena, the most evident reference is to the site of Forte Urbano at Castelfranco Emilia, inhabited from the fifth century to the first half of the fourth century BCE. The site occupied an area of about one hectare and was surrounded by an embankment and a ditch. The north–south orientation along which the structures were aligned (canals, internal paths, and buildings' foundations) reflects the wider layout criteria of the surrounding agricultural landscape: D. Locatelli in *Atlante* 2009, 67–70, with references.

21 Marchesini 1999; Marvelli 1999, 46–47, includes reference to ligneous archaeological finds, i.e., elm stumps supporting vines, found in Modena and tentatively dated to the Iron Age. For agricultural fieldwork plausibly identified as a vineyard planted according to the *per sulcos* method, located at Casalecchio di Reno (Bologna), cf. Ortalli 1995, 81–82 and fig. 24.

from Bologna, and yet the *piantata bolognese* or *a cavalletto* differs from the *modenese-reggiana* type. In all cases, a *piantata* calls for the planting of supporting trees in rows, at regular intervals. As Emilio Sereni surmised many years ago, the *piantata emiliano-romagnola* is a fossil left over from the rural landscape of Etruria. The *alberate* of Aversa, typical of northern Etruscan Campania, share the same cultural matrix and very few *alberate* survive in the Arno Valley and Casentino (Arezzo) area. Among those less studied, these do not enjoy protected status as elements of the rural landscape of historical interest. If such safeguards are not forthcoming, they are destined to disappear within one generation (Figs 1.15–1.16).[22] Archaeological and archaeobotanical research attempts to correlate the *piantata* or *alberata* to the *organized landscape system*. This landscape appears at the same time as the open sites (farms) and the countryside's regular and parcelled layout. In southern Etruria, these events coincide with the passage from the Late Orientalizing period into the Archaic period (i.e., from the last quarter of the seventh century BCE to the beginning of the sixth century BCE). The intensive improvement of agriculture reflects significant changes occurring in Etruscan society and form a prelude to programmes of arable land distribution plausibly set up by cities.[23] In the area of Emilian plains, archaeobotanical data from the *terramara* of Montale have pushed back the beginnings of vine cultivation, which can now be

Figure 1.13. Surviving elements of Etruscan viticulture in the modern Italian landscape: example of the *piantata* as practised in Emilia. Marchesini 1999.

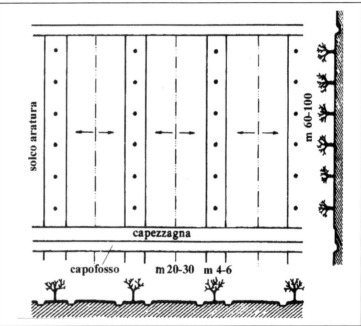

Figure 1.14. Surviving elements of Etruscan viticulture in the modern Italian landscape: graphical reconstruction of the *piantata* as practised in Emilia.

---

22 On the relationship between *piantate/alberate* with Etruscan and Roman agriculture, cf. Sereni 1964; 1987, 40–43; on *alberate* in Emilia see now Antonini and Marchesini 2017; the *alberata* as practised at Aversa is dealt with by Di Pasquale and others 2012 (including the earlier bibliography). The Tuscan *alberate* are also mentioned by Firmati and others 2015.

23 On the consequences of these changes to the rural make-up of the lands around Cerveteri, cf. Zifferero 2005b; the subdivision of central Italy's viticultural history into phases from Protohistory is set out in Ciacci and Zifferero 2007.

dated to the end of the Middle Bronze Age and the beginning of the Recent Bronze Age. We can conclude that *Vitis vinifera sativa* L., appeared in the second half of the second millennium BCE, as a consequence of the wild vine's domestication. These data also allow us to look beyond the Late Bronze Age for the selective development of vine varieties considered indigenous to the area of

Figure 1.15. Surviving elements of Etruscan viticulture in the modern Italian landscape: the *piantata aversana* before winter pruning, in the area of Casal di Principe (Caserta). Courtesy of Gaetano Di Pasquale.

Figure 1.16. Surviving elements of Etruscan viticulture in the modern Italian landscape: centuries-old vineyard supported by field maple trees near Figline Valdarno (Florence). Courtesy of Valerio Zorzi.

Figure 1.17. Details of the leaf and bunch of *Lambrusco di Sorbara* vine variety, typical of the areas of Modena and Reggio nell'Emilia. Courtesy of Giovanna Bosi.

Modena and Reggio, with significant expansions into Romagna and the areas around Mantua. The cultivars belong to the *Lambrusco* family, which is genetically related with the *Vitis vinifera* ssp. *sylvestris* (Fig. 1.17).[24] *Lambrusco* vine varieties are related to the wild varieties linguistically as well as genetically. Virgil uses the term *labrusca* to define vines growing spontaneously in field hedgerows or close to running water (i.e., *Ecl.*, v. 4–7). From this term derives the word *lambruscaia*. In central and southern Tuscany, the term is used today to describe the wild vine population growing around streams and springs. These circumstances might thus help circumscribe the selective processes in antiquity. This practice may have begun in the Late Bronze and the Early Iron Age and might have intensified during the

---

24 Cardarelli and others forthcoming; Marvelli and others 2013; Gambari 2014; on the botanical and genetic profile of *Lambrusco* vine varieties, see: Catena 2014; on genetic profile see also Scienza 2006a, 120–22 and now Scienza and Imazio 2018, 1–27.

Etruscan period. In the sixth century BCE the *piantata* was introduced, providing a typical expression of a concentrated type of colonial viticulture, practised on a wide scale.

Silvia Marvelli and others rightly suggest that the earliest wine-growing efforts in the Po Valley could also benefit from the vine varieties of Greek origin in a different way. Accumulation centres had appeared in the area of Verona and Vicenza. This was possible thanks to their proximity to the Adriatic ports of Spina and Adria. We must also remember that ancient vineyards were strongly polyvarietal. Cultivars resulting from different selections and origins were implanted there. The earliest historical indication concerning varietal circulation is offered by the central Italian origin of *Perusinia* grapes.[25] There are still doubts regarding the actual scale of production and prospective commercialization of wine produced from *Lambrusco* varieties. No vessels such as transport amphorae have been found so far to prove it was shipped over long distances. Archaeological sites in the region of Emilia have yielded many *dolia* dating to the Etruscan period. In these specific cases, it would lead us to suppose activities such as the fermentation of must and/or the conservation of wine were being carried out on a remarkable scale.[26] In any case,

it is interesting to note that funerary furnishings from the area of Bologna, Modena, and Reggio Emilia include references to wine consumption, albeit in a ritual context. These attestations date from the end of the seventh century BCE and are directly related to the Greek symposium. They demonstrate the intention of following the same consumption models first experienced by southern Etruria's aristocracies. The dumpsite of the Etruscan settlement at Forcello, near Bagnolo San Vito (Mantua), has yielded many transport amphorae, hailing from Corinth, Attica, Chios, Samos, Milos, Ionia-Massilia, and Mende. They indicate that wine of Greek provenance was highly appreciated by Etruscans living in the Po Valley (Macellari 2014; Cattaneo and De Marinis 1996).

Conclusions

The present contribution addresses and revises previously published work, updating recent data in an attempt to clarify research strategies set up through VINUM and the ArcheoVino Project. These projects set out to document the stages of the domestication of the wild vine in Italy and specifically, Etruria, highlighting the importance of archaeological methods as an irreplaceable framework for botanical and, especially, biomolecular approaches to viticulture. Valuable information about timescale, species diversification, and varietal circulation can only be ascertained through a complementary approach that uses scientific analyses within a framework provided by historical analyses. In this way, the complex trajectories of Etruscan wine production and consumption clearly emerge.

---

25 On the use of the term *labrusca* among Latin geoponic terms, cf. Sereni 1964, 149–62 and Fregoni 1991, 33–35; Marvelli and others 2013; the tendency towards oligovarietal vineyards, comprising a maximum of four or five varietals, was only reached at the end of the eighteenth century in northern Italy, as in antiquity polyvarietal vineyards were the norm: Scienza and Failla 1996, 187–89.

26 For the conservation and transport of wine, wooden barrels were introduced in first century CE in the Cisalpine area, see Cipriano 1996; the whole picture must be updated, thanks to the extraordinary find in the Alpine area of Bressanone (Bolzano), comprising of large wooden barrels still housed in a wine cellar of the ancient Raetii, and dating to the beginning of the fifth century BCE: Tecchiati and Rizzi 2014; on the spread of *dolia* in production sites in the area of Modena see

---

Ferri and Losi 1988, 29 and fig. 10; for Etruscan sites including *dolia*, see e.g., Cattani 1988, 255 and fig. 197 no. 15 (Pasano, Savignano sul Panaro); Malnati 1988b, 265 and fig. 215 nos 1–2 (Case Vandelli, Baggiovara); on the large number of *dolia* (meant for storage purposes or a wine cellar?), found at Baggiovara not far from the site of Case Vandelli, see: Locatelli 2011, 16–17.

Works Cited

Acconcia, Valeria. 2014. *Ritualità funeraria e convivialità: tra rigore e ostentazione nell'Abruzzo preromano* (Rome: Officina edizioni)

Acconcia, Valeria, and Gilda Bartoloni. 2007. 'La casa del re', in *Materiali per Populonia*, VI, ed. by Lucia Botarelli, Marta Coccoluto, and Maria Cristina Mileti (Pisa: ETS), pp. 11–29

Acconcia, Valeria, and Alessandra Piergrossi. 2021. 'L'archeologia del vino nella penisola italiana e nelle grandi isole del Tirreno tra il neolitico e la romanizzazione: tematiche, dati e approcci possibili', *Bollettino di archeologia on line*, 12.2: 183–230

Antonini, Eraldo, and Marco Marchesini. 2017. 'La piantata e la viticoltura: persistenza nel paesaggio moderno', in *'Mutina splendidissima': la città romana e la sua eredità*, ed. by Luigi Malnati, Silvia Pellegrini, Francesca Piccinini, and Cristina Stefani (Rome: De Luca), pp. 290–93

Aranguren, Biancamaria, Cristina Bellini, Marta Mariotti Lippi, Miria Mori Secci, and Paola Perazzi. 2012. 'Testimonianze dell'uso della vite nel Bronzo Medio: nuovi dati da San Lorenzo a Greve (Firenze)', in *Archeologia della vite e del vino in Toscana e nel Lazio: dalle tecniche dell'indagine archeologica alle prospettive della biologia molecolare*, ed. by Andrea Ciacci, Paola Rendini, and Andrea Zifferero (Florence: Edizioni All'Insegna del Giglio), pp. 125–31

Atlante 2003. *Atlante dei Beni Archeologici della Provincia di Modena*, I: *Pianura* (Florence: Edizioni All'Insegna del Giglio)

Atlante 2009. *Atlante dei Beni Archeologici della Provincia di Modena*, III: *Collina e Alta Pianura*, ed. by Andrea Cardarelli and Luigi Malnati (Florence: Edizioni All'Insegna del Giglio)

Bartoloni, Gilda. 2003. *Le società dell'Italia primitiva: lo studio delle necropoli e la nascita delle aristocrazie* (Rome: Carocci)

Bartoloni, Gilda, Valeria Acconcia, and Silvia ten Kortenaar. 2012. 'Viticoltura e consumo del vino in Etruria: la cultura materiale tra la fine dell'età del Ferro e l'Orientalizzante Antico', in *Archeologia della vite e del vino in Toscana e nel Lazio: dalle tecniche dell'indagine archeologica alle prospettive della biologia molecolare*, ed. by Andrea Ciacci, Paola Rendini, and Andrea Zifferero (Florence: Edizioni All'Insegna del Giglio), pp. 201–75

Bazzano 2010 = Rita Burgio, Sara Campagnari, and Luigi Malnati (eds), *Cavalieri etruschi dalle valli al Po: Tra Reno e Panaro, la valle del Samoggia nell'VIII e VII secolo a.C.* (Bologna: Aspasia)

Beijer, Arnold J. 1991. 'Impasto Pottery and Social Status in Latium Vetus in the Orientalising Period (725–575 BC): An Example from Borgo Le Ferriere (Satricum)', in *Papers of the Fourth Conference of Italian Archaeology*, II.2: *The Archaeology of Power*, ed. by Edward Herring, Ruth Whitehouse, and John Wilkins (London: Accordia Research Centre), pp. 21–39

Bellelli, Vincenzo, and Massimo Botto. 2018. 'La tomba 18 a sinistra di Via del Manganello: prime osservazioni sul sepolcro e sul suo corredo', in *Caere orientalizzante: nuove ricerche su città e necropoli*, ed. by Alessandro Naso and Massimo Botto (Rome: Quasar), pp. 305–41

Berti, Fede. 2007. 'Su un gruppo di tombe di Spina da Valle Trebba', in *Genti nel Delta da Spina a Comacchio: uomini, territorio e culto dall'antichità all'alto Medioevo* (Ferrara: Corbo), pp. 109–36

Bettelli, Marco. 2002. *Italia meridionale e mondo miceneo: ricerche su dinamiche di acculturazione e aspetti archeologici (con particolare riferimento ai versanti adriatico e ionico della penisola italiana)* (Florence: Edizioni All'Insegna del Giglio)

Bianco, Salvatore, and Addolorata Preite. 2014. 'Identificazione degli Enotri. Fonti e metodi interpretativi', *Mélanges de l'École française de Rome: antiquité*, 126.2: 1–44

Boissinot, Philippe. 2009. 'Les vignobles des environs de Mégara Hyblaea et les traces de la viticulture italienne durant l'Antiquité', *Mélanges de l'École française de Rome: antiquité*, 121.1: 83–132

Botto, Massimo. 2013. 'The Phoenicians and the Spread of Wine in the Central West Mediterranean', in *Patrimonio cultural de la vid y el vino: Vine and Wine Cultural Heritage* (Madrid: Universidad Autónoma de Madrid), pp. 103–31

——. 2016. 'La produzione del vino in Sardegna tra Sardi e Fenici: lo stato della ricerca', in *ArcheoTipico: l'archeologia come strumento per la ricostruzione del paesaggio e dell'alimentazione antica; Atti del Convegno (Viterbo 2015)*, ed. by Gian Maria Di Nocera, Alessandro Guidi, and Andrea Zifferero, *Rivista di storia dell'agricoltura*, 2016.1/2: 79–96

Braccesi, Lorenzo. 2010. *Sulle rotte di Ulisse: l'invenzione della geografia omerica* (Rome: Laterza)

Braconi, Paolo. 2012. '*In vineis arbustisque*. Il concetto di vigneto in età romana', in *Archeologia della vite e del vino in Toscana e nel Lazio: dalle tecniche dell'indagine archeologica alle prospettive della biologia molecolare*, ed. by Andrea Ciacci, Paola Rendini, and Andrea Zifferero (Florence: Edizioni All'Insegna del Giglio), pp. 291–306

Brun, Jean-Pierre. 2011. 'La produzione del vino in Magna Grecia e in Sicilia', in *La vigna di Dioniso: vite, vino e culti in Magna Grecia* (Taranto: Istituto per la storia e l'archeologia della Magna Grecia), pp. 95–142

Cardarelli, Andrea, Giovanna Bosi, Rossella Rinaldi, Mariano Ucchesu, and Gianluigi Bacchetta. Forthcoming. 'Vino o non vino? Nuovi dati sui vinaccioli della Terramara di Montale (Modena) tra la fine della media età del Bronzo e il Bronzo recente', in *Preistoria del cibo, Atti della 50ma Riunione Scientifica dell'Istituto Italiano di Preistoria e Protostoria*

Castiglione d'Orcia 2011 = Barbara Biagini (ed.), *Origini della viticoltura: atti del convegno* (Castiglione d'Orcia: Edizioni Podere Forte)

Catena, Mauro. 2014. 'Caratteristiche agronomiche dei vitigni da vino Lambrusco delle province di Modena e Reggio Emilia', in *Archeologia del lambrusco: storia delle vigne perdute*, ed. by Filippo Maria Gambari and Roberto Macellari (Reggio Emilia: Comune di Reggio Emilia), pp. 37–48

Cattaneo, Anna Chiara, and Raffaele Carlo De Marinis. 1996. 'Le anfore greche da trasporto di Adria, S. Basilio e del Forcello di Bagnolo S. Vito e il commercio del vino nell'Italia padana all'epoca della colonizzazione etrusca', in *2500 anni di cultura della vite nell'ambito alpino e cisalpino*, ed. by Gaetano Forni and Attilio Scienza (Trento: Cassa Rurale di Villazzano e Trento), pp. 317–48

Cattani, Maurizio. 1988. 'Resti di età etrusca da Pasano (Savignano sul Panaro)', in *Modena dalle origini all'anno Mille: studi di archeologia e storia*, 2 vols (Modena: Panini), I, pp. 255–57

Cerchiai, Luca, and Mariassunta Cuozzo. 2016. 'Tra Pitecusa e Pontecagnano: il consumo del vino nel rituale funebre tra Greci, Etruschi e indigeni', in *ArcheoTipico: l'archeologia come strumento per la ricostruzione del paesaggio e dell'alimentazione antica; atti del Convegno (Viterbo 2015)*, ed. by Gian Maria Di Nocera, Alessandro Guidi, and Andrea Zifferero, *Rivista di storia dell'agricoltura*, 2016.1/2: 195–207

Ciacci, Andrea. 2005. 'Il consumo del vino in Etruria: aspetti ideologici, rituali ed epigrafici', in *Vinum: un progetto per il riconoscimento della vite silvestre nel paesaggio archeologico della Toscana e del Lazio settentrionale*, ed. by Ciacci, Andrea, and Andrea Zifferero (Siena: Ci.Vin.), pp. 121–37

Ciacci, Andrea, and Andrea Zifferero (eds). 2005. *Vinum: un progetto per il riconoscimento della vite silvestre nel paesaggio archeologico della Toscana e del Lazio settentrionale* (Siena: Ci.Vin.)

——. 2007. '"Progetto VINUM": prospettive di ricerca in area populoniese', in *Materiali per Populonia*, VI, ed. by Lucia Botarelli, Marta Coccoluto, and Maria Cristina Mileti (Pisa: ETS), pp. 397–419

Ciacci, Andrea, Paola Rendini, and Andrea Zifferero (eds). 2012. *Archeologia della vite e del vino in Toscana e nel Lazio: dalle tecniche dell'indagine archeologica alle prospettive della biologia molecolare* (Florence: Edizioni All'Insegna del Giglio)

Cipriano, Silvia. 1996. 'Considerazioni sul commercio del vino in età romana', in *2500 anni di cultura della vite nell'ambito alpino e cisalpino*, ed. by Gaetano Forni and Attilio Scienza (Trento: Cassa Rurale di Villazzano e Trento), pp. 409–18

Coen, Alessandra, Fernando Gilotta, and Marina Micozzi. 2018. 'Produzioni in contesto a Monte Abatone', in *Caere orientalizzante: nuove ricerche su città e necropoli*, ed. by Alessandro Naso and Massimo Botto (Rome: Quasar), pp. 67–108

Colivicchi, Fabio. 2004. 'L'altro vino. Vino, cultura e identità nella Puglia e Basilicata anelleniche', *Siris*, 5: 23–68

Cristofani, Mauro. 1991. 'Vino e simposio nel mondo etrusco arcaico', in *Homo edens*, II: *Storie del vino: regimi, miti e pratiche dell'alimentazione nella civiltà del Mediterraneo*, ed. by Paolo Scarpi (Milan: Diapress), pp. 69–76

De Lorenzis, Gabriella, Francesco Mercati, Carlo Bergamini, Maria Francesca Cardone, Antonio Lupini, Antonio Mauceri, Angelo R. Caputo, Loredana Abbate, Maria Gabriella Barbagallo, Donato Antonacci, Francesco Sunseri, and Lucio Brancadoro. 2019. 'SNP Genotyping Elucidates the Genetic Diversity of *Magna Graecia* Grapevine Germplasm and its Historical Origin and Dissemination', *BMC Plant Biology*, 19.7: 1–15

Del Lungo, Stefano. 2016. 'Centro terziario di domesticazione: la topografia antica e la genetica in Enotria, dalle Siriche alla multivarietà viticola della Lucania', in *Basivin_SUD: la ricerca del germoplasma viticolo in Basilicata*, ed. by Vittorio Alba, Carlo Bergamini, Marica Gasparro, Francesco Mazzone, Sabino Roccotelli, Donato Antonacci, and Angelo R. Caputo (Bari: Mario Adda), pp. 37–86

Delpino, Filippo. 2002. 'Brocchette a collo obliquo dall'area etrusca', in *Etruria e Sardegna centro-settentrionale tra l'età del Bronzo Finale e l'Arcaismo: atti del 21. Convegno di studi etruschi ed italici, Sassari, Alghero, Oristano, Torralba, 13–17 ottobre 1998* (Pisa: Istituti editoriali e poligrafici internazionali), pp. 363–86

——. 2012. 'Viticoltura, produzione e consumo del vino nell'Etruria protostorica', in *Archeologia della vite e del vino in Toscana e nel Lazio: dalle tecniche dell'indagine archeologica alle prospettive della biologia molecolare*, ed. by Andrea Ciacci, Paola Rendini, and Andrea Zifferero (Florence: Edizioni All'Insegna del Giglio), pp. 189–99

Di Pasquale, Gaetano, Emilia Allevato, and Antonello Migliozzi. 2012. 'La sopravvivenza della piantata aversana: un paesaggio straordinario a rischio di estinzione', in *Archeologia della vite e del vino in Toscana e nel Lazio: dalle tecniche dell'indagine archeologica alle prospettive della biologia molecolare*, ed. by Andrea Ciacci, Paola Rendini, and Andrea Zifferero (Florence: Edizioni All'Insegna del Giglio), pp. 821–26

Di Vecchi Staraz, Manuel, Roberto Bandinelli, Maurizio Boselli, Patrice This, Jean-Michel Boursiquot, Valérie Laucou, Thierry Lacombe, and Didier Varès. 2007. 'Genetic Structuring and Parentage Analysis for Evolutionary Studies in Grapevine: Kin Group and Origins of the Cultivar Sangiovese Revealed', *Journal of the American Society for Horticultural Science*, 132.4: 514–24

Docter, Roald F. 2000. 'East Greek Fine Wares and Transport Amphorae of the 8th–5th Century BC from Carthage and Toscanos', in *Ceràmiques jònies d'època arcaica: centres de producció i comercialització al Mediterrani Occidental; actes de la Taula Rodonda celebrada a Empúries, els dies 26 al 28 de maig de 1999*, ed. by Paloma Cabrera Bonet and Marta Santos Retolaza (Barcelona: Generalitat de Catalunya), pp. 63–88

Enei, Flavio. 2001. *Progetto Ager Caeretanus: il litorale di Alsium; ricognizioni archeologiche nel territorio dei Comuni di Ladispoli, Cerveteri e Fiumicino* (Ladispoli: Comune di Ladispoli)

Failla, Osvaldo. 2007. 'Morfologia e fisiologia', in *La vite e il vino* (Bologna: ART Servizi Editoriali spa), pp. 1–45

——. 2014. 'Il vitigno: significato, origine e variabilità', in *Le frontiere nascoste della cultura del vino: atti del Seminario permanente di etnografia alpina (SPEA 14)*, ed. by Gaetano Forni, Giovanni Kezich, and Attilio Scienza, *Annali di San Michele*, 25: 115–38

Failla, Osvaldo, and Gaetano Forni (eds). 1999. *Alle radici della civiltà del vino in Sicilia* (Menfi: Cantine Settesoli)

Ferrari, Carlo, and Lucio Gambi (eds). 2000. *Un Po di terra: guida all'ambiente della bassa pianura padana e alla sua storia* (Reggio Emilia: Diabasis)

Ferri, Federica, and Anna Losi. 1988. 'La ceramica d'impasto', in *Modena dalle origini all'anno Mille: studi di archeologia e storia*, 2 vols (Modena: Panini), II, pp. 20–28

Firmati, Marco, Andrea Zifferero, Valerio Zorzi, and Gaia Ferrari Melillo. 2015. 'Scansano (GR). Progetto ArcheoVino: l'impianto del vigneto sperimentale etrusco-romano', *Notiziario della Soprintendenza per i beni archeologici della Toscana*, 11: 497–501

Forni, Gaetano. 1999. 'La tecnologia e l'economia vitivinicola della Magna Grecia e della Sicilia antica', in *Alle radici della civiltà del vino in Sicilia*, ed. by Osvaldo Failla, and Gaetano Forni (Menfi: Cantine Settesoli), pp. 131–67

——. 2012. 'La matrice euromediterranea della nostra viticoltura. La prospettiva pluridisciplinare', in *Archeologia della vite e del vino in Toscana e nel Lazio: dalle tecniche dell'indagine archeologica alle prospettive della biologia molecolare*, ed. by Andrea Ciacci, Paola Rendini, and Andrea Zifferero (Florence: Edizioni All'Insegna del Giglio), pp. 93–118

Forni, Gaetano, and Attilio Scienza (eds). 1996. *2500 anni di cultura della vite nell'ambito alpino e cisalpino* (Trento: Cassa Rurale di Villazzano e Trento)

Fregoni, Mario. 1991. *Origini della vite e della viticoltura: contributo dei popoli antichi* (Aosta: Musumeci editore)

Gambari, Filippo Maria. 2014. 'Protostoria ed archeologia del lambrusco nella Cisalpina preromana', in *Archeologia del lambrusco: storia delle vigne perdute*, ed. by Filippo Maria Gambari and Roberto Macellari (Reggio Emilia: Comune di Reggio Emilia), pp. 3–11

Giulierini, Paolo. 1999. 'Documentazione letteraria e archeologica della vitivinicoltura e della sua economia in Magna Grecia ed in Sicilia nell'epoca pre-romana', in *Alle radici della civiltà del vino in Sicilia*, ed. by Osvaldo Failla, and Gaetano Forni (Menfi: Cantine Settesoli), pp. 59–130

Gras, Michel. 1985. *Trafics tyrrhéniens archaïques* (Rome: École française de Rome)

Guidi, Alessandro. 2016. 'Pratiche conviviali in Italia tra età del Bronzo Finale ed età del Ferro', in *ArcheoTipico: l'archeologia come strumento per la ricostruzione del paesaggio e dell'alimentazione antica; atti del Convegno (Viterbo 2015)*, ed. by Gian Maria Di Nocera, Alessandro Guidi, and Andrea Zifferero, *Rivista di storia dell'agricoltura*, 2016.1/2: 133–39

Guzzo, Pier Giovanni. 2006. 'Il mare color del vino', in *Vino: tra mito e cultura*, ed. by Maria Grazia Marchetti Lungarotti and Mario Torelli (Milan: Electa), pp. 25–32

Locatelli, Daniela. 2011. 'Il popolamento dell'età del ferro nell'area di Baggiovara', in *L'insediamento etrusco e romano di Baggiovara (MO): le indagini archeologiche e archeometriche*, ed. by Donato Labate and Daniela Locatelli (Florence: Edizioni All'Insegna del Giglio), pp. 15–19

Macellari, Roberto. 2014. 'Servizi da simposio negli insediamenti etruschi del Reggiano', in *Archeologia del lambrusco: storia delle vigne perdute*, ed. by Filippo Maria Gambari and Roberto Macellari (Reggio Emilia: Comune di Reggio Emilia), pp. 13–23

Malnati, Luigi. 1988a. 'L'affermazione etrusca nel modenese e l'organizzazione del territorio', in *Modena dalle origini all'anno Mille: studi di archeologia e storia*, 2 vols (Modena: Panini), I, pp. 137–52

——. 1988b. 'Lo scavo di una fattoria etrusca a Baggiovara, località Case Vandelli', in *Modena dalle origini all'anno Mille: studi di archeologia e storia*, 2 vols (Modena: Panini), I, pp. 262–71

Marchesini, Marco. 1999. 'La piantata nel Bolognese. Sistemazione e tipologia', in *La vite maritata: storia, cultura, coltivazione, ecologia della piantata nella pianura padana* (Bologna: Comune di San Giovanni in Persiceto), pp. 53–60

Mariotti Lippi, Marta, Miria Mori Secci, and Cristina Bellini. 2012. 'L'archeobotanica e lo studio della vite nella Preistoria della Toscana', in *Archeologia della vite e del vino in Toscana e nel Lazio: dalle tecniche dell'indagine archeologica alle prospettive della biologia molecolare*, ed. by Andrea Ciacci, Paola Rendini, and Andrea Zifferero (Florence: Edizioni All'Insegna del Giglio), pp. 119–24

Marvelli, Silvia. 1999. 'Testimonianze archeobotaniche. Reperti di vite in Emilia-Romagna', in *La vite maritata: storia, cultura, coltivazione, ecologia della piantata nella pianura padana* (Bologna: Comune di San Giovanni in Persiceto), pp. 35–50

Marvelli, Silvia, Stefano De Siena, Elisabetta Rizzoli, and Marco Marchesini. 2013. 'The Origin of Grapevine Cultivation in Italy: The Archaeobotanical Evidence', *Annali di botanica*, 2013.3: 155–63

McGovern, Patrick E. 2004. *L'archeologo e l'uva: vite e vino dal Neolitico alla Grecia arcaica*, trans. by Lorenzo Argentieri (Rome: Carocci)

——. 2013. 'From East to West: The Ancient Near Eastern "Wine Culture" Travels Land and Sea', in *Patrimonio cultural de la vid y el vino: Vine and Wine Cultural Heritage* (Madrid: Universidad Autónoma de Madrid), pp. 233–41

Mersch, Christian van der. 1996. 'Vigne, vin et économie dans l'Italie du Sud grecque à l'époque archaïque', *Ostraka*, 1: 155–85

Micozzi, Marina. 2016. 'Continuità e trasformazione nei servizi da banchetto di età medio-orientalizzante: appunti da Cerveteri', in *ArcheoTipico: l'archeologia come strumento per la ricostruzione del paesaggio e dell'alimentazione antica; atti del Convegno (Viterbo 2015)*, ed. by Gian Maria Di Nocera, Alessandro Guidi, and Andrea Zifferero, *Rivista di storia dell'agricoltura*, 2016.1/2: 159–77

Modena 1988 = *Modena dalle origini all'anno Mille: studi di archeologia e storia*, 2 vols (Modena: Panini)

Moricca, Claudia, Laurent Bouby, Vincent Bonhomme, Sarah Ivorra, Guillem Pérez-Jordà, Lorenzo Nigro, Federica Spagnoli, Leonor Peña-Chocarro, Peter van Dommelen, and Laura Sadori. 2021. 'Grapes and Vines of the Phoenicians: Morphometric Analyses of Pips from Modern Varieties and Iron Age Archaeological Sites in the Western Mediterranean', *Journal of Archaeological Science: Reports*, 37: 102991

Murray, Oswin, and Manuela Tecuşan (eds). 1995. *In vino veritas* (London: British School at Rome)

Naso, Alessandro, and Massimo Botto (eds). 2018. *Caere orientalizzante: nuove ricerche su città e necropoli* (Rome: Quasar)

Neri, Diana. 2012. *Gli Etruschi tra VIII e VII secolo a.C. nel territorio di Castelfranco Emilia (MO)* (Florence: Edizioni All'Insegna del Giglio)

Neri, Sara. 2010. *Il tornio e il pennello: ceramica depurata di tradizione geometrica di epoca orientalizzante in Etruria meridionale* (Rome: Officina edizioni)

Ortalli, Jacopo. 1995. 'Bonifiche e regolamentazioni idriche nella pianura emiliana tra l'età del ferro e la tarda antichità', in *Interventi di bonifica agraria nell'Italia romana*, ed. by Lorenzo Quilici and Stefania Quilici Gigli, Atlante tematico di topografia antica, 4 (Rome: L'Erma di Bretschneider), pp. 59–86

Pecci, Alessandra. 2012. 'Potenzialità delle analisi chimiche applicate all'archeologia dei consumi alimentari: il bilancio delle conoscenze', in *Archeologia della vite e del vino in Toscana e nel Lazio: dalle tecniche dell'indagine archeologica alle prospettive della biologia molecolare*, ed. by Andrea Ciacci, Paola Rendini, and Andrea Zifferero (Florence: Edizioni All'Insegna del Giglio), pp. 153–63

Pepe, Carla. 2016. 'Giare da trasporto e ceramiche d'importazione da Vivara: contenuti e provenienze', *Scienze dell'antichità*, 22.2: 149–60

Rathje, Annette. 1983. 'A Banquet Service from the Latin City of Ficana', *Analecta Romana*, 12: 7–31

——. 2013. 'The Banquet through Etruscan History', in *The Etruscan World*, ed. by Jean MacIntosh Turfa (London: Routledge), pp. 823–40

Ravenna 2007 = Daniele Vitali (ed.), *Le fornaci e le anfore di Albinia: primi dati su produzioni e scambi dalla costa tirrenica al mondo gallico; atti del seminario internazionale, Ravenna, 6–7 maggio 2006* (Bologna: Bologna University Press)

Rendeli, Marco. 1993. *Città aperte: ambiente e paesaggio rurale organizzato nell'Etruria meridionale costiera durante l'età orientalizzante e arcaica* (Rome: Gruppo editoriale internazionale)

Rizzo, Maria Antonietta. 1990. *Le anfore da trasporto e il commercio etrusco arcaico*, I: *Complessi tombali dall'Etruria Meridionale* (Rome: De Luca)

——. 2015. *Principi etruschi: le tombe orientalizzanti di San Paolo a Cerveteri, Bollettino d'Arte*, special volume

Rojo Muñoz, Sara. 2021. 'Il vino etrusco: una concorrenza tra *grand crus?', Archeo: attualità del passato*, 439: 20–22

Ruta Serafini, Angela (ed.). 2002. *Este preromana: una città e i suoi santuari* (Treviso: Canova)

Sassatelli, Giuseppe. 2010. 'Bologna etrusca e la sua espansione nel territorio tra Reno e Panaro', in *Cavalieri etruschi dalle valli al Po: Tra Reno e Panaro, la valle del Samoggia nell'VIII e VII secolo a.C.*, ed. by Rita Burgio, Sara Campagnari, and Luigi Malnati (Bologna: Aspasia), pp. 27–36

Sassatelli, Giuseppe, and Roberto Macellari. 2002. 'Perugia, gli Umbri e la Val Padana', *Annali della fondazione per il Museo Claudio Faina*, 9: 407–34

Scali, Monica, Andrea Zifferero, and Rita Vignani. 2018. 'Distribution and Characterization of the *Vitis vinifera* L. subsp. *sylvestris* in Southern Tuscany', *Recent Patents on Biotechnology*, 12: 208–20

Scansano 2011 = Marco Firmati, Paola Rendini, and Andrea Zifferero (eds). 2011. *La valle del vino etrusco: archeologia della valle dell'Albegna in età arcaica* (Arcidosso: Effigi)

Scienza, Attilio. 2004. 'Il terzo anello: storia di un viaggio', in *La vite e l'uomo: dal rompicapo delle origini al salvataggio delle reliquie; evidenze storico-ampelografiche per ripercorrere il viaggio della vite da Oriente alle soglie dell'Occidente*, ed. by Francesco Del Zan, Osvaldo Failla, and Attilio Scienza (Gorizia: ERSA), pp. 99–148

Scienza, Attilio (ed.). 2006a. *Vitigni tradizionali ed antichi italiani: la storia, il paesaggio, la ricerca* (Siena: Ci.Vin.)

——. 2006b. *Oseleta, paradigma della viticoltura delle Venezie: analisi storico-ampelografica e risultati sperimentali* (Verona: Gruppo Tecnico Masi)

——. 2007. 'Origine e storia', in *La vite e il vino* (Bologna: ART Servizi Editoriali spa), pp. 47–87

——. 2010. 'L'origine dei vitigni coltivati: una storia interdisciplinare della cultura europea', in *'Vinum nostrum': Arte, scienza e miti del vino nelle civiltà del Mediterraneo antico*, ed. by Giovanni Di Pasquale (Florence: Giunti), pp. 24–31

——. 2013. 'Sangiovese: l'inganno delle origini', in *Il romanzo del Sangiovese*, ed. by Andrea Zanfi (Colle di Val d'Elsa: SeB Editori), pp. 10–13

Scienza, Attilio, and Osvaldo Failla. 1996. 'La circolazione dei vitigni in ambito padano-veneto ed atesino: le fonti storico-letterarie e l'approccio biologico-molecolare', in *2500 anni di cultura della vite nell'ambito alpino e cisalpino*, ed. by Gaetano Forni and Attilio Scienza (Trento: Cassa Rurale di Villazzano e Trento), pp. 185–268

Scienza, Attilio, Osvaldo Failla, Filippo Geuna, and Massimo Labra. 2000. 'Circolazione varietale antica in ambito adriatico', in *L'avventura del vino nel bacino del Mediterraneo: itinerari storici ed archeologici prima e dopo Roma*, ed. by Diego Tomasi and Chiara Cremonesi (Treviso: Istituto sperimentale per la viticoltura), pp. 185–95

Scienza, Attilio, and Osvaldo Failla. 2016. 'La circolazione varietale della vite nel Mediterraneo: lo stato della ricerca', in *ArcheoTipico: l'archeologia come strumento per la ricostruzione del paesaggio e dell'alimentazione antica; atti del Convegno (Viterbo 2015)*, ed. by Gian Maria Di Nocera, Alessandro Guidi, and Andrea Zifferero, *Rivista di storia dell'agricoltura*, 2016.1/2: 31–47

Scienza, Attilio, and Serena Imazio. 2018. *La stirpe del vino* (Milan: Sperling & Kupfer)

Sculli, Orlando. 2004. *I vitigni autoctoni della Locride* (Soveria Mannelli: Città Calabria editore)

Sereni, Emilio. 1964. 'Per la storia delle più antiche tecniche e della nomenclatura della vite e del vino in Italia', *Atti e memorie dell'Accademia toscana di scienze e lettere 'La Colombaria'*, 29: 75–204

——. 1987. *Storia del paesaggio agrario italiano* (Rome: Laterza)

Sourisseau, Jean-Christophe. 2011. 'La diffusion des vins grecs d'Occident du VIIIe au IVe s. av. J.-C., sources écrites et documents archéologiques', in *La vigna di Dioniso: vite, vino e culti in Magna Grecia* (Taranto: Istituto per la storia e l'archeologia della Magna Grecia), pp. 143–252

Tecchiati, Umberto, and Gianni Rizzi. 2014. 'La "Casa delle botti e delle ruote": scavo di un edificio incendiato del V sec. a.C. nella piana di Rosslauf a Bressanone (BZ)', in *Antichi popoli delle Alpi: sviluppi culturali durante l'età del Ferro nei territori alpini centro-orientali; Atti della giornata di studi internazionale, 1 maggio 2010, Sanzeno, Trento*, ed. by Rosa Roncador and Franco Nicolis (Trento: Provincia Autonoma di Trento), pp. 73–103

Ten Kortenaar, Silvia. 2011. *Il colore e la materia: tra tradizione e innovazione nella produzione dell'impasto rosso nell'Italia medio-tirrenica* (Rome: Officina edizioni)

Tomasi, Diego, and Chiara Cremonesi (eds). 2000. *L'avventura del vino nel bacino del Mediterraneo: itinerari storici ed archeologici prima e dopo Roma* (Treviso: Istituto sperimentale per la viticoltura)

Torelli, Mario. 2000. 'Primi appunti per un'antropologia del vino degli Etruschi', in *L'avventura del vino nel bacino del Mediterraneo: itinerari storici ed archeologici prima e dopo Roma*, ed. by Diego Tomasi and Chiara Cremonesi (Treviso: Istituto sperimentale per la viticoltura), pp. 89–100

Viglietti, Cristiano. 2011. *Il limite del bisogno: antropologia economica di Roma arcaica* (Bologna: Il Mulino)

Vignani, Rita, Elisa Paolucci, Monica Scali, Jacopo Bigliazzi, Mauro Cresti, and Valerio Zorzi. 2012. 'Il "Progetto ArcheoVino": caratteri e genoma della vite silvestre in Maremma', in *Archeologia della vite e del vino in Toscana e nel Lazio: dalle tecniche dell'indagine archeologica alle prospettive della biologia molecolare*, ed. by Andrea Ciacci, Paola Rendini, and Andrea Zifferero (Florence: Edizioni All'Insegna del Giglio), pp. 653–62

Villing, Alexandra. 2021. 'Spicing Wine at the Symposion: Fact or Fiction? Some Critical Thoughts on Material Aspects of Commensality in the Early Iron Age and Archaic Mediterranean World', *The Journal of Hellenic Studies*, 141: 1–30

Vouillamoz, José F., Antonella Monaco, Laura Costantini, Marco Stefanini, Attilio Scienza, and Maria Stella Grando. 2007. 'The Parentage of "Sangiovese", the Most Important Italian Wine Grape', *Vitis*, 46: 19–22

Vouillamoz, José F., Antonella Monaco, Laura Costantini, Jessica Zambanini, Marco Stefanini, Attilio Scienza, and Maria Stella Grando. 2008. 'Il Sangiovese è per metà figlio del Calabrese di Montenuovo', *L'Informatore Agrario*, 5: 59–62

Zifferero, Andrea. 2005a. 'La produzione e il commercio del vino in Etruria', in *Vinum: un progetto per il riconoscimento della vite silvestre nel paesaggio archeologico della Toscana e del Lazio settentrionale*, ed. by Ciacci, Andrea, and Andrea Zifferero (Siena: Ci.Vin.), pp. 97–120

——. 2005b. 'La formazione del tessuto rurale nell'agro cerite: una proposta di lettura', in *Dinamiche di sviluppo delle città nell'Etruria meridionale: Veio, Caere, Tarquinia, Vulci; Atti del XXIII Convegno di studi etruschi ed italici, Roma, Veio, Cerveteri/Pyrgi, Tarquinia, Tuscania, Vulci, Viterbo, 1–6 ottobre 2001* (Pisa: Istituti editoriali e poligrafici internazionali), pp. 257–72

——. 2016. 'Archeologia e circolazione varietale: prospettive di ricerca e valorizzazione del paesaggio agrario in Italia centrale', in *ArcheoTipico: l'archeologia come strumento per la ricostruzione del paesaggio e dell'alimentazione antica; Atti del Convegno (Viterbo 2015)*, ed. by Gian Maria Di Nocera, Alessandro Guidi, and Andrea Zifferero, *Rivista di storia dell'agricoltura*, 2016.1/2: 13–30

——. 2017a. 'Le attività artigianali nel territorio vulcente: la Valle dell'Albegna e Marsiliana', in *Gli artigiani e la città, Officine e aree produttive tra VIII e III sec. a.C. nell'Italia centrale tirrenica: atti della giornata di studi, British School at Rome, 11 gennaio 2016*, ed. by Maria Cristina Biella, Roberta Cascino, Antonio Francesco Ferrandes, and Martina Revello Lami, *Scienze dell'antichità*, 23.2: 311–29

——. 2017b. 'Il paesaggio del vino a *Mutina*: circolazione varietale, produzione e consumo', in *'Mutina splendidissima': la città romana e la sua eredità*, ed. by Luigi Malnati, Silvia Pellegrini, Francesca Piccinini, and Cristina Stefani (Rome: De Luca), pp. 275–84

SARAH WHITCHER KANSA

2. Butchery, Meat Distribution, and Ritual Dining in Etruscan Poggio Civitate (Murlo)

Introduction

Faunal remains from archaeological sites can be classified and described in several dimensions, including biological taxonomy, anatomy, and fragmentation, among many other attributes. Documentation and interpretation of these attributes enables zooarchaeological analysis to provide a rich source of evidence in the exploration of economic, social, and symbolic practices in ancient societies. As demonstrated in this paper, even observations of anatomical siding in bone specimens may reveal patterns that relate to ancient ritualized behaviours.

Side preferencing is not typically reported from first-millennium BCE habitation contexts in the Mediterranean. Although assigning specific animal parts and sides is well attested in ancient Greek and Roman sacrificial contexts, side preference has not been observed in non-sacrificial contexts (Ekroth 2007). Side preference also has not been noted in Etruscan contexts, despite Etruria's long participation and integration in wider Mediterranean cultural developments. Given the proximity of the Etruscan world to ancient Greek and Roman practices, it would not be surprising to see this binary. Much of what we know about Etruscan ritual behaviour comes from funerary and sanctuary contexts, which provide abundant evidence for rituals, but which are often focused on elites and only

reflect behaviours related to death and deposition. This study explores a rare case of side selection observed in a comparison of elite and non-elite contexts at an Etruscan habitation site. The site of Poggio Civitate (Murlo) in central Tuscany provides an opportunity to explore a settlement which includes both elite and non-elite inhabitants living together at the site from the eighth–sixth centuries BCE. We observed a marked difference in the relative proportions of right- and left-sided elements in the elite and non-elite areas. We use this evidence to explore how animals contributed to the preparation and execution of ritual meals among the site's elite inhabitants to mark and advance their social standing.

Background

A preference for right-sided animal portions, especially sheep and goats, for sacrifice to gods and heroes is well documented in the ancient Mediterranean world, through texts and to a lesser extent through faunal remains excavated at archaeological sites. Examples include Davis's (2008) observations on fauna at the archaic (eighth–sixth century BCE) Temple of Apollo (Kourion, Cyprus), where he found a clear preference for right-sided elements. In discussing

Sarah Whitcher Kansa Executive Director, The Alexandria Archive Institute (Open Context) (skansa@berkeley.edu)

Consumption, Ritual, Art and Society: Interpretive Approaches and Recent Discoveries of Food and Drink in Etruria, ed. by Lisa Pieraccini and Laurel Taylor, NAA, 2 (Turnhout, 2023), pp. 41–56   BREPOLS ❦ PUBLISHERS   10.1484/M.NAA-EB.5.132804

the dominance of right-sided portions in a temple context at Iron Age Zincirli (Turkey), Hermann notes:

> In the eastern Mediterranean, the right side of the animal, and particularly the right fore- or hind limb, was often considered the portion suitable for offering to the gods and consumption by the priests, leaving the left side to be consumed by lay people. This is attested both in the Old Testament [...] and in contemporary Iron Age archaeological remains from Israel, Greece, and Cyprus. (Hermann 2014, 55)

MacKinnon (2013, 140) provides an overview of cases from ancient Greek contexts where this is the case, and also highlights particular exceptions, such as Nemea, where left-sided elements were preferred and appear to have been at least partly associated with underworld deities. Similarly, Rask (2014) found among sacrificial assemblages in Europe that right-sided elements of the shoulder and forelimb appear to have been preferentially selected over left-sided elements in sacrificial assemblages. These side preferences in sacrificial contexts can be seen as reflecting a duality where 'right side normally equals positive qualities: heavenly, good, sacred' (MacKinnon 2013, 140). This can be seen as related to right-handed dominance in humans, which has led to social and religious constructs favouring the right side (Rask 2014, 251), including in language, where 'sinister' comes from the Latin word meaning 'on the left side'. In discussing how zooarchaeology can provide evidence for this distinction, Rask (2014, 251) points out:

> Presumably, either side carries equal importance if the cultural focus is strictly upon the animal as a meat-producing, symmetrical organism. However, if a greater emphasis is placed on the symbolic nature of right and left as good and bad, respectively, deliberate side selection may transpire.

The Greeks and Romans alike appear to have had beliefs that the right/left duality extended to good/evil, god/mortal, and sacred/profane. A side preference is found in Roman beliefs but has not been observed in zooarchaeological remains (MacKinnon 2010). Sorrentino (1989) points to a predominance of 'lean' forelimb bones in Roman burials and highlights the key role pigs played as Roman funerary offerings but does not observe a side preference.

Animals were used in sacrifice and ritual in the Etruscan period, and there is evidence from funerary and sanctuary contexts for whole animals or animal parts being used in sacrifice and various other ritual and religious behaviours. A range of species documented at Etruscan sanctuaries may relate to the deity being honoured, including sheep, goats, pigs (and piglets), chickens, and cattle, but also dogs and a variety of wild animals such as deer, foxes, and tortoises (Rask 2014; Rafanelli 2013). However, faunal studies from this period do not report a side preference in sacrifice and ritual. As the left/right duality was a key part of both Greek and Roman belief systems, we can expect it to have also been a part of the Etruscan world-view, though it may not be as apparent given the lack of Etruscan textual sources. Furthermore, if this duality did exist, can we extend it beyond its use in sacrifices to gods and heroes and see it as pertaining also to differences such as elite/common and rich/poor?

In Etruria, much of what we know about ritual comes from funerary contexts, which have better preservation (such as of paintings and artefacts) than habitation sites. A key problem is that this evidence leads us to consider ritual only for elites — those who were interred in the elaborate funerary contexts. This also pushes us to consider ritual only in the context of death. This study explores ritual behaviours in the context of the *living* and attempts to extend the right/left duality beyond sacrificial settings and into ritual meals carried out by Etruscan elites at Poggio Civitate. Drawing on faunal analyses

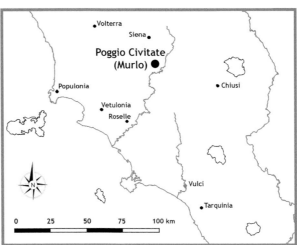

Figure 2.1. Map of Tuscany showing the location of Poggio Civitate and other major Etruscan settlements. Kansa and Tuck 2021.

from two distinct areas that can be seen as related to elites and non-elites, this study explores how particular meat cuts may have been used in ritualized meals to regularly reaffirm the status of the elites at the site.

Defining Ritual

Ritual is difficult to both define and recognize in the archaeological record. In this study, I follow Chaix's (2003) definition of ritual as rule-governed and consistently replicated over time. I add that ritual is not necessarily related to religious practices or beliefs about divinity or the supernatural. Brushing one's teeth twice a day can be seen as a ritual. Butchering an animal carcass following a series of steps is also a ritual. Thus, ritual can be seen as informing and shaping daily practice (Russell 2011, 53). In zooarchaeology, this means that we should not only look at 'special' deposits from discrete events (such as a complete animal sacrificed and included in a burial context) as evidence of ritual practices, but we need to expand this to consider how rule-governed, repeated practices over long periods of time would be reflected in the zooarchaeological record.

Discerning rituals in the zooarchaeological record is particularly challenging at a habitation site, where various activities involving many people over time create refuse that builds up and obscures discrete practices. It may be impossible to identify frequent rituals such as daily meals because the remains of these activities form the broad patterns we observe in the faunal remains across a site, especially if depositional and post-depositional processes muddle assemblages. However, we may have some hope in distinguishing ritual behaviours by comparing faunal assemblages between areas of a site inhabited by different groups of people. We are fortunate at Poggio Civitate to have two such distinct areas where several lines of evidence have pointed to elite and non-elite activity. As a habitation site, Poggio Civitate provides a different perspective than that provided by funerary archaeological remains — that of a living settlement with the remains of repeated practices of butchery, meat distribution, and meals consumed in different functional areas of the site. This invites us to investigate not only the nature of ritual meals but also their location and participants, to explore the 'consumption scapes' (Kistler 2017, 195) of these ritual behaviours that have left traces in the archaeological record.

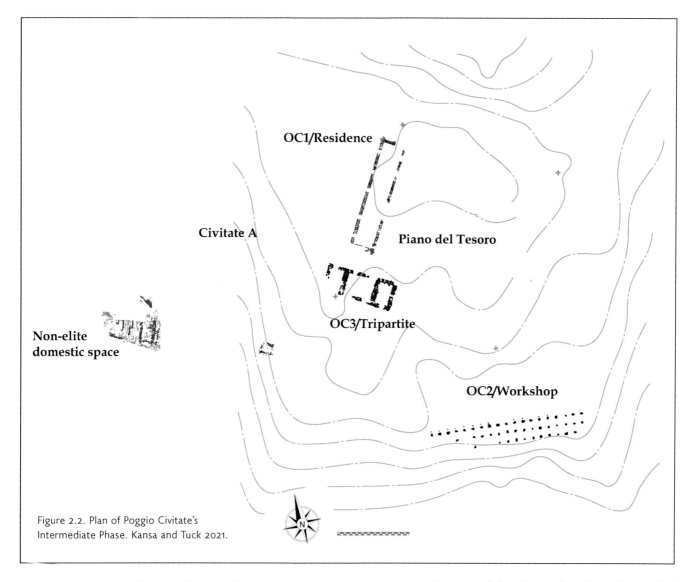

Figure 2.2. Plan of Poggio Civitate's Intermediate Phase. Kansa and Tuck 2021.

Elite and Non-elite Spaces at Poggio Civitate

Poggio Civitate is located approximately 25 km south of the modern city of Siena, Italy (Fig. 2.1). Inhabited from the late eighth to the end of the sixth centuries BCE, Poggio Civitate is a rare example of an Etruscan settlement with a co-occurrence of elite and non-elite occupation. The site experienced three major phases of monumental building and development before it was suddenly wiped out in the final years of the sixth century BCE. The site's near-abandonment at that point left a clear archaeological record of the intermediate phase of development (Tuck 2017). The intermediate phase (Orientalizing period) dates from approximately 675–550 BCE to the end of the seventh or beginning of the sixth century BCE (Nielsen and Tuck 2001). It consisted of three monumental structures on a plateau (Piano del Tesoro) that represented different aspects of elite obligation and behaviour (Fig. 2.2). Orientalizing Complex Building 1/Residence (OC1/Residence) served as the domicile for the community's elite family, preserving evidence of imported and locally manufactured luxury items as well as a range of cooking wares and banquet equipment. The total volume of banqueting equipment recovered from the building's environs, including bronze vessels, imported Greek wares, and local fine wares, as well as humbler ceramic types, could have easily accommodated dozens of participants (see discussion in Berkin 2003, 119–26), suggesting that one feature of life at Poggio Civitate involved the community's elite family providing for and engaging in communal banqueting (Tuck 2021). Immediately adjacent to the south and perpendicular to the OC1/Residence was a structure with a tripartite division of interior space, Orientalizing Complex Building 3/Tripartite (OC3/Tripartite). While this building was not as well preserved as the OC1/Residence, materials collected from its preserved floor surface along with its overall architectural design suggest it served as a religious structure or was an early form of temple (Nielsen and Tuck 2001). Recent zooarchaeological analysis on the faunal remains from this building identified among the remains a shed milk tooth from an equid (Kansa and MacKinnon 2014), suggesting that the building or its immediate surroundings may have served as a stable at some point, possibly for the horses associated with elite hunting. Finally, positioned along the southern edge of the Piano del Tesoro was Orientalizing Complex Building 2/Workshop (OC2/Workshop). This structure housed various manufacturing spaces, including the production of architectural roofing materials, small-scale bronze casting, ceramic production, fibre processing and weaving, as well as the processing of animals for food and other products (Tuck 2014).

Five decades of excavations at the site have produced an abundance of material cultural and faunal remains. Spatial differences observed across the site in the species represented and their distribution in the elite and non-elite areas have been the focus of ongoing study (Kansa and Tuck 2023). Such differences are evident among other material types, as well, such as the occurrence of spindle-whorls of different sizes that suggest different types of weaving activities took place in the elite and non-elite areas (Tuck 2021, fig. 11.8).

The Zooarchaeological Assemblage

Since 2012, the author has undertaken a systematic analysis of faunal remains from more than fifty years of excavation since the mid-1960s at Poggio Civitate. Analysis is ongoing and the current analysed assemblage includes more than fourteen thousand specimens, making it one of the largest Etruscan animal bone assemblages analysed to date and comparable to the assemblage from the slightly later (sixth–fourth century) Etruscan city at Forcello at the northernmost extent of Etruscan civilization (Trentacoste 2014). All data are published and available open access in the Murlo project database in Open Context (Tuck 2012).[1]

Ongoing zooarchaeological analysis at Poggio Civitate follows methods detailed in Kansa and MacKinnon (2014). Recorded specimens include those that could be identified to skeletal element and taxon (such as genus or species). Ribs and vertebrae were recorded but only to a size category (such as 'large mammal'). Fragments that could not be identified to element and taxon were counted and recorded in groups according to fragment size (i.e., 'Less than 5 cm'). Every identified specimen includes context information, a unique bone number, and observations on taxon, element, side, fragmentation, skeletal area, sex, age, cut marks, gnaw marks, pathologies, burning, and measurements. All results presented here are based on a slightly modified count of the number of identified specimens (NISP), where each specimen is counted as representing one individual except in cases

---

1 <https://opencontext.org/projects/DF043419-F23B-41DA-7E4D-EE52AF22F92F> [accessed 10 January 2023].

Table 2.1. Relative occurrence and number of individual specimens (showing percentage and NISP counts with articulating and pairing specimens removed) by taxon in the OC1/Residence and the OC2/Workshop, compared to all specimens identified across the remainder of the faunal assemblage (which are largely from non-elite contexts).

Taxon	OC1/Residence	OC2/Workshop	*Other Areas*
Cattle (*Bos taurus*)	30.6% (550)	19.0% (339)	*16.6% (1085)*
Sheep or Goat (*Ovis aries / Capra hircus*)	21.7% (389)	25.8% (460)	*26.7% (1748)*
Pig (*Sus scrofa dom.*)	35.4% (636)	45.1% (805)	*46.8% (3065)*
Dog (*Canis familiaris*)	2.2% (40)	2.7% (48)	*2.2% (145)*
Equid (*Equus* sp.)	0.9% (17)	1.2% (21)	*0.4% (29)*
Red deer (*Cervus elaphus*)	4.8% (87)	2.6% (47)	*1.8% (118)*
Roe deer (*Capreolus capreolus*)	0.3% (6)	0.1% (1)	*0.1% (7)*
Boar (*Sus scrofa*)	2.5% (45)	1.3% (23)	*1.8% (116)*
Fox (*Vulpes vulpes*)	0.1% (2)	0.3% (5)	*0.2% (11)*
Hare (*Lepus* spp.)	0.2% (4)	0.2% (4)	*0.5% (36)*
Wolf (*Canis lupus*)	0.1% (1)	-	*0.02% (1)*
Cat (*Felis* spp.)	-	0.1% (2)	*0.1% (5)*
Badger (*Meles meles*)	0.1% (2)	-	*0.03% (2)*
Bear (*Ursus arctos*)	0.1% (1)	-	-
Beaver (*Castor fiber*)	-	-	*0.02% (1)*
Goat, wild (*Capra* spp.)	-	-	*0.03% (2)*
Cattle, wild (*Bos primigenius*)	0.1% (1)	-	-
Rodent	0.2% (3)	0.1% (1)	*0.1% (7)*
Bird	0.4% (7)	1.3% (23)	*1.7% (114)*
Tortoise/Turtle	0.2% (4)	0.4% (7)	*0.8% (54)*
Fish	-	-	*0.1% (4)*
Total NISP	**1795**	**1786**	***6550***
Total domestic mammals	91% (1632)	95% (1673)	*95% (6072)*
Total wild mammals	9% (152)	5% (83)	*5% (306)*

where specimens clearly articulated or were paired (left- and right-sided elements likely from the same individual). In those cases, the specimens were recorded separately but counted together as a single individual (NISP=1) to avoid intentional over-quantification. This method was undertaken on a context-specific level; that is, no attempt was made to pair or articulate bones from different contexts.

Because excavations have occurred at Poggio Civitate for many decades and involved different teams, it is to be expected that excavation strategies would not be consistent. In an entirely hand-collected assemblage like this, a particular concern for the faunal remains is differential collection of bones, where large or 'interesting' bones might be collected more often than small or broken bones. This could result in an overrepresentation of large animals such as cattle and deer. To address this possible collection bias, Kansa and MacKinnon (2014) performed some simple tests and found that fragment size did not change significantly over time; that is, there is a similar proportion of very small fragments to larger fragments and complete bones in all excavation areas. They also found that about 35 per cent of the assemblage is made up of non-identifiable fragments from all areas across all decades. These indications of relatively consistent collection practices over time and space increase our confidence of being able to compare the faunal assemblages recovered in different areas of the site by different teams over the years.

The majority of the faunal remains from all areas of Poggio Civitate analysed to date (Table 2.1) comes from domestic pigs (*Sus scrofa domesticus*), sheep (*Ovis aries*), and cattle (*Bos taurus*). These are common domestic animals kept for a wide range of additional products such as milk, wool, labour, and dung while alive and, at later point, slaughtered for meat, hides, grease, sinews, and bones for tool-making and other products. Sheep were herded locally and exploited for wool (Trentacoste and others 2020; Gleba 2007), while beef from prime-age cattle may have contributed to occasional feasts (Kansa and MacKinnon 2014). Wild animals, which make up less than 10 per cent of the total assemblage, would have been hunted or trapped for sport or industrial activities. Although their overall numbers are low, there is a marked difference in wild taxa in different areas; namely, the relative proportion of large wild mammals from the OC1/Residence is nearly twice that from the OC2/Workshop, which not only has fewer large wild mammals but also the majority of all bird bones found across the site. Ongoing research explores the role of wild animals in elite hunting and trophy display (Kansa and Tuck 2023) and the industrial uses of animal products in different areas of the site. Analysis and visualization of the artefacts and ecofacts recovered at Poggio Civitate, including the research presented here, point to evidence for elite activities like hunting and banqueting associated with the OC1/Residence, while the OC2/Workshop was a place where more mundane industrial activities took place.

Zooarchaeological data for the current analysis are associated with the OC1/Residence and OC2/Workshop contexts (Fig. 2.2). The OC1/Residence trenches include those located both within the area of the OC1/Residence as well as along the northern flank of the plateau where debris from the building was placed prior to the construction of the subsequent (archaic) phase of construction in an attempt to level the area. The OC2/Workshop data include the trenches that encompass the floor area of the workshop building as well as areas immediately to the north and south of the structure where debris associated with the daily industrial activities was recovered. The area to the north of the OC2/Workshop appears to have been an open, flat area where manufacturing practices occurred in conjunction with the workshop space, while the area to its south was where materials appear to have washed downhill after the OC2/Workshop's destruction. While animal remains included in this study are recovered from all these areas, high concentrations are found both immediately north of the OC2/Workshop and to the immediate north-east of the OC1/Residence, perhaps indicating these areas were used for refuse associated with activities housed in the structures. These together make up approximately 3500 of the specimens identified to at least the genus level (Table 2.1).

All trenches were georeferenced by Taylor Oshan during the 2014–2018 field seasons and spatial data were linked to the project database so that individual faunal specimens can be visualized in a map interface on Open Context. The current discussion uses Open Context's mapping tools to explore spatial differences in the faunal remains between the OC1/Residence and the OC2/Workshop.

Figure 2.3. An example of a split vertebra from Poggio Civitate, showing division of the carcass into left and right sides as one stage of the butchery process. Image credit: Anthony Tuck 'Photo B of Bone PC-07797 from Italy/Poggio Civitate/Tesoro North Flank/Tesoro North Flank 1/2003, ID: 498/Locus 2/PC-07797' (2017). In *Murlo*. Anthony Tuck (ed.), Open Context: <http://opencontext.org/media/93a42a7c-4de1-4f06-b307-53c124c6a68f> [accessed 10 January 2023].

Evidence for Carcass Splitting and Side Selection

This study reports on 706 specimens from the OC1/Residence and 907 specimens from the OC2/Workshop representing the main skeletal elements that could be sided and that came from cattle, sheep/goat, or pigs (Table 2.2). Of these, forty-three specimens show indications of burning, representing 2 per cent of the OC1/Residence specimens and 3 per cent of the OC2/Workshop specimens. A greater proportion (14 per cent or 105 specimens) of bones from the OC1/Residence have cut marks than observed among the specimens from the OC2/Workshop (9 per cent or sixty-nine specimens). Only 2 per cent of the specimens from both areas show evidence of gnawing, suggesting little disturbance from scavengers and rodents. Fragmentation is about equal across both areas, with roughly the same proportions of small fragments as larger and complete bones. Among the common domestic food mammals, the OC1/Residence has a predominance of specimens identified as coming from females (twenty-one females vs. eight males), while the OC2/Workshop has a balance of sexes, with eight females and six males. Females are more valuable animals because they are kept for breeding, so a higher proportion of them in the food refuse in the OC1/Residence may indicate 'costly signalling' associated with elite status displays.

The broader Poggio Civitate faunal assemblage reveals strong evidence for a regular practice of splitting animal carcasses into left and right portions as part of the butchery process. Vertebrae are regularly chopped cleanly through (Fig. 2.3), representing a lengthwise split down the carcass. Cut marks were observed on nearly 20 per cent of the 1224 vertebrae in the full assemblage, and most reflect splitting in this manner. Thus, we have direct evidence for left and right carcass portions, which would have been further divided in the butchery process into meat cuts.

Among the elements that could be sided, left and right elements occur in both the OC1/Residence and the OC2/Workshop (Table 2.2). Most elements show only slight differences in the occurrence of left and right sides. However, the ulna stands out as having a strong statistically significant difference particularly for sheep/goat but also for pigs (Table 2.3 and Figs 2.4–2.5) and to a lesser extent cattle though the cattle numbers are too small to be reliable. Right-sided ulnae occur in both the OC1/Residence and the OC2/Workshop, but there are fewer in the OC2/Workshop. In the case of left-sided ulnae, there are far fewer in the OC1/Residence than the OC2/Workshop. In the case of sheep, left-sided ulnae are nearly absent in the OC1/Residence and right-sided ulnae are nearly absent in the OC2/Workshop. Thus, the data suggest that, at least in the case of this one skeletal element, the left side was avoided by the inhabitants of the OC1/Residence.

In sheep and pigs, the portion of meat that contains the ulna is the fore shank. The ulna in this joint is tightly grouped with the distal humerus and the proximal radius, making up the elbow joint. In Tuscan restaurants today, this portion or lamb or pork (*stinco di agnello/maiale*) can be found on most menus. In the case of lamb, one shank weighs one half to one pound, which would serve one person generously. Thus, this is

Table 2.2. Count of elements from the primary domestic taxa that could be identified to left or right side from the OC1/Residence (n = 706; data source: <https://n2t.net/ark:/28722/k2pc3dm0s>) and the OC2/Workshop (n = 907; data source: <https://n2t.net/ark:/28722/k2jq1d57s>).

Element	Cattle		Pig		Sheep/Goat	
	OC1/ Residence	OC2/ Workshop	OC1/ Residence	OC2/ Workshop	OC1/ Residence	OC2/ Workshop
Scapula						
Left	2	2	22	29	6	6
Right	6	3	18	22	5	17
Humerus						
Left	7	1	42	33	18	32
Right	4	5	44	40	17	28
Radius						
Left	4	6	17	29	27	30
Right	9	8	13	24	25	41
Ulna						
Left	6	5	17	45	3	13
Right	5	1	28	32	13	3
Carpal						
Left	3	7	2	5	2	5
Right	6	7	0	4	6	2
Pelvis						
Left	10	10	17	22	15	19
Right	3	6	19	20	9	18
Femur						
Left	2	2	12	9	7	11
Right	2	5	9	9	3	14
Tibia						
Left	4	8	27	30	20	30
Right	6	3	25	29	19	40
Astragalus						
Left	11	11	7	16	8	10
Right	10	14	12	7	10	13
Calcaneus						
Left	5	3	11	19	9	8
Right	11	7	16	15	10	14
TOTAL	**116**	**114**	**358**	**439**	**232**	**354**

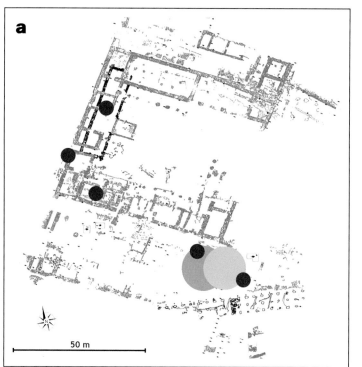
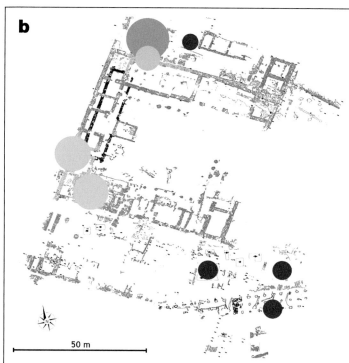

Figure 2.4. Heat map of Poggio Civitate, showing the occurrence of sheep/goat left-sided ulnae (a) and right-sided ulnae (b) in the OC1/Residence and OC2/Workshop. Figure by author.

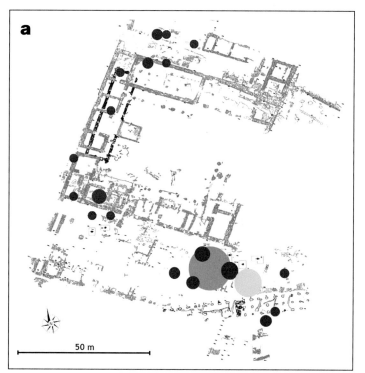
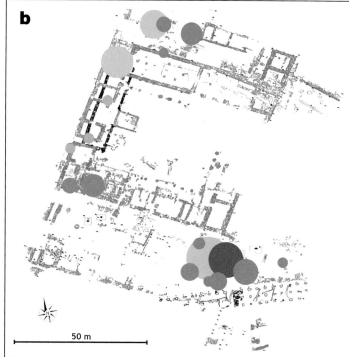

Figure 2.5. Heat map of Poggio Civitate, showing the occurrence of pig left-sided ulnae (a) and right-sided ulnae (b) in the OC1/Residence and OC2/Workshop. Figure by author.

Table 2.3. Chi-square tests on left and right ulnae for sheep/goat and pigs in the OC1/Residence and the OC2/Workshop at Poggio Civitate. An alpha level of 0.05 was used for both tests.

Sheep/Goat Ulna Counts			
Actual	Left	Right	Total
OC1/Residence	3	13	16
OC2/Workshop	13	3	16
	16	16	32
Expected	Left	Right	Total
OC1/Residence	8	8	16
OC2/Workshop	8	8	16
	16	16	32
$p < 0.001$			
Pig Ulna Counts			
Actual	Left	Right	Total
OC1/Residence	17	28	45
OC2/Workshop	45	32	77
	62	60	122
Expected	Left	Right	Total
OC1/Residence	23	22	45
OC2/Workshop	39	38	77
	62	60	122
$p < 0.03$			

a portion of meat that reflects an individual meal rather than a large-scale feast. Interestingly, we do not see the same left-right patterning that we see in the ulna in the other elements that would be clustered in this meat portion (the distal humerus and proximal radius). There is no clear explanation for why this pattern emerges only in the ulnae, unless ulnae were removed from their tight grouping with the radius and humerus and used for some unknown purpose beyond food.

Ritual Dining at Poggio Civitate

Ritual meals were just one of the ways that the elites set themselves apart (and/or were set apart by others) at Poggio Civitate. As excavations at Poggio Civitate continue, there is mounting evidence for the presence of an elite group

of people at the site. This is well attested in architectural remains, iconography, and ceramics from the OC1/Residence. In fact, Poggio Civitate boasts one of the few examples of a secular banquet, depicted in a series of archaic decorative frieze plaques from the (non-funerary) Archaic-period building that followed the OC1 and OC2 occupation. The activities depicted on the Murlo plaques which decorated the building may relate to the events that took place at the site, such as banqueting, processions, horse races, and assemblies (Rathje 2007; also see Tuck and Glennie 2020 for a detailed description and interpretation of the various scenes). That these activities are depicted on plaques suggests they occurred regularly and signalled the importance of a certain group of people, likely those associated with the building they adorned. Taylor (Chapter

3) highlights the private, exclusionary nature of diacritical feasts that reinforced elite social status in her discussion of the banqueting frieze plaques from Poggio Civitate.

More recently, faunal analysis has provided evidence for trophy hunting and more frequent consumption of beef from valuable prime-aged cows, suggesting large-scale feasts and ostentatious displays of wealth and wasteful consumption (Kansa and Tuck 2023). We can now also add evidence for smaller, frequent ritual meals featuring right-sided cuts of lamb and sometimes pork, also focusing on costly females of these species. These smaller ritual meals likely took place behind closed doors in the OC1/Residence, perhaps in a room adorned with hunting trophies, adding to their exclusivity.

This is not to say that non-elites did not consume this cut of meat. Indeed, we find ample evidence of the bones from the fore shank in the OC2/Workshop. The fact that we see no side distinction in meals associated with the OC2/Workshop suggests that the meat portions did not carry the same symbolic weight as they did in the OC1/Residence. The pattern observed in the OC1/Residence may reflect occasional ritualized meals, perhaps to mark a special occasion or visitor. The selected portion of meat may have had little to do with the actual nutritional value of the food and more with the cultural significance of certain food preferences or avoidances, body parts, or taxa, among a group of people (Bartosiewicz 1997).

It is notable that the OC1/Residence assemblage also has nearly double the relative proportion of cattle than the OC2/Workshop (Table 2.1), as well as a higher proportion of deer. The cattle bones are from prime-age animals, suggesting that more beef was processed and consumed in this elite area of the site than in other areas. The cattle ulnae showed a weak left-right pattern that matches that observed for sheep/goat and pigs. With a larger sample size, this pattern may become stronger. Alternatively, cattle may have

not been used in the same way as sheep and pigs because of their potential to provide a massive amount of meat ideal for a large-scale, collective banquet (Tuck 2021), while the shank portions were well suited to more intimate dining with small groups.

In his analysis of a faunal assemblage from a medieval-period high-status residence at Launceston Castle (England), Simon Davis argued that the choice of meat appeared to refer to a stratum of society:

> It was apparently customary in Medieval England for the aristocracy to be offered what was considered the choice part of the hunted animal — its haunch. Perhaps it was not a ritual in the conventional sense but something that might be called 'almost ritual' — homage paid to the nobility. (Davis 2008, 65)

Similarly, perhaps giving elites at Poggio Civitate a specific meat portion and side can be seen as an extension of special offerings that would be made to gods and heroes in Greek settings, where left portions would be avoided because of their negative associations.

The patterning we have observed here points to a ritualized practice of butchery and distribution, where it was seen as important to keep track of the animal side for certain cuts of meat. This raises the question of how butchery was carried out and who kept track of these particular portions. Assuming the discard of meal refuse occurred near the location of consumption, the abundance of right-sided portions and apparent avoidance of left-sided portions (especially in the case of sheep) in the OC1/Residence points to discreet meals taking place regularly in one location. A communal banquet involving beef would produce large amounts of refuse that might end up discarded in many locations if many people were involved in its consumption. In contrast, the small fore shank portions of sheep/goat and pigs observed here suggest private, elite meals that left a pattern in the refuse only at the OC1/Residence.

It is important to recognize that rituals, defined as practices that are rule-governed and consistently replicated over time, were not necessarily exclusive to the elites at Poggio Civitate. Certainly, common people had rituals beyond the funerary realm — rituals around seasonal activities, births, and marriages. While the current study provides evidence that points to ritual dining in the elite residence, similar practices may have also occurred in the non-elite contexts, but the evidence may be obscured by the nature of the refuse associated with that area. The many different kinds of economic activities that took place locally at Poggio Civitate would require a large number of people doing various kinds of work to support the site's elite residents. The refuse associated with the OC1/Residence, coming from a small population of people associated with that area, may therefore provide a more focused picture of the activities taking place in the OC1/Residence. The OC2/Workshop, in contrast, may reflect a more mixed deposit with refuse from many more people and diverse activities.

Finally, the inhabitants of Poggio Civitate certainly engaged in other ritual practices beyond meals, even if they are more difficult to identify at a large settlement site. When it is possible to see aspects of elite display beyond the realm of funerary ideology, hunting appears to be an important feature of how elites communicated status within the community of Poggio Civitate (Kansa and Tuck 2023). Indeed, hunting itself can be described as a ritualized activity, which is imbued with meaning about roles and expectations, traditional dress, and other trappings, as well as related feasts and festivities. Although not necessarily a religious ritual, the hunt itself can be a showy display that reinforces social status and brings prestige to participants, much like banquets and ritual meals.

Conclusions and Future Directions

This study has shown that we can extend the right/left duality observed in sacrificial contexts to a habitation site. We have evidence for both left and right ulnae in the faunal assemblage, but spatially they map differently in different functional areas. The signature is weakened by the other habitation debris over many years, but certain patterns are clear — namely, the statistically significant and nearly exclusive occurrence of right-sided ulnae of sheep in the OC1/Residence. We can only speculate on whether the right side was demanded by the elites themselves or was given to them by butchers as a sort of 'tribute' in recognition of their social standing. If expected by the elites, the occasional use of these small meat portions suggests that this was not for large-scale, publicly visible feasts. Rather, it implies small, likely private meals perhaps to honour a guest or to mark a special occasion. If, on the other hand, the right-sided meat portions were set aside by butchers or others overseeing meat distribution, this intentional practice would suggest a sort of 'offering' to the elites. Selecting a specific side in butchery may not be easily apparent to the public (MacKinnon 2010), so selection of the right side in this case was likely mediated by a butcher or similarly experienced individual, as an intentional message to the elites in the OC1/Residence.

This is not to say that non-elites did not have ritual dining practices. Certainly, non-elites also marked occasions with special meals common across many cultural and social settings. However, we do not see such practices marked by a side preference in the OC2/Workshop assemblage as we do in the OC1/Residence. Non-elites may have followed other rituals that we have not yet detected in the zooarchaeological assemblage.

We also cannot be certain that these remains do not have religious or sacrificial relevance. While we make a case here for ritual meals, the lack of stratigraphic resolution in the earlier decades of excavation at the site raises other possibilities. Although less likely, it is important to consider these remains may relate to potential religious activities associated with the adjacent OC3/Tripartite building. Perhaps the right sides of sheep and sometimes pigs were brought to the building as offerings. Beyond the layout of the building that suggests it was a temple, however, there is no evidence for religious activities in the sparse archaeological remains from OC3/Tripartite area (although see recent evidence presented in Tuck and Glennie 2020). Among the faunal remains attributed to OC3/Tripartite building, we do not see the right-side preference that we observe in the OC1/Residence (although this may be due to the very small sample size of identified specimens from this area). Furthermore, a lack of burning on the animal bones from OC3/Tripartite building and from the site in general suggests the assemblage does not contain burnt offerings. However, a large fragment of an altar found at the bottom of a well in another excavation area during the 2015 season with traces of blood on its upper surface (Tuck and others 2016; Tuck and Glennie 2020) provides new evidence for possible sacrificial activities at the site at least during the subsequent Archaic period.

Regardless of the source of the side preference, the association of 'right' with qualities like 'good' and 'powerful' likely reinforced status and prestige distinctions that we see in other aspects of the iconography, material culture, and faunal remains at Poggio Civitate. MacKinnon (2010, 256) highlighted the need for more exploration of the 'connection of ritual dining, and the relationship of side choice to banquet participants and honourees (divine or mortal)' and this study provides a rare window into how ritual dining may have been used to reinforce social status during the Orientalizing period at this site through the association of 'right' with 'elite' or 'special'. Although the longer-term habitation of the site has certainly muted the patterns, this study and others drawing on the same faunal assemblage have shown that some clear spatial differences can be detected between the different areas of the site. Further exploration of ritual dining at Poggio Civitate itself is merited, as well as investigations for evidence from other habitation (non-funerary) sites that may support ritual dining practices among elites and non-elites alike. Importantly, this is the type of information which is often lost in the typical reporting practices of summary statistics. More analysts recording bone siding at other Etruscan sites will certainly help reveal more patterning allowing for a broader understanding of faunal remains in Etruria.

Works Cited

Bartosiewicz, Laszlo. 1997. 'This Little Piggy Went to Market … An Archaeozoological Study of Modern Meat Values', *Journal of European Archaeology*, 5.1: 170–82 <https://doi.org/10.1179/096576697800703610>

Berkin, Jon. 2003. *The Orientalizing Bucchero from the Lower Building at Poggio Civitate (Murlo)*, Archaeological Institute of America Monographs, n.s., 6 (Philadelphia: University of Pennsylvania Museum of Archaeology and Anthropology)

Chaix, Louis. 2003. 'La découpe de l'agneau: un rite funéraire à Kerma (Soudan) vers 2000 av. J.-C.', *Revue archéologique de Picardie*, 21: 219–24

Davis, Simon. 2008. '"Thou Shalt Take of the Ram … the Right Thigh; for It Is a Ram of Consecration …" Some Zoo-archaeological Examples of Body-Part Preferences', in *Uomini, piante e animali nella dimensione del sacro: atti del Seminario di studi di bioarcheologia, Cavallino (Lecce) 28–29 giugno 2002*, ed. by Francesco D'Andria, Jacopo De Grossi Mazzorin, and Girolamo Fiorentino (Bari: Edipuglia), pp. 63–70

Ekroth, Gunnel. 2007. 'Meat in Ancient Greece: Sacrificial, Sacred or Secular?', *Food and History*, 5: 249–72

Gleba, Margarita. 2007. 'Textile Production in Early Etruscan Italy: Working towards a Better Understanding of the Craft in its Historic, Social, and Economic Contexts', *Etruscan Studies*, 10.1: 1–9

Herrmann, Virginia R. 2014. 'The Katumuwa Stele in Archaeological Context', in *Remembrance of Me: Feasting with the Dead in the Ancient Middle East*, ed. by Virginia Herrmann and David Schloen, Oriental Institute Museum Publications, 37 (Chicago: Oriental Institute of the University of Chicago), pp. 49–56 <https://oi.uchicago.edu/sites/oi.uchicago.edu/files/uploads/shared/docs/oimp37.pdf> [accessed 10 January 2023]

Kansa, Sarah Whitcher, and Michael MacKinnon. 2014. 'Etruscan Economics: Forty-Five Years of Faunal Remains from Poggio Civitate', *Etruscan Studies*, 17.1: 63–87 <https://doi.org/10.1515/etst-2014-0001>

Kansa, Sarah Whitcher, and Anthony Tuck. 2023. 'Where the Wild Things Are: Etruscan Hunting and Trophy Display at Poggio Civitate (Murlo)', *European Journal of Archaeology*, 26.1: 81–100 <https://doi.org/10.1017/eaa.2022.28>

Kistler, Erich. 2017. 'Feasts. Wine and Society, Eighth-Sixth Centuries BCE', in *Etruscology*, ed. by Alessandro Naso (Berlin: De Gruyter), pp. 195–206 <https://doi.org/10.1515/9781934078495-013>

MacKinnon, Michael. 2010. '"Left" Is "Right": The Symbolism behind Side Choice among Ancient Animal Sacrifices', in *Anthropological Approaches to Zooarchaeology: Colonialism, Complexity and Animal Transformations*, ed. by Douglas Campana, Pam Crabtree, Susan deFrance, Justin Lev-Tov, and Alice Choyke (Oxford: Oxbow), pp. 250–58

—— . 2013. '"Side" Matters: Animal Offerings at Ancient Nemea', in *Bones, Behaviour and Belief: The Zooarchaeological Evidence as a Source for Ritual Practice in Ancient Greece and Beyond*, ed. by Gunnel Ekroth and Jenny Wallensten (Stockholm: Swedish Institute in Athens), pp. 129–47

Nielsen, Erik, and Anthony Tuck. 2001. 'An Orientalizing Period Complex at Poggio Civitate (Murlo): A Preliminary View', *Etruscan Studies* 8: 35–64

Phillips, Kyle M. Jr. 1973. 'Bryn Mawr College Excavations in Tuscany, 1972', *American Journal of Archaeology*, 77.3: 319–26

Pieraccini, Lisa. 2014. 'The Ever Elusive Etruscan Egg', *Etruscan Studies*, 17.2: 267–92 <https://doi.org/10.1515/etst-2014-0015>

Rafanelli, Simona. 2013. 'Etruscan Religious Rituals: The Archaeological Evidence', in *The Etruscan World*, ed. by Jean MacIntosh Turfa (London: Routledge), pp. 566–93

Rask, Kathryn. 2014. 'Etruscan Animal Bones and their Implications for Sacrificial Studies', *History of Religions* 53.3: 269–312 <https://doi.org/10.1086/674242>

Rathje, Annette. 2007. 'Murlo, Images and Archaeology', *Etruscan Studies*, 10.1: 175–84

Russell, Nerissa. 2011. *Social Zooarchaeology: Humans and Animals in Prehistory* (Cambridge: Cambridge University Press)

Sorrentino, Claudio. 1989. 'Il *Sus scrofa L.* come offerta funebre: la sua distribuzione nelle tombe della necropoli romana del "Cantone" a Collelongo (L'Aquila, Abruzzo, Italia)', in *Animal et pratiques religieuses: les manifestations matérielles*, ed. by Patrice Méniel, *Anthropozoologica*, 3: 119–26

Trentacoste, Angela C. 2014. 'The Etruscans and their Animals: The Zooarchaeology of Forcello di Bagnolo San Vito (Mantova)' (unpublished doctoral thesis, University of Sheffield)

Trentacoste, Angela C., Emma Lightfoot, P. J. Le Roux, Michael Buckley, Sarah W. Kansa, C. Esposito, and Margarita Gleba. 2020. 'Heading for the Hills? A Multi-isotope Study of Sheep Management in First-Millennium BC Italy', *Journal of Archaeological Science: Reports*, 29 (102036) <https://doi.org/10.1016/j.jasrep.2019.102036>

Tuck, Anthony. 2012. 'Murlo', *Open Context* <https://doi.org/10.6078/M77P8W98>

——. 2014. 'Manufacturing at Poggio Civitate: Elite Consumption and Social Organization in the Etruscan 7th Century', *Etruscan Studies*, 17.2: 13–39

——. 2017. 'The Evolution and Political Use of Elite Domestic Architecture at Poggio Civitate (Murlo)', *Journal of Roman Archaeology*, 30: 227–43 <https://doi.org/10.1017/S1047759400074092>

——. 2021. 'Resource and Ritual: Manufacturing and Production at Poggio Civitate', in *Making Cities: Economies of Production and Urbanization in Mediterranean Europe, 1000–500 BC*, ed. by Margarita Gleba, Beatriz Marín-Aguilera, and Bela Dimova (Cambridge: McDonald Institute for Archaeological Research), pp. 147–60

Tuck, Anthony, Ann Glennie, Kate Kreindler, Eoin O'Donoghue, and Cara Polisini. 2016. '2015 Excavations at Poggio Civitate and Vescovado di Murlo (Provincia di Siena)', *Etruscan Studies*, 19.1: 87–148 <https://doi.org/10.1515/etst-2015-0024>

Tuck, Anthony, and Ann Glennie. 2020. 'The Archaic Aristocracy: The Case of Murlo (Poggio Civitate)', *Annali della Fondazione per il Museo Claudio Faina*, 27: 573–600

LAUREL TAYLOR

3. Beyond the Banquet, Beyond the Tomb

Typologies of Feasting in Etruscan Visual and Material Culture

Introduction

From the Villanovan through the Late Etruscan period, banqueting imagery occurs across multiple categories of Etruscan artefacts, in both funerary and non-funerary contexts and, with over one hundred representations, constitutes one of the most numerous themes in Etruscan imagery. The iconography of these scenes is fairly formulaic with figures reclining on dining couches, typically surrounded by the accoutrements of feasting — vessels, servants, and musicians — all factors that have contributed to the identification of such images as 'banquets'. Yet, perhaps because of this standard visual formula, scholars have often tended to elide 'banqueting' scenes from funerary contexts with those from non-funerary contexts, potentially obscuring significant differences in critical details and symbolic value. Using Michael Dietler's typologies of feasting and commensal modes (Dietler 1990; 1996; 1999; and 2001) this paper explores the social and ritual meaning of the 'banquet' in Etruscan visual language during the sixth and fifth centuries BCE and presents a more nuanced reading of consumption iconography. Banquet scenes from mortuary contexts frequently present vessels for serving and consuming wine yet rarely depict food items or food-associated vessels. Conversely, feasting scenes from non-funerary contexts often depict distinct and diverse food items as well as drinking equipment. Legible vessel types in, for example, the Archaic-period terracotta plaques from Murlo and Aquarossa may signal diacritical or exclusionary feasting, a performative behaviour intended to display status among elites. Finally, this paper considers how the symbolic visual language of the plaques may also help us better understand ritual feasting within the specific architectural contexts in which these plaques were discovered.

The Feast

Commensal events can signal social, cultural, religious, and political identity and so it is perhaps no surprise that banqueting is a visual motif that occupies an important place within Etruscan iconography (De Marinis 1961; Cristofani 1987; Cerchiai and d'Agostino 2004; and Small 1971). The 'banquet' appears in tombs, on plaques, mirrors, reliefs, and ceramic vessels, with the vast majority of scenes dating from the mid–late sixth century through the fifth century BCE. De Marinis (1961), the first Etruscologist to systematically study the Etruscan banquet, categorized banqueting images as either a funerary

Laurel Taylor Senior Lecturer, Departments of Art and Art History and of Classics, University of North Carolina Asheville (ltaylor@unca.edu)

Consumption, Ritual, Art and Society: Interpretive Approaches and Recent Discoveries of Food and Drink in Etruria, ed. by Lisa Pieraccini and Laurel Taylor, NAA, 2 (Turnhout, 2023), pp. 57–76   BREPOLS ⊗ PUBLISHERS   10.1484/M.NAA-EB.5.132805

rite, a scene from daily life, or the continuation of earthly pleasures into the afterlife (see also Mitterlechner 2016). Since then, scholars have noted the indebtedness of Etruscan banqueting practice and imagery to Near Eastern models (Colivicchi 2017; Rathje 1990; 1994; 2004; and 2007) and/or Greek models (Torelli 1997 and Dentzer 1982).[1] While such approaches can reveal influence as well as critical differences in gender and culture, I propose to shift perspective here away from this particular type of comparative approach and instead consider how typologies of feasting may help us think more critically about what is depicted or not in these banquet scenes and why.

Feasting, the communal consumption of food and drink as an extraordinary and ritualized activity, is replete with symbolic action and potential. Feasts can, among myriad possibilities, work to mobilize labour; link humans to gods or ancestors; enact reciprocity; facilitate redistribution; and reify cultural or political capital. Anthropologically oriented approaches to feasting can provide a critical theoretical framework for situating commensal events within their ritual, social, and political contexts.[2] While the analytical utility of feasting can be approached from diverse theoretical orientations, it is Dietler's framework that I find most relevant for this analysis because of his focus on the socio-political dimension of feasting. Dietler singles out three primary modes of institutional feasting all defined by specific

bonds of mutual obligation between host and guests or between the feasters themselves. In the patron-role feast, a commensal event founded on asymmetrical power relations, the host cultivates bonds of obligation and superiority in relation to his guests through hospitality. Such feasts legitimize and institutionalize fixed relations of asymmetrical power, such as with Inca rulers who would give elaborate feasts in return for labour (Jennings 2004; Bray 2003). In the empowering or entrepreneurial feast, the host manipulates hospitality towards the acquisition of symbolic capital that can be used to influence larger groups (Dietler 2001). Typically associated with social hierarchies not clearly defined by inheritance, these feasts allow egalitarian elites — chiefs, kinship units, or even whole communities — to exploit social fluidity and opportunity for symbolic capital. Diacritical feasting, the remaining category, is exclusionary, incorporating only certain segments of the population and thus reinforcing inequalities. Exclusionary feasting is typically marked by differentiated cuisine and/or styles of consumption. This can include exotic, expensive, or complexly prepared foods as well as specific food service and consumption vessels. Such vessels can be made from expensive materials, may be imports, and/or exploit new forms or decorations. Notably, the diacritical feast is often also associated with architectonically distinguished settings that serve to 'frame' elite consumption. While the patron-role and entrepreneurial feasts typically emphasize quantity of food and drink, the diacritical shifts to quality — of taste, style, and/or setting (Dietler 2001, 85). Notably, many cultures have simultaneously employed two or more of these types of feasting modes for different purposes.

Identifying these diverse types of feasting is most readily and securely accomplished through ethnographic observation and many contemporary ethnographies have contributed to a wider understanding of feasting modes in the recent and distant past. Dietler (2001), for example,

---

1 For a critical overview of the 'Greekness' of these scenes, see Small 1994. For a comparative look at feasting modes in the archaic Greek world, see Wecowski 2014.

2 Over the past two decades, scholars addressing the analytical utility of feasting have generated a significant and fruitful body of scholarship and theoretical models. While these are too numerous to outline here, two recent and thorough overviews of the history of feasting studies and the various theoretical orientations and classifications can be found in Hayden 2014 and in Hayden and Villeneuve 2011. See also Bray 2003; Dietler 1996; and Dietler and Hayden 2001a.

uses ethnographies of various agrarian African societies to elucidate his theoretical constructs and their analytical utility for archaeological application. While direct observation may provide more conclusive confirmation of the feasting purpose, archaeological and visual evidence can also yield certain insights. Schmandt Besserat, for example, has looked at Mesopotamian feasting iconography on the Standard of UR, seals, and plaques, for example, and noted an exclusive focus on the economic aspects, that is, a visual emphasis on quantity in which feasts were the 'fulcrum of state distribution economy' (Schmandt Besserat 2001, 402). The visual emphasis in Mesopotamian imagery is frequently also reflected by textual evidence. Similarly, diverse categories of evidence — visual, archaeological, and botanical — from various ancient Maya sites hint at the critical role of exclusionary feasting in maintaining Mayan polities (LeCount 2001; Rice 2009, 78–79; and Lamoureux-St Hilaire 2020 though many other types of feasting occurred within Maya culture (Lohse and others 2013; Staller 2010; and LeCount 2001).

Can such close readings of banqueting images in Etruscan archaic art vis-à-vis archaeological evidence also point towards diverse types of feasting? While speculative, my intent here is to consider various lines of evidence — the internal visual evidence, the related archaeological evidence, and the contextual or architectural evidence — to move beyond the banquet and consider how non-funerary scenes may reflect specific types of commensal practice.[3] Before considering the Archaic-period terracotta plaques from non-funerary contexts such as Poggio Civitate and Acquarossa that feature

---

3   Dietler and Hayden 2001b, 3–11 discuss how archaeological evidence can be used to identify modes of feasting (as do many of the chapters in the volume). See also Rosenwig 2007 for the ways iconography and architecture reveal diacritical aspects of feasting among the Olmec in early Mesoamerica.

banqueting imagery, a brief overview of how the banquet is visually constructed in funerary contexts during this same period is important (see Pieraccini, *infra*). It is necessary to understand what is depicted and, importantly, not depicted in funerary banquets if we are to examine how such discretionary inclusion and exclusion of details may reveal specific types of feasting in non-funerary banquet images.

Banqueting Imagery in Archaic-Period Tombs

That the banquet occupied a primary position within tomb painting is evidenced both by the frequency of its representation as well as its spatial placement within compositional schemes. Around fifty banquet scenes have been preserved in painted tombs from Tarquinia, Cerveteri, Chiusi, Orvieto, and Sarteano spanning over two hundred years from the late sixth century to the late fourth BCE. (With nearly forty tombs depicting banquets, Tarquinia boasts the most numerous, the earliest of which include the Bartoccini tomb and the Tomb of the Lionesses (*c.* 530–520 BCE) and the latest the Tomb of Shields (*c.* 350).) Nearly all these banquet scenes are located prominently opposite the entrance in the main compositional space, in the gable and, on occasion, occupying the lateral walls (Figs 3.1–3.2).

While archaeological evidence attests to the importance of food within funerary ritual (see Tuck 1994 and Pieraccini 2000), close examination of these scenes reveals that food is very rarely depicted in the Archaic period and the vast majority reference drink only. Forty out of some fifty reference drinking through equipment that is varied in both vessel shape and size with large kraters and a wide variety of drinking and pouring vessels including kylikes, oinochoai, and shallow, wide drinking bowls. Drinking or, at least the allusion to wine, is often a thematic

Figure 3.1. A banquet scene on the back wall of the Tomb of the Triclinium (early fifth BCE), Tarquinia. Courtesy of the Soprintendenza Archeologia, Belle Arti e Paesaggio per la provincia di Viterbo e l'Etruria Meridionale.

Figure 3.2. Tomb of Hunting and Fishing, Tarquinia, c. 510 BCE. After Weber-Lehmann 1985, taf. 5, fig. 4.

Figure 3.3. Detail showing egg, Tomb of the Lionesses, Tarquinia, c. 520 BCE. After Pieraccini 2000, fig. 10.

component of these scenes. Despite this, it is interesting to note that not all figures equally participate; only men hold drinking vessels and so while women feature prominently in the majority of banqueting scenes, their tangible association with drinking seems absent.[4] Why this would be so consistent and if it, in fact, reflects some lived reality is uncertain. What is clear, however, is that women in non-funerary banqueting scenes are frequently depicted holding drinking vessels, a detail that I would argue is not random but, indeed, tied to the elite status of these women and exclusionary feasts in which they participate.

Another curious feature of these tomb paintings is that, while we refer to these scenes as 'banquets', food does not visibly play a part in these images. Aside from the later and singular Golini I tomb (c. 350–330 BCE) which depicts a kitchen prep scene and an underworld banquet with Hades and Persephone (Sarti 2017; Steingräber 2006, 211–14; and Barbieri 1987), tomb paintings generally avoid the depiction of both food and food-related vessels. During the sixth and fifth centuries, only nine reference food for certain.[5] What is most remarkable is perhaps not the small number but that when a food item is shown it is

always recognizable as an egg (Fig. 3.3) (Pieraccini 2014 and 2000). Though some scholars have noted that these objects could be a bread or fruit, the small size, oval shape, and consistency of colour all suggest eggs. Their visual prominence is highlighted by vivid gestural action in which the figure holds it prominently or passes it to another figure. As Pieraccini (2014, 289) notes, their appearance in tombs references life and rebirth and it is interesting to compare these to a banquet scene from an archaic funerary urn from Chiusi (Jannot 2010, fig. 13) where two pomegranates (whole and unprepared) appear below a kline, another use of food to reference the afterlife and rebirth. Only a single tomb from this period (the Tomb of the Triclinium at Tarquinia) shows food-related vessels. Thus, while drinking — or at least the allusion to it and then only by men — is commonly featured in these painted banquet scenes, food is not something that was visually critical.

Though many commonalities exist between banqueting imagery from funerary contexts and non-funerary contexts, critical nuances can be distinguished, in particular as they relate to food, food containers, held objects, and gender. Such differences in visual language, I would argue, should not be ignored as they may be employed to signal diverse types of feasts, especially ones that, in the case of non-funerary images, reflect the socio-political dimension of feasting. While actual funerary feasts were likely more private affairs (Pieraccini 2003, 172) feasts in other contexts — as many Etruscan scholars concur — were the most conspicuous expression of status, power, and lifestyle for the elite. How these events may have been visually translated into feasting imagery is explored below.

---

4 It is possible that a female figure in the Tomb of the Biclinium at Tarquinia (late fifth century BCE) held a rhyton in her hand. Discovered in the eighteenth century but no longer surviving, the reconstruction of the tomb shows a number of fanciful details making this detail unlikely.

5 These include the following tombs from Tarquinia: the Tomb of the Lionesses (c. 520 BCE); the Tomb of the Frontoncino (510–500 BCE); the Tomb of the Bigas (mid-fifth century); the Tomb of the Leopards (480 BCE); the Tomb of the Triclinium (470 BCE); the Tomb of the Maiden (late fifth century BCE); the Tomb of the Blue Demons (late fifth century BCE); the Tomb of the Biclinium (late fifth century BCE); and the Tomb of the Black Sow (late fifth century). The later Tomb of the Shields (c. 350 BCE) also features food items. A nineteenth-century *lucido* of the Tomb of the Triclinium at Cerveteri (late fourth century BCE) shows food items that were likely added during the rendering and not present in the original.

Figure 3.4. Banquet frieze, Poggio Civitate, c. 575–550 BCE. Drawing by author after Small 1971, fig. 1.

Terracotta Plaques and Elite Feasting

One of the richest sources of non-funerary feasting images comes from a series of terracotta plaques dating to the Archaic period and found at a number of important sites such as Murlo and Acquarossa and in Rome, just to name a few.[6] Originally associated with buildings that were most certainly connected with elite families, these low-relief square and rectangular friezes were part of more extensive series of friezes depicting, among other images, horse races, processions, dancing, assemblies, and — in a couple of instances — mythological figures. In a recent study of these, Roth-Murray (2007) demonstrates how these plaques reflect a shared elite ideology as well as networks of elite interaction through the use of identical matrices between certain cities. Identical plaques found in Veii, Rome, and Velletri, for example, and made from the same matrix may reflect alliances between the ruling elite of these cities as do plaques from Acquarossa and Tuscania made from a different matrix but identical to one another. While each city may have different combinations of images, the terracotta plaques as a whole reflect an elite ideology specific to this moment in the Archaic period; the ruling class engaged in behaviours (feasting, chariot racing, assembling) that distinguished themselves within society and, thus, legitimized and reinforced their power (Torelli 2000 and 1988). As Roth-Murray (2007, 136) notes, the imagery in the frieze plaques reflects 'shared understandings of elite social roles'. The display of such imagery in monumental buildings constructed at the behest of the elite is clear even while in some cases the actual function of the building may be debatable. Many of these structures are linked, however, by their shared monumentality, decoration, restrictive access, and dominate courtyards as well as by archaeological evidence suggesting feasting, gatherings, and craft production (Strandberg Olofsson 1984 and 1996; Cristofani 1987; Edlund 1987; Rathje 1994; Riva and Stoddart 1996; Izzet 2000; Meyers 2014;

---

6 To date, these have been found at Poggio Civitate, Acquarossa, Tarquinia, Veii, Rome, Velletri, Tuscania, Poggio Buco, Castelnuovo Berardegna, Castellina del Marangone, Roselle, and Caere-Vigna Parocchiale. In some cases (such as at Tarquinia, Veii, and Rome), there are multiple find-spots for the plaques.

and Roth-Murray 2007). Whether residential, cultic, or some combination of these and other functions, the physical structures and contexts of these plaques were ones inextricably tied to elite control and the imagery of the plaques reflected such elite ideology and linked them to these spaces (Roth-Murray 2007, 143–44). Here I focus primarily on the better preserved terracotta plaques from the monumental complexes at Poggio Civitate and Acquarossa, with brief reference to plaques preserved from other sites.

The well-known banquet plaques from Poggio Civitate (Fig. 3.4), the earliest of all terracotta plaques, are part of a series of revetment plaques that includes horse races, assemblies, and procession scenes all associated with the Archaic Building complex (Tuck 2020; Small 1994; Rathje 2007; von Mehren 1993; Winter 2009). At least ninety friezes of the four scenes adorned the building complex, most likely on both the interior and exterior of the building, a roughly 60 × 60 m monumental square building with a central colonnaded courtyard (von Mehren 1993; Rathje 2007; Small 1971 and 1994). The plaques preserve very little paint today, but their original white painted background with details added in red (and possibly other colours) would have contributed to their visibility. The banquet scene shows two couples, each reclining on a kline and flanked on either side by a standing servant. In the centre is a large cauldron presumably for wine while in front of each kline appear food-laden tables with a single dog crouching under each. The standing figure in the centre of the image facing the right kline holds their arms in such a way as to indicate that they may have originally held a double flute the details of which would have been added in paint but are now lost. All these details — servants, lavish food and drink displays, music, dogs — signify the aristocratic context of the scene.

One of the most striking aspects in the banquet plaques is the level of specificity. Though terracotta as a medium makes it difficult to

Figure 3.5. Umbro-Etruscan terracotta food votive set from Todi, third century BCE, University of Pennsylvania Museum of Anthropology and Archaeology, MS 1407, 1409–23, 1425–27. Photo by author.

achieve fine detail, great attention has been devoted to the careful rendering of banqueting equipment. In the centre is an elaborate stand with a large cauldron, wine pitchers carried by servants, diverse drinking vessels, and assorted containers for serving and eating food. On the left side of the image is a table that holds a shallow bowl with slanting oval objects, two high-footed plates, and a high-footed bowl with round items inside. On the right table, also in front of the kline, similar objects appear, including a slim, high-footed plate, a high-footed bowl containing round objects, a broad plate, a bowl with slanted objects, and a cup. The abundance of foodstuffs is remarkable and deliberate attention has been devoted to making these foods formally distinct from one another. It remains, however, difficult to distinguish what exactly are these oval, round, and slanted foods. Perhaps the oval-shaped objects are eggs while the slanted and round objects may be types of bread and/or fruit. A comparison with an Umbro-Etruscan third-century terracotta votive set of foodstuffs (Fig. 3.5) shows a similar range of food shapes. Rathje (1994 and 2007), who has remarked on the similarities between these plaques and Neo-Assyrian banquet plaques, notes that similarly shaped objects on the Neo-

Figure 3.6. Vessels, Banquet frieze, Poggio Civitate, c. 575–550 BCE. Drawing by author after Small 1971, fig. 1.

Assyrian plaques are fruit and should be read as such here.[7] Whatever these are, their appearance here is important — they signal the opulence and display of elite feasting.

Complementing the foodstuffs are the various types of drinking equipment held by the figures. Not only are these easily legible, they also have correlates in the archaeological record at Poggio Civitate and elsewhere in Etruria. The male reclining figures and the servant to the left hold hemispherical drinking bowls (Fig. 3.6 — vessels circled) often seen also in Near Eastern banquet scenes where their use signals elite consumption (Rathje 2007, 178). These are morphologically distinct from the Ionian drinking cups held by the women, a form that Poletti Ecclesia has also recently tied to ceremonial usage (Poletti Ecclesia 2002). The servant depicted on the right seems to hold a third type of vessel, one that appears to be a skyphos. The effort to represent distinctly legible vessel types, especially imported forms, is particularly notable as equipment is often a marker of diacritical feasting (Dietler 2001).

The transformation in consumption patterns and the demand for new luxury ceramics are well-known hallmarks of the previous century (Riva 2006 and Naso 2000) and attested at Poggio Civitate by the large amount of banqueting equipment found at the site (Berkin 2003 and Tuck 1994). As noted by Small (1971, 53) in her studies of this scene and by Berkin (2003, 119–25) in his study of the Orientalizing ceramics at Poggio Civitate, excavations in the lower building have yielded many ceramic fragments — such as the Ionian cups and high-footed plates — of the same shapes as vessels represented on plaques as well as two bronze cauldrons similar to that scene on the plaque (cf. Rathje 1983 on similar forms from Ficana; Berkin 2003, 119–25). The simple drinking bowl held by the men and servant on the left is a type known from the

---

7 It is interesting to compare these to food items depicted on a bronze mirror in the Villa Giulia where there is a similar interest in showing diverse food items (possible eggs, fruit, and/or bread) and vessels on a table in front of a kline (Pieraccini 2000, fig. 1). As mirrors were likely part of everyday life before deposited in the grave, such emphasis on the opulence of the feast and elite behaviour in the mirror has much in common with the plaques.

Figure 3.7. Banquet plaque from the 'Veii-Rome-Velletri' series. Drawing by author after Bruun 1993, fig. 2.

Near East, both imported to Italy as well as imitated in bronze and precious metal (Rathje 2007). Changing patterns of ceramic import consumption as well as specialized drinking, pouring, and mixing equipment are markers frequently associated with diacritical feasting.[8] And as many scholars have often noted (Dietler 2020; Arnold 1999; Pieraccini 2011; and Rathje 2007), the acquisition and proper consumption of wine (and the depiction thereof) is intended to convey rank, status, and/or authority.[9]

The access to and proper consumption of wine is a diacritical device that distinguishes one from peers and inferiors. As Dietler (1990, 391) notes, drinking is a 'social practice through which relations of economic and political power in a society are reflected and manipulated'. The depiction of specialized and imported forms of drinking equipment, the use of which begins in the seventh century BCE and continues on in the sixth century, has great visual resonance as a signifier of status. An emphasis on multiple types of drinking vessels in the plaques from Poggio Civitate is an attempt, in my opinion, to amplify and reinforce the visual impact of such specialized knowledge. Multiple drinking vessels may reference diverse beverages, a hierarchical distinction (Rathje 1994, 97), or specific moments in a feast that simply get conflated in a single snapshot as in the plaque. As Berkin (2003, 119–26) comments, it is impossible to know what a 'standard' banquet service was per person (indeed as many as six different drinking types were found in the lower building) though he estimates that between twenty and fifty people could have been accommodated based on the number recovered. Of similar importance for this analysis is that women in this and in many other terracotta plaques hold drinking vessels. In the terracotta banquet plaques from Velletri, Tarquinia, Rome, and Veii, all of which use the same matrix (known as the 'VRV' series), each of the two women holds a different type of drinking vessel (Colonna 2001; Fortunati 1993; Downey 1995; and Roth-Murray 2007). On the well-preserved example from Velletri (Fig. 3.7), the woman on the left kline holds what looks to be a kylix in her left hand and a flower or food object in her right while her companion holds a rhyton in his left hand. On the right couch, the woman holds a type of deep skyphos. In banquet imagery from funerary contexts women hold eggs but not drinking vessels. Their association with drinking in these non-funerary images is,

---

8 Junker 2001, in an analysis of feasting in the Philippines, demonstrates how a careful examination of regional patterns of ceramic import consumption can reveal evidence of diacritical feasting. Cf. Haggis 2007.
9 Pieraccini 2011, 128 notes the symbolic association between wine and the dead in funerary contexts, as perhaps connected to immortality and rebirth. This is, to me, quite distinct from its consumption in the context of non-funerary feasts where it expresses status and authority.

Figure 3.8. Detail of banquet plaque, Type C, Acquarossa, mid-sixth century BCE. Drawing by author.

I argue, significant.[10] Greek authors of the Late Classical period (cf. the well-known observation by Theopompus, Athenaeus XII. 517d) were shocked by the participation of Etruscan women in banquets and, moreover, in wine drinking. Aristocratic Etruscan women, however, enjoyed substantial freedom in their actions, a phenomenon confirmed by visual as well as inscriptional evidence; inscriptions on numerous vases confirm their agency as consumers and dispensers of wine (Colonna 1980 and Cristofani 1991). The depiction of these women with drinking vessels is not gratuitous but meant to signal their active participation in elite feasting rituals.

The banquet plaques from Acquarossa, like those from Poggio Civitate, come from a building complex that was monumental in size and character (Strandberg Olofsson 1984; 1989; 1994; and 2006). Located in Zone F, the complex consisted of two main porticoed buildings — A (10 m in length) and C (25 m in length) — arranged at a right angle to one another and decorated with numerous terracotta revetments. The banquet frieze was part of a decorative programme different from that at Poggio Civitate but equally rich in its imagery. The series includes a dancing scene as well as two different processions with Herakles, one with the Cretan bull and the other with the Nemean lion, scenes perhaps intended to evoke associations between a ruling figure or family at Acquarossa and the legendary hero (Strandberg Olofsson 1994).

While sharing many elements with the banquet scene from Poggio Civitate and the VRV series, the Acquarossa plaques (and identical plaques from Tuscania) feature some differences, notably in the number of figures as well as other details. The image shows, from the left, a flutist, a kline with three figures and dog crouching underneath, a lyre player in the centre, a second kline also with three figures and dog underneath, and then a final figure serving wine from a large cauldron. On each kline a woman is in the centre flanked by men on each side. The male figures on the far left of each kline and the one on the far right of the right kline hold a type of kylix that may be a Komast cup, a form popular around 580–560 and exported widely from mainland Greece and Ionia (Brijder 1983). Located in front of each kline is a table filled with a variety of shallow bowls and plates though unlike in the plaques from Poggio Civitate, no actual foodstuffs appear in the vessels and, instead, food or food-related items are shown held by some of the banqueters. The male figures on the far left hold long thin objects (Fig. 3.8) that may be a knives (Small 1994, 43; Colivicchi 2017, 213) or, more likely, pieces of bread or meat similar to shapes seen in the terracotta votive set mentioned above (Pieraccini 2003, 117–18 fig. 71 for a parallel on a Caeretan stamped brazier). On similar plaques from Tarquinia, male figures hold identical objects. Quite distinct is the flat, oblong object held by the other two figures (Fig. 3.8). Though not easily identifiable, the object is clearly not an egg but perhaps a piece of bread, a cake, or a piece of fruit. In both cases, these objects — however identified as food or a food-related object — never appear in banquet scenes from tomb paintings. It is worth noting also that most figures depicted in the terracotta

---

10 On alcohol, identity, and gender, see Dietler 2006.

plaques hold some sort of object — a vessel, food, knives, flowers — while only about a third of the figures from funerary banquets hold objects (mostly cups and the rare egg). The inclusion of such items in the terracotta revetment plaques is significant, meant to signal the opulence of the elite feast and the actual consumption of foodstuffs.

The clear emphasis on food in these plaques as a diacritical device finds important parallels in the zooarchaeological record. In a study of the faunal remains from Poggio Civitate dating to the seventh century BCE, Kansa and MacKinnon (2014) documented a higher proportion of cattle, deer, and large wild animals (boar, bear, and wolf) in association with the elite residence than in other areas of the site. The zooarchaeological evidence in association with banqueting paraphernalia is, as they note, highly significant as the consumption of these animals would have signalled elite status to the larger community at Poggio Civitate (see Kansa, this volume).

Staging the Feast

This last section considers the relationship between the plaques and their architectural contexts. As noted above, all of these plaques come from structures that are monumental in scale and/or decoration though the actual function of many of these structures is of some debate. In the case of Poggio Civitate and Acquarossa, both complexes were preceded by more modest buildings which were monumentalized during the Archaic period with the addition of complex iconography. This has suggested to many scholars that these are elite residential areas and/or areas of aristocratic activity (cf. Meyers 2014). Other theories, in addition to that of being the residence of an aristocratic clan, include identification as temples, administrative or civic complexes, political meeting-places, sites of cultic activity, festal or initiation sites, and mercantile or trading

centres.[11] Their architectural features do seem to indicate they were constructed at the behest of some political, religious, and/or elite group and indeed, it is quite likely that these complexes were multifunctional (perhaps in both a synchronic and diachronic sense) incorporating many of the functions outlined above. What perhaps may be a more fruitful avenue of inquiry is thinking about how the features of these complexes compare to other sites or contexts where diacritical feasts are known to have been held and how this may help understand the context of the plaques. A look at lowland Classic Maya royal compounds, the locus of much documented feasting, is instructive here.

A frequent feature of diacritical feasting is the use of architectonic elaboration and/or spatial differentiation that serves to frame elite consumption. The degree of accessibility and restriction are also often features embedded in the architectural context of exclusionary feasting areas. As noted by LeCount, diacritical feasts are often held in or near private and controlled areas in order to reinforce social distance away from the larger community whereas more inclusionary feasts occur in areas more open or more accessible to the community (LeCount 2001, 935). As the institution of kingship spread in Mesoamerica during the Preclassical period, many Maya royal compounds grew incrementally as successive kings enlarged and modified the structures to accommodate a variety of activities.[12] While these

---

11 For an overview of theories related to Acquarossa, see Strandberg-Olofsson 1994. See also Wikander and Wikander 1990 and Säflund and Frazer 1993. For Poggio Civitate, see, among others, Philips 1993; Cristofani 1975; Tuck 2017 and 2006; Torelli 2000; Rathje 2007, Macintosh Turfa and Steinmayer 2002. See de Grummond 1997 who problematizes the interpretive issue as it relates to the evidence. See Roth-Murray 2007 for the evidence and theories regarding the contexts of plaques from other sites.

12 On Preclassic royal compounds, see Clark and Hansen 2001 and Spencer and Redmond 2004. On Classic-period and later compounds, see Evans 2004; Inomata

68 LAUREL TAYLOR

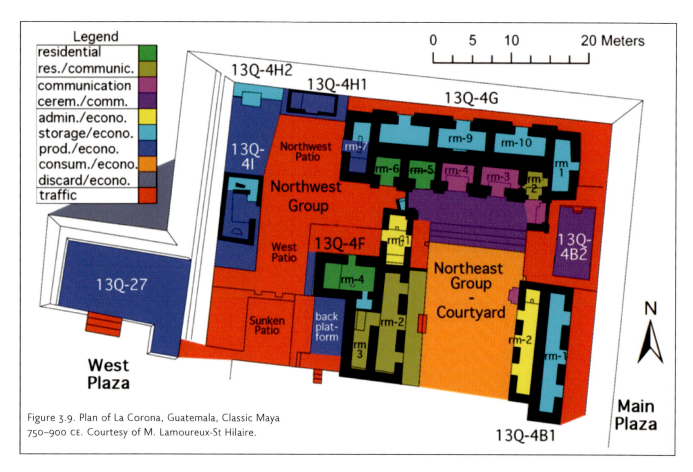

Figure 3.9. Plan of La Corona, Guatemala, Classic Maya 750–900 CE. Courtesy of M. Lamoureux-St Hilaire.

Figure 3.10. Archaic Building Complex, Poggio Civitate. 'Phase 2 Reconstruction from Italy/Poggio Civitate' (2012). In *Murlo*. Anthony Tuck (ed.), Open Context: <https://opencontext.org/media/68AFAD53-179E-4C0C-74FB-036755D796AA> [accessed 10 January 2023].

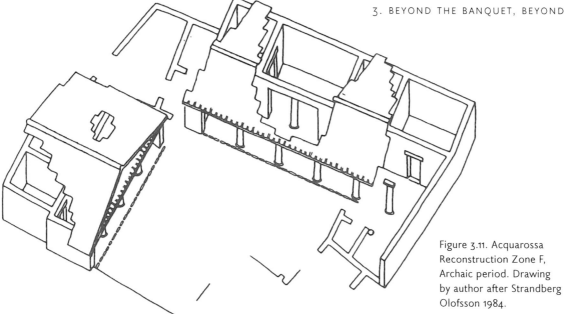

Figure 3.11. Acquarossa Reconstruction Zone F, Archaic period. Drawing by author after Strandberg Olofsson 1984.

walled compounds display variation in size, form, and room configuration, many are defined by the presence of a central courtyard and, in some cases like the well-preserved palace at Palenque, multiple courtyards. These royal complexes make use of monumental stages with politically charged art for courtly feasts but also contain spatial sequences that could accommodate groups of different sizes, ranging from the more public in large central courtyards to more private rooms within the interior. The royal compound of La Corona in the highlands of Guatemala (Fig. 3.9) demonstrates how spatial sequencing could be employed to accommodate a spectrum of feasts. The excavator Lamoureux-St Hilaire (2018, 35) who has studied the botanical, architectural, and iconographical evidence of feasting at La Corona, demonstrates that the political apparatus of Classic Maya royal courts was dependent upon these architectural complexes that could accommodate more inclusive feasting events in large courtyards to more exclusive diacritical events aimed at political networking in the more private areas. Classic Maya-period painted vessels depict elite individuals within these settings (LeCount 1996), vases in hand and platters stacked with food in ways that are reminiscent of the banqueting plaques from Poggio Civitate and Acquarossa.

The formal features of Poggio Civitate (Fig. 3.10) and Acquarossa (Fig. 3.11) are in many respects congruent with the spatial sequences in Maya royal compounds. This is not to suggest that these reflect some sort of parallel institution of kingship but simply that the spatial sequences have some important analogies. Clearly the archaic building complexes at Poggio Civitate and at Acquarossa each exhibit remarkable formal and material features that mark them as distinct from other more modest buildings in their larger surroundings. At Poggio Civitate, the monumental, colonnaded courtyard features a large, central space with controlled access as well as smaller, more intimate surrounding rooms. The monumental complex at Acquarossa, while smaller, was a unified spatial area, emphasized through the decoration of the facades of the two buildings facing the courtyard and a precinct wall in the south (Strandberg Olofsson 1994, 138). Scholars have attempted to identify specific dining areas at these sites, but, as with the Maya

and Houston 2000; 2001; Sheehy 1996; Smith 2017; and Redmond and Spencer 2017.

royal compounds, both monumental complexes could have accommodated groups of different size and composition in and around the courtyard.[13] As Strandberg-Olofsson notes about Acquarossa, whether the building complex is interpreted as cultic, palatial, festal, and/or multifunctional, the best-attested use of this area is banqueting, confirmed by the discovery of numerous Ionian drinking cups as well as storage, serving, and other drinking vessels.[14]

Conclusion

This paper attempts to provide a more nuanced reading of the Etruscan 'banquet' by parsing the elements included in feasting images from funerary contexts versus non-funerary contexts.

---

13 At Acquarossa, dining areas have been suggested by Bergquist 1973, Strandberg Olofsson 1996; and Torelli 1988. At Poggio Civitate, Rystedt 1984 and Berkin 2003 have attempted to identify dining areas.

14 Strandberg-Olofsson 1994, 143. She does note that the area must be connected to a ruler, whether living there or not and that the complex may have been both residential at some point as well as having cultic function.

In the case of the latter, artisans who created the terracotta plaques were concerned with the depiction not only of specialized drinking equipment but with the clear and often abundant presence of food and, notably, with the active participation of elite women in consuming wine. As F. Colivicchi (2017, 210) has noted

> the banquet became one of the most important venues for the representation and reproduction of the power of Orientalizing and Archaic aristocracies and the complex dynamics of social relationship of these periods, both vertically, between the highest ranks of the clan and their dependents, and horizontally, between different clans of the same or other communities.

Diacritical feasting functions as an exclusionary, commensal event as well as an important conduit of communication in which the exchange of information and ideas between such horizontal elites can occur (Dietler 1990 and 1996). The terracotta plaques discussed here employ a visual language that vividly expresses and confirms this exclusive elite status that manifests itself through feasting rituals.

Works Cited

Andren, Arvid. 1940. *Architectural Terracottas from Etrusco-Italic Temples* (Lund: Gleerup)

Arnold, Bettina. 1999. '"Drinking the Feast": Alcohol and the Legitimation of Power in Celtic Europe', *Cambridge Archaeological Journal*, 9: 71–93

Barbieri, Gabriella. 1987. 'La Tomba Golini I e la cista di Bruxelles: due rapresentazioni di "cucina"', in *L'Alimentazione nel mondo antico: gli Etruschi*, ed. by Gabriella Barbieri (Rome: Istituto poligrafico), pp. 49–53

Berkin, John. 2003. *The Orientalizing Bucchero from the Lower Building at Poggio Civitate (Murlo)* (Boston: University of Pennsylvania Museum of Archaeology and Anthropology)

Bergquist, Birgitta. 1973. 'Was There a Formal Dining Room, Sacred or Civic on the Acropolis of Acquarossa?', *Opusula Romana*, 9: 21–34

Blake, Emma. 2005. 'The Material Expression of Cult, Ritual, and Feasting', in *The Archaeology of Mediterranean Prehistory*, ed. by Emma Blake and A. Bernard Knapp (Oxford: Wiley Blackwell), pp. 102–29

Bray, Tamara. 2003. 'To Dine Splendidly', in *The Archaeology and Politics of Food and Feasting in Early States and Empires*, ed. by Tamara Bray (Boston: Springer), pp. 93–142

Brijder, Herman A. G., and G. Strietman. 1983. *Siana Cups I and Komast Cups* (Amsterdam: Allard Pierson Museum)

Brothwell, Don, and Patricia Brothwell. 1998. *Food in Antiquity* (London: John Hopkins University Press)

Bruun, Christer. 1993. 'Herakles and the Tyrants: An Archaic Frieze from Velletri', in *Deliciae fictiles: Proceedings of the First International Conference on Central Italic Architectural Terracottas at the Swedish Institute in Rome, 10–12 December 1990*, I (Stockholm: Åström), pp. 267–75

Cerchiai, Luca, and Bruno d'Agostino. 2004. 'l banchetto e il simposio nel mondo etrusco', *Thesarus cultus et rituum antiquorum (ThesCRA)*, 2: 254–67

Clark, John E., and Richard Hansen. 2001. 'The Architecture of Early Kingship: Comparative Perspectives on the Origins of the Maya Royal Court', in *Royal Courts of the Ancient Maya*, II: *Data and Case Studies*, ed. by TakeshiInomata and Stephen D. Houston (Boulder: Westview), pp. 1–45

Colivicchi, Fabio. 2017. 'Banqueting and Food', in *Etruscology*, ed. by Alessandro Naso (Berlin: De Gruyter), pp. 207–20

Colonna, Giovanni. 1980. 'Graeco more bibere: l'iscrizione della tomba 115 dell'Osteria dell'Osa', *Archeologia Laziale*, 3, *QuadAEI*, 4: 51–55

——. 2001. 'Portonaccio', in *Veio, Cerveteri, Vulci: città d'Etruria a confronto*, ed. by Anna Maria Moretti Sgubini (Rome: L'Erma di Bretschneider), pp. 37–66

Cristofani, Mauro. 1975. 'Considerazioni su Poggio Civitate (Murlo, Siena)', *Prospettiva*, 1: 9–17

——. 1987. 'Il banchetto in Etruria', in *L'Alimentatione nel mondo antico: gli Etruschi*, ed. by Gabriella Barbieri (Rome: Istituto poligrafico e Zecca dello stato), pp. 123–32

——. 1991. 'Vino e simposio nel mondo etrusco arcaico', in *Homo Edens*, II: *Storie del vino*, ed. by P. Scarpi (Milan: Diapress), pp. 69–76

de Grummond, Nancy. 1997. 'Poggio Civitate, a Turning Point', *Etruscan Studies*, 4: 23–39

De Marinis, Simonetta. 1961. *La tipologia del banchetto nell'arte Etrusca arcaica* (Rome: L'Erma di Bretschneider)

Dentzer, Jean-Marie. 1982. *Le motif du banquet couché dans le Proche-Orient et dans le monde grec du VIle au IVᵉ siècle avant J.-C.* (Rome: École française de Rome)

De Puma, Richard, and Jocelyn Penny Small (eds). 1994. *Murlo and the Etruscans: Art and Society in Ancient Etruria* (Madison: University of Wisconsin Press)

Dietler, Michael. 1990. 'Driven by Drink: The Role of Drinking in the Political Economy and the Case of Early Iron Age France', *Journal of Anthropological Archaeology*, 9: 352–406

——. 1996. 'Feast and Commensal Politics in the Political Economy: Food, Power and Status in Prehistoric Europe', in *Food and the Status Quest: An Interdisciplinary Perspective*, ed. by Polly Wiesner and Wulf Schiefenhovel (Providence: Berghahn), pp. 87–126

——. 1999. 'Rituals of Commensality and the Politics of State Formation in the "Princely" Societies of Early Iron Age Europe', in *Les princes de la protohistoire et l'émergence de l'État: actes de la table ronde internationale organisée par le Centre Jean Bérard et l'École française de Rome Naples, 27–29 octobre 1994* (Rome: École française de Rome), pp. 135–52

——. 2001. 'Theorizing the Feast: Rituals of Consumption, Commensal Politics, and Power in African Contexts', in *Feasts: Archaeological and Ethnographic Perspectives on Food, Politics, and Power*, ed. by Michael Dietler and Brian Hayden (Washington, DC: Smithsonian Institution), pp. 65–114

——. 2006. 'Alcohol: Anthropological/Archaeological Perspectives', *Annual Review of Anthropology*, 35: 229–49

——. 2020. 'Alcohol as Embodied Material Culture: Anthropological Reflections on the Deep Entanglement of Humans and Alcohol', in *Alcohol and Humans: A Long and Social Affair*, ed. by Robin I. M. Dunbar and Kimberley Hockings (Oxford: Oxford University Press), pp. 299–319

Dietler, Michael, and Brian Hayden (eds). 2001a. *Feasts: Archaeological and Ethnographic Perspectives on Food, Politics, and Power* (Washington, DC: Smithsonian Institution)

——. 2001b. 'Digesting the Feast: Good to Eat, Good to Drink, Good to Think', in *Feasts: Archaeological and Ethnographic Perspectives on Food, Politics, and Power*, ed. by Michael Dietler and Brian Hayden (Washington, DC: Smithsonian Institution), pp. 1–20

Downey, Susan. 1993. 'Archaic Architectural Terracottas from the Regia', in *Deliciae fictiles, I: Proceedings of the First International Conference on Central Italic Architectural Terracottas at the Swedish Institute in Rome, 10–12 December 1990*, ed. by Eva Rystedt and Charlotte Wikander (Stockholm: Åström), pp. 233–48

——. 1995. *Architectural Terracottas from the Regia*, Papers and Monographs of the American Academy in Rome, 30 (Ann Arbor: University of Michigan Press)

Edlund, Ingrid. 1987. *The Gods and the Place* (Stockholm: Åström)

Edlund-Berry, Ingrid, Giovanna Greco, and John Kenfield (eds). 2006. *Deliciae fictiles, III: Architectural Terracottas in Ancient Italy: New Discoveries and Interpretations* (Oxford: Oxbow)

Evans, Susan Toby. 2004. *Ancient Mexico and Central America* (London: Thames & Hudson)

Fortunati, Francesca Romana. 1993. 'Il tempio delle Stimmate di Velletri: il rivestimento arcaico e considerazioni sul Sistema decorativo', in *Deliciae fictiles, I: Proceedings of the First International Conference on Central Italic Architectural Terracottas at the Swedish Institute in Rome, 10–12 December 1990*, ed. by Eva Rystedt and Charlotte Wikander (Stockholm: Åström), pp. 256–65

Gaultier, Francoise. 1993. 'Terrecotte architettoniche arcaiche da Tuscania: le collezione del Louvre e gli scavi recenti nella necropolis dell'Ara del Tufo', in *Deliciae fictiles, I: Proceedings of the First International Conference on Central Italic Architectural Terracottas at the Swedish Institute in Rome, 10–12 December 1990*, ed. by Eva Rystedt and Charlotte Wikander (Stockholm: Åström), pp. 183–91

Grignon, Claude. 2001. 'Commensality and Social Morphology: An Essay of Typology', in *Food, Drink and Identity: Cooking, Eating and Drinking in Europe since the Middle Ages*, ed. by Peter Scholliers (Oxford: Berg), pp. 23–33

Haggis, Donald. 2007. 'Stylistic Diversity and Diacritical Feasting at Protopalatial Petras: A Preliminary Analysis of the Lakkos Deposit', *American Journal of Archaeology*, 111.4: 715–75

Hague Sinos, Rebecca. 1994. 'Godlike Men. A Discussion of the Murlo Procession Frieze', in *Murlo and the Etruscans: Art and Society in Ancient Etruria*, ed. by Richard Daniel De Puma and Jocelyn P. Small (Wisconsin: University of Wisconsin Press), pp. 100–17

Hayden, Brian. 1996. 'Feasting in Prehistoric and Traditional Societies', in *Food and the Status Quest: An Interdisciplinary Perspective*, ed. by Polly Wiessner and Wulf Schiefenhövel (Oxford: Berghahn), pp. 127–47

——. 2001. 'Fabulous Feasts – a Prolegomenon to the Importance of Feasting', in *Feasts: Archaeological and Ethnographic Perspectives on Food, Politics, and Power*, ed. by Michael Dietler and Brian Hayden (Washington, DC: Smithsonian Institution Press), pp. 23–64

——. 2014. *The Power of Feasts: From Prehistory to the Present* (Cambridge: Cambridge University Press)

Hayden, Brian, and Suzanne Villeneuve. 2011. 'A Century of Feasting Studies', *Annual Review of Anthropology*, 40: 433–49

Hill, Shaun. 2006. 'The Social Context of Eating', in *Food in the Ancient World*, ed. by John M. Wilkins and Shaun Hill (Oxford: Blackwell), pp. 41–78

Inomata, Takeshi, and Stephen D. Houston (eds). 2000. *Royal Courts of the Ancient Maya*, I: *Theories, Themes, and Comparisons* (Boulder: Westview)

——. (eds). 2001. *Royal Courts of the Ancient Maya*, II: *Case Studies* (Boulder: Westview)

Izzet, Vedia. 2000. 'Tuscan Order: The Development of Etruscan Sanctuary Architecture', in *Religion in Archaic and Republican Rome and Italy*, ed. by Edward Bispham and Christopher J. Smith (Edinburgh: Edinburgh University Press), pp. 34–53

Jannot, Jean-René. 2010. 'Les reliefs de Chiusi: mise à jour de nos connaissances', *Les Mélanges de l'École française de Rome: antiquité*, 122.1: 51–72

Jennings, Justin. 2004. 'La Chichera y El Patrón: Chicha and the Energetics of Feasting in the Prehistoric Andes', *Archeological Papers of the American Anthropological Association*, 14: 241–59

Junker, Laura. 2001. 'The Evolution of Ritual Feasting Systems', in *Feasts: Archaeological and Ethnographic Perspectives on Food, Politics, and Power*, ed. by Michael Dietler and Brian Hayden (Washington, DC: Smithsonian Institution), pp. 267–310

Kansa, Sarah Whitcher, and Michael MacKinnon. 2014. 'Etruscan Economics: Forty-Five Years of Faunal Remains from Poggio Civitate', *Etruscan Studies*, 17.1: 63–87

Lamoureux-St-Hilaire, Maxime. 2020. '9. Talking Feasts: Classic Maya Commensal Politics at La Corona', in *Her Cup for Sweet Cacao: Food in Ancient Maya Society*, ed. by Traci Ardren (Austin: University of Texas Press), pp. 243–73

LeCount, Lisa Jeanne. 1996. 'Pottery and Power: Feasting, Gifting, and Displaying Wealth among the Late and Terminal Classic Lowland Maya' (unpublished doctoral thesis, University of California, Los Angeles)

——. 2001. 'Like Water for Chocolate: Feasting and Political Ritual among the Late Classic Maya at Xunantunich, Belize', *American Anthropologist*, 103: 935–53

Lohse, Jon C. 2013. *Classic Maya Political Ecology: Resource Management, Class Histories, and Political Change in Northwestern Belize* (Los Angeles: Cotsen Institute of Archaeology Press, University of California)

Lohse, Jon C., Kerry Sagebiel, and Joanne Baron. 2013. 'The Ball Game, Community Ceremony, and Political Development in Northwestern Belize', in *Classic Maya Political Ecology: Resource Management, Class Histories, and Political Change in Northwestern Belize*, ed. by Jon C. Lohse (Los Angeles: Cotsen Institute of Archaeology Press, University of California), pp. 99–127

Macintosh Turfa, Jean, and Alwin G. Steinmayer, Jr. 2002. 'Interpreting Early Etruscan Structures: The Question of Murlo', *Papers of the British School at Rome*, 70: 1–28

Maggiani, Adriano, and Vincnezo Bellelli. 2006. 'Terrecotte architettoniche da Cerveteri (Vigna Parrocchiale): nuove acquisizioni', in *Deliciae fictiles*, III: *Architectural Terracottas in Ancient Italy: New Discoveries and Interpretations*, ed. by Ingrid Edlund-Berry, Giovanna Greco, and John Kenfield (Oxford: Oxbow), pp. 83–96

Mehren, Margit von. 1993. 'The Murlo Frieze Plaques. Considerations on their Distribution and Number', in *Deliciae fictiles*, I: *Proceedings of the First International Conference on Central Italic Architectural Terracottas at the Swedish Institute in Rome, 10–12 December 1990*, ed. by Eva Rystedt and Charlotte Wikander (Stockholm: Åström), pp. 139–45

Meyers, Gretchen. 2014. 'Introduction: The Experience of Monumentality in Etruscan and Early Roman Architecture', in *Monumentality in Etruscan and Early Roman Architecture: Ideology and Innovation*, ed. by Ingrid Edlund-Berry, Michael Thomas, and Gretchen Meyers (Austin: University of Texas Press), pp. 1–20

Mitterlechner, Tira. 2016. 'The Banquet in Etruscan Funerary Art and its Underlying Meaning', in *Dining and Death: Interdisciplinary Perspectives on the 'Funerary Banquet' in Ancient Art, Burial and Belief*, ed. by Catherine Draycott and Maria Stamatopoulou (Peeters: Leuven), pp. 523–52

Moretti Sgubini, Anna Maria, and Laura Ricciardi. 1993. 'Le terrecotte architettoniche di Tuscania', in *Deliciae fictiles*, I: *Proceedings of the First International Conference on Central Italic Architectural Terracottas at the Swedish Institute in Rome, 10–12 December 1990*, ed. by Eva Rystedt and Charlotte Wikander (Stockholm: Åström), pp. 163–81

Naso, Alessandro. 2000. 'The Etruscan Aristocracy in the Orientalizing Period: Culture, Economy, Relations', in *The Etruscans*, ed. by Mario Torelli (London: Thames and Hudson), pp. 111–39

Phillips, Kyle Meredith. 1993. *In the Hills of Tuscany: Recent Excavations at the Etruscan Site of Poggio Civitate (Murlo Siena)* (Philadelphia: University Museum University of Pennsylvania)

Pieraccini, Lisa. 2000. 'Families, Feasting, and Funerals: Funerary Ritual at Ancient Caere', *Etruscan Studies*, 7.1: 35–50

——. 2003. *Around the Hearth: Caeretan Cylinder-Stamped Braziers* (Rome: L'Erma di Bretschneider)

——. 2011. 'The Wonders of Wine in Etruria', in *The Archaeology of Sanctuaries and Ritual in Etruria*, ed. by Nancy T. de Grummond and Ingrid Edlund-Berry, Journal of Roman Archaeology, Supplementary Series (Portsmouth, RI: Journal of Roman Archaeology), pp. 127–37

——. 2014. 'The Ever Elusive Etruscan Egg', *Etruscan Studies*, 17.2: 267–92

Poletti Ecclesia, Elena. 2002. 'Coppe Ioniche', in *Cerveteri: importazioni e contesti nelle necropolis*, ed. by Giovanna Bagnasco Gianni (Bologna: Cisalpino), pp. 559–77

Rathje, Annette. 1983. 'A Banquet Service from the Latin City of Ficana', *Analecta Romana Instituti Danici*, 12: 7–29

——. 1988. 'Manners and Customs in Orientalizing Central Italy: Influence from the Near East', *Acta Hyperborea*, 1: 81–90

——. 1990. 'The Adoption of the Homeric Banquet in Central Italy in the Orientalizing Period', in *Sympotica: A Symposium on the Symposium*, ed. by Oswyn Murray (Oxford: Clarendon), pp. 279–88

——. 1994. 'Banquet and Ideology: Some New Considerations about Banqueting at Poggio Civitate', in *Murlo and the Etruscans: Art and Society in Ancient Etruria*, ed. by Richard De Puma and Jocelyn Penny Small (Wisconsin: University of Wisconsin Press), pp. 95–99

——. 2007. 'Murlo, Images and Archaeology', *Etruscan Studies*, 10: 175–84

Redmond, Elsa, and Charles Spencer. 2017. 'Ancient Palace Complex (300–100 BC) Discovered in the Valley of Oaxaca, Mexico', *Proceedings of the National Academy of Sciences*, 114: 3805–14

Rice, Prudence. 2009. 'On Classic Maya Political Economies', *Journal of Anthropological Archaeology*, 28: 70–84

Riva, Corinna. 2006. 'The Orientalizing Period in Etruria: Sophisticated Communities', in *Orientalization: Multidisciplinary Approaches to Change in the Ancient Mediterranean*, ed. by Corinna Riva and Nicholas C. Vella (London: Equinox), pp. 110–34

Riva, Corinna, and Simon Stoddart. 1996. 'Ritual Landscapes in Archaic Etruria', in *Approaches to the Study of Ritual*, ed. by John B. Wilkins (London: Accordia Research Institute), pp. 9–110

Rosenwig, Robert. 2007. 'Beyond Identifying Elites: Feasting as a Means to Understand Early Middle Formative Society on the Pacific Coast of Mexico', *Journal of Anthropological Archaeology*, 26: 1–27

Roth-Murray, Carrie. 2007. 'Elite Interaction in Archaic Etruria: Exploring the Exchange Networks of Terracotta Figured Frieze Plaques', *Journal of Mediterranean Studies*, 17.1: 135–60

Rystedt, Eva, and Charlotte Wikander (eds). 1993. *Deliciae fictiles*, I: *Proceedings of the First International Conference on Central Italic Architectural Terracottas at the Swedish Institute in Rome, 10–12 December 1990* (Stockholm: Åström)

Säflund, Gösta, and Peter Frazer. 1993. *Etruscan Imagery: Symbol and Meaning* (Partille: Åström)

Sarti, Susanna. 2017. 'Tomba Golini I', in *Dipingere l'Etruria: le riproduzioni delle pitture etrusche di Augusto Guido Gatti*, ed. by Lucrezia Cuniglio, Natacha Lubtchansky, and Susanna Sarti, Archeologia, n.s., 5 (Venosa: Osanna)

Sassatelli, Giuseppe. 1999. 'The Diet of the Etruscans', in *Food: A Culinary History from Antiquity to the Present*, ed. by Jean-Louis Flandrin and Massimo Montanari (New York: Columbia University Press), pp. 106–12

Scheffer, Charlotte. 1987. 'Forni e fornelli Etruschi in eta Arcaia', in *L'Alimentatione nel mondo antico: gli Etruschi*, ed. by Gabriella Barbieri (Rome: Istituto poligrafico e Zecca dello stato), pp. 97–105

Schmandt Besserat, Denise. 2001. 'Feasting in the Ancient Near East', in *Feasts: Archaeological and Ethnographic Perspectives on Food, Politics, and Power*, ed. by Michael Dietler and Brian Hayden (Washington, DC: Smithsonian Institution Press), pp. 391–403

Sheehy, James J. 1996. 'Ethnographic Analogy and the Royal Household in 8th Century Copan', in *Arqueología Mesoamericana: Homenaje a William T. Sanders*, II, ed. by Alba Guadalupe Mastache, Jeffrey R. Parsons, Robert S. Santley, and Mari Carmen Serra Puche (Mexico City: Instituto nacional de antropología e historia), pp. 253–76

Small, Jocelyn Penny. 1971. 'The Banquet Frieze from Poggio Civitate', *Studi etruschi*, 39: 25–61

——. 1994. 'Eat, Drink and be Merry: Etruscan Banquets', in *Murlo and the Etruscans: Art and Society in Ancient Etruria*, ed. by Richard De Puma and Jocelyn Penny Small (Wisconsin: University of Wisconsin Press), pp. 85–94

Smith, Michael. 2017. 'The Teotihuacan Anomaly: The Historical Trajectory of Urban Design in Ancient Central Mexico', *Open Archaeology*, 3: 175–93

Spencer, Charles, and Elsa Redmond. 2004. 'Primary State Formation in Mesoamerica', *Annual Review of Anthropology*, 33: 173–99

Staller, John E. 2010. 'Ethnohistoric Sources on Foodways, Feasts, and Festivals in Mesoamerica', in *Pre-Columbian Foodways*, ed. by John E. Staller and Michael B. Carrasco (New York: Springer), pp. 23–69

Steingräber, Stephan. 2006. *Abundance of Life: Etruscan Wall Painting* (Los Angeles: Getty Publications)

Stopponi, Simonetta (ed.). 1985. *Case e palazzi d'Etruria* (Milan: Electa)

Strandberg Olofsson, Margareta. 1984. *Acquarossa: Results of Excavations Conducted by the Swedish Institute of Classical Studies at Rome and the Soprintendenza alle Antichità dell'Etruria Meridionale, v.1: The Head Antefixes and Relief Plaques: A Reconstruction of a Terracotta Decorations and its Architectural Setting*, Skrifter utgivna av Svenska Institutet i Rom, 4°, 38.1 (Stockholm: Aström)

——. 1989. 'On the Reconstruction of the Monumental Area at Acquarossa', *Opusula Romana*, 17.12: 163–83

——. 1994. 'Some Interpretational Aspects of the Acquarossa/Tuscania Mould-Made Terracottas and their Architectural Context', in *Opus mixtum: Essays in Ancient Art and Society* (Stockholm: Aström), pp. 135–47

——. 2006. 'Herakles Revisited. On the Interpretation of the Mould-Made Architectural Terracottas from Acquarossa', in *Deliciae fictiles*, III: *Architectural Terracottas in Ancient Italy: New Discoveries and Interpretations*, ed. by Ingrid Edlund-Berry, Giovanna Greco, and John Kenfield (Oxford: Oxbow), pp. 122–29

Torelli, Mario. 1988. 'Le popolazioni dell'Italia antica: società e forme del potere', in *Storia di Roma*, I: *Roma in Italia*, ed. by Arnaldo Momigliano and Aldo Schiavone (Turin: Einaudi), pp. 53–74

——. 1997. *Il rango, il rito e l'immagine alle origini della rappresentazione storica romana* (Milan: Electa)

——. 2000. 'Le Regiae etrusche e laziali tra Orientalizzante e Arcaismo', in *Principi etruschi tra Mediterraneo ed Europa*, Museo Civico archeologico di Bologna (Venice: Marsilio), pp. 67–78

Tuck, Anthony. 1994. 'The Etruscan Seated Banquet: Villanovan Ritual and Etruscan Iconography', *American Journal of Archaeology*, 98: 617–28

——. 2006. 'The Social and Political Context of the 7th Century Architectural Terracottas at Poggio Civitate (Murlo)', in *Deliciae fictiles*, III: *Architectural Terracottas in Ancient Italy: New Discoveries and Interpretations*, ed. by Ingrid Edlund-Berry, Giovanna Greco, and John Kenfield (Oxford: Oxbow), pp. 130–35

——. 2017. 'The Evolution and Political Use of Elite Domestic Architecture at Poggio Civitate (Murlo)', *Journal of Roman Archaeology*, 30: 227–43

Tuck, Anthony, and Ann Glennie. 2020. 'The Archaic Aristocracy: The Case of Murlo (Poggio Civitate)', *Annali della Fondazione per il Museo Claudio Faina*, 27: 573–600

Weber-Lehmann, Cornelia. 1985. 'Spätarchaische Gelagenbilder in Tarquinia', *Römische Mitteilungen*, 92: 19–44

Wecowski, Marek. 2014. *The Rise of the Greek Aristocratic Banquet* (Oxford: Oxford University Press)

Wiessner, Polly, and Wulf Schiefenhövel (eds). 1996. *Food and the Status Quest: An Interdisciplinary Perspective* (Oxford: Berghahn)

Wikander, Charlotte, and Örjan Wikander. 1990. 'The Early Monumental Complex at Acquarossa', *Opuscula Romana*, 18: 189–205

Winter, Nancy. 2009. *Symbols of Wealth and Power: Architectural Terracotta Decoration in Etruria and Central Italy, 640–510 B.C.* (Ann Arbor: University of Michigan Press)

LISA C. PIERACCINI

4. Dining with the Dead

Visual Meals, Memory, and Symbolic Consumption in Etruscan Tomb Painting

Food and drink sustain us in life – why not also in death?[1]

Introduction

Food, life, and death share a precarious relationship — we often forget how intricately connected they are in ancient and even modern cultures (Cann 2018a; 2018b; Hastorf 2017; Haland 2012; Dietler and Hayden 2010; Hayden 2009; Hamilakis 1998). When it comes to understanding how food and death are complexly woven into ancient society, especially a culture like the Etruscans, the careful reading and interpretation of their art can offer fascinating visual clues (especially valuable since their literature has not survived).[2] Etruscan tomb painting presents a particularly unique class of narrative art that showcases images of feasting and dining within a funerary context. The iconic visual programmes of Etruscan tomb walls dating from the sixth to fourth centuries BCE often consisted of the conventional banquet, but how did these images capture moments of the living and feed the dead (Fig. 3.1, this volume)?[3]

So much work has been done on describing the banquet, that the 'symbolic' feast has often been missed. The reclining couples, the nude servants, and the colourful blankets, pillows, and clothing form part of the painted funerary canon of elite Etruscan culture. But the semiotic, sensory, temporal, and mnemonic aspects, not to mention the gastropolitics of food imagery as painted on Etruscan tomb walls have not been the subject of intense study — especially important as food and funerary practices make up such an original core feature of Etruscan society. Dining imagery in painted tombs not only explains deeply rooted social and mortuary customs and rituals, but also emphasizes the collective practices and socioeconomic facets of feasting in Etruscan mortuary practice. This chapter, thus, seeks to examine the visual culture of food and drink from Etruscan painted tombs dating to the sixth to fourth centuries BCE. It looks at how wall painting mediated, interacted with, and negotiated a visual food and drink culture based on activities of the living that were actively transferred to and performed in the realm of the dead. It examines archaeological

---

1 Cann 2018b, 4; for more on modern and ancient cross-cultural perspectives related to eating and death, see Cann 2018ab; Dietler and Hayden 2010; Hayden 2009.
2 For more on Etruscan art and food, see: Cristofani 1987; Cianferoni 2005; Menotti 2005; Rathje 2013; 1994; Riva 2010; Pieraccini 2000; 2013; 2014; Di Nocera and others 2016.
3 For more on Etruscan banquet ideology, see: Colivicchi 2018; Cianferoni 2005; Menotti 2005; Rastrelli 2005;

Riva 2010; Rathje 2013; 1994; Pieraccini 2000; Small 1994; Tuck 1994; Cristofani 1987.

Lisa C. Pieraccini History of Art, University of California, Berkeley (lisap@berkeley.edu)

data of food from offerings left in tombs and compares this evidence to the visual programmes in wall paintings. While the 'banquet' may be an aristocratic convention in Etruscan art and culture more broadly, the feasting imagery within these mortuary spaces reveals valuable insight into the power of dining and its symbolic agency in funerary décor, performativity, memory making, and bereavement rituals in Etruria.

A series of questions seem fitting for such a study. What sort of food items appear in Etruscan tomb painting and do they match the archaeological record? Why are certain food items, such as eggs held out in the hands of banqueters? Upon entering a tomb to inter a loved one, did family members stare in the darkly lit tombs at the painted banquet scenes and reflect on past feasting with the deceased? Did these painted scenes nourish the corpse as it lay dormant in the tomb? And finally, what did it mean to engage in visual consumption of painted feasts on tomb walls during the funeral ritual? A study of this sort is interdisciplinary and multifaceted and my brief paper touches only on certain characteristics of what is a much larger study. But I hope to shed light on the larger cultural, funeral, and ritual aspects of dining imagery in wall paintings. For the sake of casting a wide net regarding the definition of 'shared meals', I use the terms banquet, dining, and feasting interchangeably in this study. With more attention than ever on visual descriptions of painted tomb narratives along with careful analysis of organic materials found in tombs, it is time we explore food and drink beyond the descriptive paradigm.

Gastropolitics of Etruscan Funerals and Feasts

On both a global and historical level, food *is* culture. There is no escaping the multidimensional powerful dynamic that revolves around food and its consumption. The cause of wars, famines, migrations, and empires, food has played a central role in the development and livelihood of human evolution. Food, the basis of life, is also a marker of death. Yet, it is only recently that the study of food has gained a strong foothold in ancient Mediterranean studies.[4] Certainly, within the context of elite painted tombs in Etruria, food art is deeply connected to aristocratic ideologies, practices, and customs. It mirrors the very society that it depicted — a society which, by the early seventh century BCE, had established a prestigious food culture showcasing how food and drink functioned as conduits expressing luxury and prestige (van der Veen 2003). Gastropolitics (the economic and political forces at play with respect to why certain foods were valued by the Etruscan elite) played a vital role in how foods within dining/feasting/banqueting scenes were produced, consumed, and nourished the living and the dead. In this way, food and drink were used as semiotic markers — aristocrats depicted certain foods because they signified social hierarchies, status, power, wealth, and family prestige. Examining feasting and mortuary dining equipment as painted on tomb walls allows for a profound awareness of their visual agency and symbolic use and consumption. Firstly, some unpacking is necessary — painted tombs were a part of an exclusive group of Etruscan funerary décor, as the majority of Etruscans could not afford such lavish proclivities. Likewise, painted tombs appear to be a phenomenon of southern Etruria more generally, so there is a regional aspect

---

4 See Draycott and Stamatopoulou 2016 for the funerary banquet in ancient art. For food in the ancient world, see Wilkins and Nadeau 2015 (although oddly a chapter on the Etruscan banquet is not included); Hamilakis 1998 for Bronze Age Greek mortuary customs and eating as well as Haland 2012 for contemporary and ancient Greek funerary food rituals. See Ikram 2008 for Egyptian funerals and the dead; and for ancient Rome, see Lindsay 1998; Dunbabin 2003. No doubt there is a direct connection between Etruscan banqueting rituals and those of early Rome — future work in this area will surely shed more light on the topic.

to this type of decorative funerary expression. Tombs were entered by a small group of family members — they were private chambers (not public) created for the deceased and his/her family. The Etruscans spent a good amount of their lives preparing for death, especially the elite who commissioned custom-built tomb chambers to last an eternity. Moreover, the décor would have ideally been chosen by the deceased before he/she perished and was the final stop of the lavish funerary procession. The time and resources spent on the construction and decoration of a tomb were substantial investments and provided an insurance policy against oblivion. At sites like ancient Caere, large tumuli were status markers in the funerary landscape. The tumuli would be visible by all, but the inner tomb chambers were an exclusive space for reintegrating the deceased through feasting activities (Cann 2018a; Hayden 2014). The painted banquets accompanied by other material offerings transformed the sepulchre into a material and visual memory box. It was not enough to simply place prestige food items in the tomb as offerings (offerings that would decompose and break-down). The painted meals, I suggest, promised an eternal and infinite feast. The interior decoration had an active visual agency that kept the deceased metaphorically satiated. Socioeconomic factors made it possible for elite Etruscans to flex their status vis-à-vis food and drink in the tomb. Thus, such painted images of dining were negotiated and visually consumed as crucial components of these highly mediated memory archives.

Food Art and Offerings in Etruscan Tombs

Although the banquet is depicted in a variety of mediums in Etruscan art and over a long period of time (see Taylor Chapter 3)[5] — it is often challenging to identify specific food items in great detail — and tomb paintings are no exception. Perhaps a mere suggestion of a cake or loaf of bread is rendered or sometimes indiscernible fruits (figs, plums, pomegranates, quince, grapes) are partially sticking out of vessels — *food seems hidden in plain sight*. What *is* clearly conveyed in these wall paintings, however, is that food is prepared, presented, served, and consumed (especially seen in the fifth century BCE and beyond). The performativity of the painted meals, in regard to dining, feasting, and banqueting, is clearly communicated within the larger scope of the composition and through visual cues in the form of banqueting equipment and gestures. Just because we do not see the specific type of fruit, bread, or cake, does not mean these foods were not present — these paintings undoubtedly convey feasting. These food visuals are performative in that they depict a 'selected reality' and cultural construct embedded within social values which allowed loved ones a means for honouring, remembering, and engaging with the dead. By looking at the archaeological evidence found in tombs alongside the identifiable food items depicted on wall paintings some important facets of funerary food culture begin to emerge. For starters, wine vessels (clay and metal) permeate the feasting scenes overall with either pitchers, drinking cups, large containers for mixing wine, or a combination of all of these.[6] These vessels have a binary aspect in that they are desirable luxury and utilitarian objects (especially the larger vessels for mixing wine) and they contain/hold a prestigious commodity, namely wine. Tarquinian tombs such as the Tomb of the Lionesses, Tomb of the Augurs, Tomb of Hunting and Fishing, Tomb of the Chariots, Tomb of the Triclinium, Tomb of the Funerary Bed, Tomb of the Leopards, Tomb 5513, Tomb of the Ship, Tomb of the Shields, the Querciola Tomb I, and

---

5 For further discussion, see Colivicchi 2018; Rastrelli 2005; Rathje 1994.

6 For more on vessels and eating and drinking in Etruscan funerary practice, see Riva 2010.

Figure 4.1. Detail of Larth Velcha and his wife on the back wall of the Tomb of the Shields (mid-fourth century BCE), Tarquinia. © Museo Nazionale Etrusco di Villa Giulia. Archivio fotografico. Fotografo Mauro Benedetti.

the Tomb of the Warrior (just to name some) all feature vases that reference wine drinking. It is the one liquid (indicated by its containers) that is ever-present throughout tomb offerings and tomb paintings and as such, holds a special place as the quintessential divine liquid of the funerary world (see Zifferero Chapter 1). However, wine is not depicted in the act of being poured or consumed in wall paintings — a topic I will address shortly. It is such a part of the aristocratic banquet paradigm that in its funerary context, it is understood as a symbolic liquid — the intoxicating aspect of wine serving as a communicative vehicle between mortal and immortal and the living and the dead (Ciacci and Zifferero 2005; Cristofani 1987; Pieraccini 2011). Grape seeds have survived in the archaeological record in various tombs — one interesting example can

be seen in Tomb G at Casale Marittimo, where grapes were wrapped in linen along with hazelnuts and a pomegranate (Rastrelli 2005). Questions about grapes continue to pique curiosity — do the grapes in funerary wall paintings have the same symbolic import as wine? We can only speculate that regardless of fermentation, grapes were a valued fruit. The grapes painted on the 'funerary banquet' table in the fourth-century BCE Tomb of the Shields at Tarquinia and the Golini Tomb I in Orvieto strongly suggest their luxury status as a fruit (Giulierini 2005; Rastrelli 2005; Menotti 2005). They may be specific to a season, namely the fall, for example in the Tomb of the Shields (although it is difficult for us to know), or as a vital ingredient of the aristocratic mortuary meal (Fig. 4.1). Regardless, in this tomb they are displayed in a frozen moment of the meal shared by husband and wife. They may also perform as a visual construct in the tomb for Larth and his wife to consume in the afterlife. The grapes form part of an elite 'mortuary meal plan', as the Velcha family were one of the leading political entities in Tarquinia in the fourth century BCE (we know this from the inscriptions inside of the tomb) (Maggiani 2005).

It is not surprising to see the combination of grapes, grain, and olives (the great 'Mediterranean triad') in the archaeological record in tombs as well as in tomb painting. Grains have been found inside tombs, especially in containers as part of the funerary deposit for provisions for the afterlife (Colivicchi 2017). Analysis of grains in tombs is increasing, but we should not forget the many large containers placed in tombs that were for containing grains, such as the large storage jars (pithoi) from sites like Caere (Ridgway 2010). The various small cakes or loaves seen on a myriad of diverse media (bronze mirrors, vase painting, wall painting) suggest that some form of bread was consumed by the Etruscans as early as the seventh century BCE. An early example can be seen on the Montescudaio cinerary urn where a man sits at a table with a female servant — a

Figure 4.2. A modern reconstruction of a banquet scene on the back wall of the Tomb of the Triclinium, Tarquinia by Julie Wolf.

wine vessel is placed near the table laden with food items — the two oblong objects have regularly been described as *focaccia* or a type of bread (Menotti 2005). In a tomb in Verrucchio three well-preserved tables, left for a funerary meal for the family or for the deceased, had vases containing traces of rabbit, fish, hazelnuts, grapes, honey, and bread (Cianferoni 2005). Similar 'loaves' are seen in the Tarquinian Tomb of the Shields (Fig. 4.1). The loaves are placed alongside other food items such as grapes in front of the deceased, Larth Velcha and his wife. Smaller loaves, buns, or cakes may be painted in some of the dishes on the banquet table in the Tomb of the Triclinium dating to the fifth century BCE at Tarquinia (Fig. 3.1). Thanks to the nineteenth-century *lucido* by Carlo Ruspi, details of small round food items can be seen in the painting as they are carefully arranged in several dishes (Fig. 4.2).

In fact, some of the very small round objects appear to be olives. Olives have been found on numerous occasions in the archaeological record in Etruria. One of the most significant examples, to date, is the Giglio shipwreck where Etruscan storage vessels were packed with olives — presumably on their way out of Etruria as precious cargo (Bound and Vallintine 1983). Olives are also found in tombs (or at least the olive pits are found). One need only look at the Tomb of the Olives at Cerveteri where a substantial hoard of olives dating to the mid-sixth century BCE were discovered in a large basin (Sassatelli 2013). In terms of wall painting, it is tempting to see olives in the trees, such as on the left wall of the Tomb of the Leopards in Tarquinia where black dots strongly suggest the small fruit. However, these trees, like many trees featured in Etruscan tomb paintings, are most likely laurel trees (*laurus nobilis*) — their seasonal black berries resemble olives. Today Etruscan necropoleis, like that of ancient Caere (modern Cerveteri), are inundated with indigenous laurel trees. Their use in Etruscan cuisine, as a flavour enhancer, may be understood with future analysis of trace organic materials in tombs.

Bronze cheese graters were placed in the tombs of wealthy males in the seventh century BCE indicating that cheese was produced (Ridgway 1997; 2009).[7] However, it is difficult to identify cheese on painted tomb walls. However, in the fourth-century BCE Tomb of the Reliefs at Cerveteri, a circular item depicted on one of the upper right columns has been identified by J. Heurgon (1964) as a cheese basket of sorts, while H. Blank argues that it is a type of cushion/pillow (Blank 1987). Whatever the case, the fact that cheese graters existed in Etruria signifies the production and consumption of cheese, at least within the Etruscan elite (as the tombs found with the graters indicate). While cheese graters have not been easily identified in tomb paintings, their small size and bronze colour may render such detection challenging. However, tomb paintings which feature dishes on the banquet tables clearly with food inside, such as the Tomb of the Triclinium, Tomb of the Shields, and the Querciola Tomb I at Tarquinia, may in fact contain an assortment of foods such as cheese, bread, olives, grapes, figs, pomegranates, and nuts.

Due to an increase in zooarchaeological studies we know much more about meat in a funerary context. Even food deposits in humble burials dating to the Iron Age are found (Bertani 1995; Minniti 2012). Likewise, the technology for cooking meats, such as spits, knives, cauldrons, and firedogs found in seventh-century BCE tombs strongly suggests that meat was left in some elite tomb chambers, and this is supported by recent

animal remains recently identified in Etruscan tombs (Minniti 2012; Maini and Curci 2013; Prato and Tecchiati 2015). The usual ancient Mediterranean suspects are present, sheep, goat, pig, oxen, and the occasional chicken and even a few examples of fish (Minniti 2012; Bertani 1995; see Maras Chapter 5). In fact, in a wall painting from the Tomb of the Inscriptions at Tarquinia, a fascinating image shows a fish held out over a table (see Maras Chapter 5, Fig. 5.6; Giulierini 2005). What I find most interesting about these recent studies is the knowledge we have gained about the great variety of animals employed for offerings. Likewise, the butchery of the animals, specifically the cuts of pork, usually the ribs, placed in tombs reveals fascinating patterns of funerary practice.[8] All of these animal remains, and I only mention a few, tell us a great deal about meat offerings and consumption in a mortuary context; whether as a food item for the afterlife, a votive offering for the deceased, or a combination of the two, meat was an integral part of elite funerary *carte du jour* in Etruria. Meats were expensive proteins — a prestige food item probably few could afford on a regular basis (Colivicchi 2018; Giulierini 2005). The quintessential illustration of meat on a tomb wall comes from the fourth-century BCE Golini Tomb I in Orvieto, where we find a butcher's scene (Fig. 4.3). In this fascinating painting the artist has depicted a series of animals as they hang from the butcher's rack: wild rabbit, duck, goat, and an ox. The decapitated head of the ox, painted as if placed on the ground, looks up in a lively manner to its own severed torso — a snippet of Etruscan humour. And yet, the ox may

---

7 These bronze graters, another technological advancement and identity marker in Etruscan tombs, appear to be gender specific, discovered, thus far, in predominantly, if not exclusively, male tombs. See Ridgway 2009.

8 The consistent choice of the same portions of pork ribs are found at sites like Monterenzio Vecchio south of Bologna (Maini and Curci 2013). Moreover, there is a long history of pork and funerary deposits seen in proto-Etruscan sites like Villa Bruschi Falgari (Minniti 2012). Chickens too have been found in tombs, see Prato and Tecchiati 2015.

be reflecting on its own, soon to be, consumed state once the feasting begins.

The Golini Tomb I is a truly remarkable example of the preparation of food — it's our only surviving wall painting which depicts such activities. On the left-side wall, both female and male slaves work behind a counter preparing food (including grapes and pomegranates). A flute player adds music to the activities while a male servant is engaged in food preparation in a large basin (perhaps kneading bread or working with a pestle) (Fig. 4.4). The *preparation* of a banquet for this tomb owner was significant for the deceased or his/her family — as the choice of tomb décor was deeply personal and shaped by the socio-political constructs of the time.

There is one particular food item which can be clearly identified and which appears for over two hundred years in Etruscan tomb painting, namely eggs (Pieraccini 2014). Small and portable, eggs are representative of life itself — the eggshell literally contains life. Eggs retained a distinct place at the Tarquinian funerary banquet — being held, passed, exchanged, and/or displayed (e.g., Tomb of the Lionesses, Tomb of the Leopards, Tomb of the Maiden; Tomb of the Shields; Tomb of the Chariots) — and the Golini Tomb I at Orvieto (Menotti 2005). In fact, they are the only food item we see handled. At times, the eggs are literally held out for the viewer to observe — either marking the deceased or someone honouring/wishing well the deceased (see Fig. 4.5). Food rituals are complex affairs and, in the case of the egg, it appears that protocols of gestures were in place. Not only are eggs depicted within a ritualized context, but within a performative framework. As a potential 'indicator' of the deceased or the loved one of the deceased, the Etruscan egg was a highly semiotic device in elite tomb painting (Figs 4.5–4.6). It is handled and held because it is a signifier. Eggs transcended the boundaries of consumption to social indicator with performative agency. They may have wielded mnemonic power like the feasts (prompting a

Figure 4.3. Detail of the entry wall of the Golini Tomb I (mid-fourth century BCE) Orvieto. An ox head looks up at its hanging torso on a butcher's block. Immagini riprodotte su gentile concessione della Soprintendenza Archeologio, Belle Arti e Paesaggio dell'Umbria.

Figure 4.4. Detail of the left side of the Golini Tomb I depicting the preparation of a banquet (mid-fourth century BCE) Orvieto. Courtesy of the Soprintendenza Archeologia, Belle Arti e Paesaggio per la provincia di Viterbo e l'Etruria Meridionale.

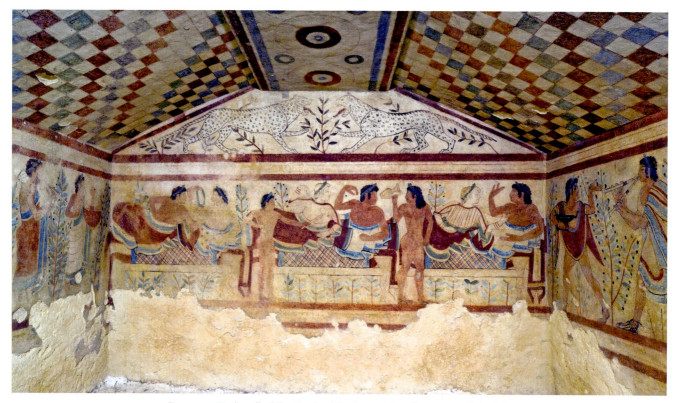

Figure 4.5. Back wall of the Tomb of the Leopards — the man on right side holds out an egg (early fifth century BCE, Tarquinia). © Museo Nazionale Etrusco di Villa Giulia. Archivio fotografico. Fotografo Mauro Benedetti.

Figure 4.6. Back wall of the Tomb of the Chariots — the man on the left holds out an egg (fifth century BCE), Tarquinia. © Museo Nazionale Etrusco di Villa Giulia. Archivio fotografico. Fotografo Mauro Benedetti.

sensory reaction by the viewer). Because eggs are one of the few identifiable food items and held out in special gestures, they can be understood through many lenses, i.e., as a vital symbol of life, death, and fertility, as portable funerary food, a transformative symbolic nutrient (eating/offering of the egg), as well as a votive.

The archaeological data concerning eggs, even though presumed fragile, does not disappoint, as eggs have been uncovered in Etruscan tombs throughout Etruria, but famously known inside a Caeretan brazier in the Maroi Tomb III at Cerveteri (Pieraccini 2003; 2013; 2014) (Fig. 4.7).[9] Placed in this manner, that is, left roasting on hot coals, the eggs were also food items for the feast in the tomb for the living and the dead. It is not difficult to see them as symbolic tokens or votives for a safe journey to the afterlife. Eggs maintained a cache of emblematic import as ritualized cuisine and indicators of life, death, and rebirth. Recent finds in Etruria reveal eggs in the Tolle necropolis at Chianciano Terme (Rastrelli 2005, 47) and nearby quail eggs were found in a bucchero vessel from a seventh-century BCE tomb (Rastrelli 2005).

Visual Meals, Symbolic Consumption, and Memory

Even though it is difficult at times to discern the exact food items painted on tomb walls, the painted banquet scenes with furniture (*klinai*, blankets, pillows, tables, candle stands, etc.) and feasting accoutrements (dishes, cups, vessels for mixing wine, knives, spits, braziers, etc.) indicate that food was present for consumption

Figure 4.7. Photograph of a Caeretan brazier with eggs left roasting on coals from the Maroi Tomb III (sixth century BCE), Cerveteri. © Museo Nazionale Etrusco di Villa Giulia. Archivio fotografico. Fotografo Mauro Benedetti.

inside the many vessels and on the tables in these funerary paintings. That we do not see the act of drinking and eating in Etruscan tomb painting may suggest details of elite 'norms' in society (as they do today in our own culture, where elites who commission their own portraits do not show themselves chewing and drinking). In other words, masticating food and drinking wine are not necessary to visually imply and communicate feasting and drinking, but the display of a feast is. The food and drink thus far discussed are not difficult to recognize in the overall funerary visual rhetoric in Etruria. As far as archaeological material and food, we must remember that non-organic artefacts are the traditional 'stars' of the 'material culture show' in the field of ancient Mediterranean studies more broadly. The stone monuments, civic centres, temples, gateways, and more take up a large part of the academic conversation. But here, both visual and organic material, not to mention the built environment of the tomb, come together to underscore the substantial and deeply symbolic role of funerary dining for elite Etruscans. The visual power of these meals indicates how Etruscans established their own

---

9 Moreover, the brazier is a good example of hybrid technology as a cooking and heating device, as it functioned in the home as a hearth, in sanctuaries and temples as a mini altar, and in the tomb in multifaceted ways, i.e., as a hearth, mini altar, and funerary hot plate where eggs were placed on hot coals and roasted, see Pieraccini 2003; 2013.

food materiality and culture as well as how they perpetuated and sustained its long-term funerary practice. The privacy of tomb chambers lends itself to confining these spaces to small groups of family members and loved ones allowed into the tomb chamber during the funerary ritual and deposition of the deceased. Once inside, food and memory played a vital role. As Hamilakis (1998, 16) has argued, 'memory should not be treated as a passive container of experiences but as an active process of recording, retaining'. In this light, family members would be triggered by the painted visuals of feasting and prompted to 'remember' their loved one within the construct of dining/banqueting. The mnemonic, emotional, and sensory power of food becomes a powerful device for expressing a wide range of human feelings, especially within a funerary context where customs of the living merge with those of the dying (Hamilakis 1998). After such rituals in a tomb, the door of the tomb would be shut and sealed, opened only when depositing another family member (for example a spouse). The recycled funerary space, along with the painted images, not to mention the decomposed body and offerings of food, coalesced to make the internal space of the tomb an interactive experience. Here, life (those entering), death (the rotting body and decomposed food from the previous burial) and eating (painted feasts on the walls and fresh food offerings) overlap in fascinating ways. Further still, when family members re-entered tombs generation after generation, they may have relished these painted feasts even more as vintage 'snapshots' of long-enduring customs.[10] To what extent non-elites expressed mourning

and funerary rituals through food is a challenging topic due to the practice of cremation and buried ash-urns, but it is not difficult to envision that foods were a vital part of mortuary customs regardless of status and wealth.

Thus, I argue, these paintings acted as 'graphic meals' visually consumed by the small community entering the tomb, but more importantly, for the deceased to enjoy and 'feed on' in the afterlife — this gives new meaning to the colloquial expression, 'dying to eat'. To this end, the journey to the afterlife, full of ancestors, combined with visual feasting and food left in the tomb — allowed for a sort of a symbolic reunion where life, food, and death were blended in deeply meaningful ways. Further, if we look at these tombs as liminal spaces where the deceased could indulge in earthly pleasures, then the images of dining/feasting/banqueting work to simultaneously nourish the living *and* the deceased where everyone engages in 'dining with the dead'. The meals painted on tomb walls need not be replenished — as they were fixed and constant fodder for the deceased.

Conclusion

Food allows us to understand agriculture, economics, religion, ritual, gender, identity, politics, and the complicated process of death. The merging of Etruscan food culture studies with analysis of food imagery, as seen in painted tombs deepens our understanding of food, consumption, ritual, memory, and funerary practice. Not only, these paintings were an original expression of Etruscan culture. The twentieth century saw, unfortunately, the routine disposal of food and decomposed materials in Etruscan tombs. The majority of some of our most important tombs to date were excavated at a time when organic materials were simply discarded or not considered worthy of study — we would know much more about food offerings if advanced methods for excavating tombs had been

---

10 We must keep in mind that wall paintings underground could have been intimately tied to paintings in aristocratic homes above ground (although evidence of this has not fully emerged). But still, it is important to remember that Etruscan artists must have been painting scenes of feasting *above ground* in sanctuaries, civic centres, and private homes, etc.

employed. Thankfully, the twenty-first century has encouraged innovative approaches and advanced technological developments that greatly enrich our knowledge of organic materials, expanding our understanding of so many aspects of Etruscan culture, ritual, and art. Even the smallest traces of food materials, difficult to pin down in the archaeological record, can now be studied. The intersectionality of the painted meals on tomb walls with the organic discoveries from tombs promises a new understanding of how we view funerals, food, and feasting in Etruria. Shared meals, whether funerary or not, allow us to explore the internal shape of Etruscan society. When it comes to looking at food items in Etruscan funerary practice, the tombs provide much more than a 'grocery list' for consumption. The individual food items, their presentation, how they are handled, or not, their performativity, all combine to reveal how food functioned within religious, funerary, ritual, and secular contexts.

We tend to set our markers of 'civilization' based on accomplishments seen in text and stone. The prose and poetry, civic monuments and religious structures, towns, cities, and roads have traditionally been the cultural, historical, and artistic barometers in the field of ancient Mediterranean studies. We often miss the core meaning of what 'civilization' means when we pass up the evidence of something so common as the preparing, presenting, and sharing of a meal. Traditional scholarship of the ancient Mediterranean has looked for evidence of socio-political structures, identity, and power in tangible markers predominately from colonizing imperial systems, when in fact, the experience of a meal speaks to the very essence of what it means to be human in all cultures across the globe (Jones 2007). For the Etruscans, food imagery mediated, pacified, and communicated with the dead *and* the living. Painted meals on Etruscan tomb walls evoked memory, exercised gastropolitics, and negotiated food semiotics in ways that made the funeral of a loved one a more comforting and interactive experience — giving evocative meaning to the term, 'dining with the dead'.

Works Cited

Bertani, M. G. 1995. 'Il banchetto dei morti nel Etruria padana (IX–IV secolo a.C.)', *Studi etruschi*, 56: 255–69

Blank, H. 1987. 'Utensili della cucina etrusca', in *L'alimentazione nel mondo antico: gli etruschi*, ed. by Gabriella Barbieri (Rome: Istituto poligrafico e Zecca dello stato), pp. 107–17

Bound, Mensun, and R. Vallintine. 1983. 'A Wreck of Possible Etruscan Origin off Giglio Island', *International Journal of Nautical Archaeology*, 12.2: 113–22

Cann, Candi (ed.). 2018a. *Dying to Eat: Cross-Cultural Perspectives on Food, Death, and the Afterlife* (Lexington: University Press of Kentucky)

——. 2018b. 'Starters: The Role of Food in Bereavement and Memorialization', in *Dying to Eat: Cross-Cultural Perspectives on Food, Death, and the Afterlife*, ed. by Candi Cann (Lexington: University Press of Kentucky), pp. 1–14

Ciacci, Andrea, and Andrea Zifferero. 2005. *Vinum: un progetto per il riconoscimento della vita silvestre nel paesaggio archeologico della Toscana e del Lazio settentrionale* (Siena: Cl.Vin.)

Cianferoni, Giuseppina C. (ed.). 2005. *Cibi e sapori nel mondo antico* (Florence: National Archaeological Museum)

Colivicchi, Fabio. 2017. 'Banqueting and Food', in *Etruscology*, ed. by Alessandro Naso (Berlin: De Gruyter), pp. 207–20

Cristofani, Mauro. 1987. 'Il banchetto in Etruria', in *L'Alimentatione nel mondo antico: gli Etruschi*, ed. by Gabriella Barbieri (Rome: Istituto poligrafico e Zecca dello stato), pp. 123–32

Dietler, Michael. 1996. 'Feast and Commensal Politics in the Political Economy: Food, Power and Status in Prehistoric Europe', in *Food and the Status Quest: An Interdisciplinary Perspective*, ed. by Polly Wiesner and Wulf Schiefenhovel (Providence: Berghahn), pp. 87–126

Dietler, Michael, and Brian Hayden (eds). 2010. *Feasts: Archaeological and Ethnographic Perspectives on Food, Politics, and Power* (Washington, DC: Smithsonian Institution)

Di Nocera, Gian Maria, Alessandro Guidi, and Andrea Zifferero (eds). 2016. *ArcheoTipico: l'archeologia come strumento per la ricostruzione del paesaggio e dall'alimentazione antica; atti del Convegno (Viterbo 2015)*, Rivista di storia dell'agricoltura (Florence: Le lettere)

Draycott, Catherine M., and Maria Stamatopoulou (eds). 2016. *Dining and Death: Interdisciplinary Perspectives of the 'Funerary Banquet' in Ancient Art, Burial and Belief* (Leuven: Peeters)

Dunbabin, Katherine M. D. 2003. *The Roman Banquet: Images of Conviviality* (Cambridge: Cambridge University Press)

Giulierini, Paolo. 2005. 'Il cibo in Etruria: produzione e consumi', in *Cibo e sapori nel mondo antico: Firenze, Museo Archeologico Nazionale 18 Marzo 2005-15 Gennaio 2006*, ed. by Giuseppina C. Cianferoni (Livorno: Sillabe), pp. 66–78

Haland, Evy J. 2012. 'When the Dead Ensure the Food. Death and the Regeneration of the Life through Festivals, Food and Social Gathering during the Ritual Year in Modern and Ancient Greece', *Cosmos*, 28: 309–46

Hamilakis, Yannis. 1998. 'Eating the Dead: Mortuary Feasting and the Politics of Memory in the Aegean Bronze Age Societies', in *Cemetery and Society in the Aegean Bronze Age Societies*, ed. by Keith Branigan (Sheffield: Sheffield Academic Press), pp. 115–32

Hastorf, Christine A. 2017. *The Social Archaeology of Food: Thinking about Eating from Prehistory to the Present* (Cambridge: Cambridge University Press)

Hayden, Brian. 2009. 'Funerals as Feasts: Why Are They So Important?', *Cambridge Archaeology Journal*, 19: 29–52

——. 2014. *The Power of Feasts: From Prehistory to the Present* (Cambridge: Cambridge University Press)

Hayden, Brian, and Suzanne Villeneuve. 2011. 'A Century of Feasting Studies', *Annual Review of Anthropology*, 40: 433–49

Heurgon, Jacques. 1964. *Daily Life of the Etruscans* (London: Weisenfeld and Nicolson)

Ikram, Salima. 2008. 'Food and Funerals: Sustaining the Dead for Eternity', *Polish Archaeology in the Mediterranean*, 20: 361–71

Jones, Martin. 2007. *Feast: Why Humans Share Food* (Oxford: Oxford University Press)

Lindsay, Hugh. 1998. 'Eating with the Dead: The Roman Funerary Banquet', in *Meals in a Social Context*, ed. by Inge Nielsen and Hanne S. Nielsen (Oxford: Oxford University Press), pp. 67–80

Maini, Elena, and Antonio Curci. 2013. 'The Food of the Dead: Alimentary Offerings in the Etruscan-Celtic Necropolis of Monterenzio Vecchio', *Anthropozoologica*, 48.2: 341–54

Maggiani, Andrea. 2005. 'Simmetrie architettoniche, dissimmetrie rappresentative. Osservando le pitture della Tomba degli Scudi di Tarquinia', in *Pittura parietale, pittura vascolare: ricerche in corso tra Etruria e Campania; atti Convegno Santa Maria Capua Vetere*, ed. by Fernando Gilotta (Naples: Arte Tipografica Editrice), pp. 115–32

Menotti, Elena Maria. 2005. *Cibo: vita e cultura nella collezioni del Museo archeologico nazionale di Mantova* (Mantua: Tre Lune)

Minniti, Claudia. 2012. 'Offerte rituali di cibo animale in contesti funerari dell' Etruria e del Lazio nella prima eta' del Ferro', in *Atti del 6° Convegno nazionale di archeozoologia: Centro visitatori del Parco dell'Orecchiella, 21–24 maggio 2009, San Romano in Garfagnana - Lucca*, ed. by Jacopo De Grossi Mazzorin, Daniela Saccà, and Carlo Tozzi (Pisa: Universita di Pisa), pp. 153–61

Pieraccini, Lisa. 2000. 'Families, Feasting, and Funerals: Funerary Ritual at Ancient Caere', *Etruscan Studies*, 7.1: 35–50

——. 2003. *Around the Hearth: Caeretan Cylinder-Stamped Braziers* (Rome: L'Erma di Bretschneider)

——. 2011. 'The Wonders of Wine in Etruria', in *The Archaeology of Sanctuaries and Ritual in Etruria*, ed. by Nancy T. de Grummond and Ingrid Edlund-Berry, Journal of Roman Archaeology, Supplementary Series (Portsmouth, RI: Journal of Roman Archaeology), pp. 127–37

——. 2013. 'Food and Drink in the Etruscan World', in *The Etruscan World*, ed. by Jean M. Turfa (New York: Routledge), pp. 812–22

——. 2014. 'The Ever Elusive Etruscan Egg', *Etruscan Studies*, 17.2: 267–92

Prato, Ornella, and Umberto Tecchiati. 2015. 'Sulla deposizione di Gallus gallus nella tomba 4 UniMi della necropolis estrusco/romano di "le Morre" di Tarquinia', in *Atti 8° Convegno nazionale di Archeozoologia (Lecce, 2015)*, ed. by Jacopo De Grossi Mazzorin, Ivana Fiore, and Claudia Minniti (Lecce: Università del Salento Terrenato), pp. 321–24

Rathje, Annette. 1983. 'A Banquet Service from the Latin City of Ficana', *Analecta Romana Instituti Danici*, 12: 7–29

——. 1988. 'Manners and Customs in Orientalizing Central Italy: Influence from the Near East', in *East and West: Cultural Relations in the Ancient World*, ed. by Tobias Fischer-Hansen, Acta Hyperborea, 1 (Copenhagen: Museum Tusculanum Press), pp. 81–90

——. 1990. 'The Adoption of the Homeric Banquet in Central Italy in the Orientalizing Period', in *Sympotica: A Symposium on the Symposium*, ed. by Oswyn Murray (Oxford: Clarendon), pp. 279–88

——. 1994. 'Banquet and Ideology: Some New Considerations about Banqueting at Poggio Civitate', in *Murlo and the Etruscans: Art and Society in Ancient Etruria*, ed. by Richard De Puma and Jocelyn Penny Small (Wisconsin: University of Wisconsin Press), pp. 95–99

——. 2013. 'The Banquet through Etruscan History', in *The Etruscan World*, ed. by Jean M. Turfa (New York: Routledge), pp. 823–30

Rastrelli, Anna. 2005. 'Il banchetto in Etruria: le rappresentazioni', in *Cibo e sapori nel mondo antico: Firenze, Museo Archeologico Nazionale 18 Marzo 2005-15 Gennaio 2006*, ed. by Giuseppina C. Cianferoni (Livorno: Sillabe), pp. 44–55

Ridgway, David. 1997. 'Nestor's Cup and the Etruscans', *Oxford Journal of Archaeology*, 16.3: 325–44

——. 2009. 'La coppa di Nestore e una grattugia da Vulci', in *Etruria e Italia preromana*, ed. by Stefano Bruni (Rome: Fabrizio Serra), pp. 789–91

Ridgway, Francesca R. S. 2010. *Pithoi Stampigliati Ceretani: una classe originale di ceramica etrusca*, ed. by Francesca R. Serra Ridgway and Lisa Pieraccini (Rome: L'Erma di Bretschneider)

Riva, Corinna. 2010. 'Nuove tecnologie del se': il banchetto rituale collettivo in Etruria', *Saguntum extra*, 9: 69–80

Sassatelli, Giuseppe. 2013. 'The Diet of the Etruscans', in *Food: A Cultural History from Antiquity to the Present*, ed. by Jean-Louis Flandrin, Massimo Montanari, and Albert Sonnenfeld (New York: Columbia University Press), pp. 106–12

Small, Jocelyn P. 1994. 'East, Drink and "Be Merry" Etruscan Banquets', in *Society in Ancient Etruria*, ed. by Richard De Puma and Jocelyn Penny Small (Madison: University of Wisconsin Press), pp. 85–94

Smith, Monica L. 2015. 'Feasts and their Failures', *The Journal of Archaeological Method and Theory*, 22: 1215–37

Steingräber, Stephan. 2006. *Abundance of Life: Etruscan Wall Painting* (Los Angeles: Getty Publications)

Tuck, Anthony. 1994. 'The Etruscan Seated Banquet: Villanovan Ritual and Etruscan Iconography', *American Journal of Archaeology*, 98: 617–28

Veen, Marijke van der. 2003. 'When Is Food a Luxury?', *World Archaeology*, 34.3: 405–27

Wilkins, John, and Robin Nadeau (eds). 2015. *A Companion to Food in the Ancient World* (Chichester: Wiley Blackwell)

DANIELE F. MARAS

5. Fish and Rituals

Working Notes on Religious Practices
Involving Fish in Ancient Etruria

Too Many Fish in the Sea (and Too Few in Context)

The Etruscans were famous throughout antiquity as a seafaring people, with a special reputation for piracy and in certain historical periods even exercising a real thalassocracy — that is to say, a maritime supremacy on the seas surrounding the Italian Peninsula (Cristofani 1983; Gras 1985; Cherici 2006; Bruni 2013; Pommey 2017, 371–72; see further Gianfrotta 1988 and Turfa 2012, 146–48). Apparently, such specialization began already in the Early Iron Age, contemporary with the earliest formation of proto-urban settlements (synoecism) in the areas of the future Etruscan metropolises (di Gennaro 2000; Pacciarelli 2000, 170–76; Mandolesi 2014, 200–01). In fact, while in the Late Bronze Age only sparse and small villages are attested on the seashore in southern Etruria, by the Early Iron Age a large port settlement was founded at the site of Saline (salt-works) of Tarquinia (Mandolesi 2014). Recent surveys in the difficult environment of the salt-works (which were used until the late twentieth century and which currently host a wild-life reservoir) show that habitation and production sites were spread uniformly in an elongated stretch around sixty

hectares wide and one kilometre long on the coastline, as evidenced by a number of pottery sherds of the Villanovan period.

This settlement has been interpreted in connection with the proto-urban centre of Tarquinia, as a working place for the exploitation of the coast for salt production, sea-trade, and fishing (Annoscia and others 2019, 227–28). Later, in the Orientalizing period, the settlement at Saline shrank and a few aristocratic families seem to have taken control of the shore with its resources (Borzillo and Maras 2021), at least until the end of the seventh and the first half of the sixth centuries BCE, when East Greek traders started to frequent the site of Gravisca (Fiorini and Torelli 2017, 257–61 and 276–79). A similar interest in seafaring and international trade from the late eighth to the sixth centuries is attested at Caere and Vulci, with outstanding imports from the Near East and the Aegean providing evidence for the decisive projection of the south Etruscan cities towards the sea (Bruni 2013, 761–63; Michetti 2016, 73; 2017, 394–98).

Indeed, confirmation of this seafaring culture can be seen in the earliest references to the Etruscans in Greek which reference the sea, such as the verses of Hesiod's *Theogony* (1011–16), where they are said to live far off in the 'Sacred Islands' (Ampolo 2000, 29; Ercolani 2012):

---

* A heartfelt thanks to all the colleagues and friends who have discussed with me many of the arguments tackled in this paper, with special thanks to Giovanna Bagnasco Gianni, Valeria Beolchini, Lucio Fiorini, and Angela Trentacoste

---

Daniele F. Maras Soprintendenza Archeologia Belle Arti e Paesaggio per la provincia di Viterbo
e l'Etruria meridionale (danielefederico.maras@beniculturali.it)

Κίρκη δ᾽, Ἡελίου θυγάτηρ Ὑπεριονίδαο, γείνατ᾽
Ὀδυσσῆος ταλασίφρονος ἐν φιλότητι Ἄγριον ἠδὲ
Λατῖνον ἀμύμονά τε κρατερόν τε· [Τηλέγονον
δ᾽ ἄρ᾽ ἔτικτε διὰ χρυσέην Ἀφροδίτην.] οἳ
δή τοι μάλα τῆλε μυχῷ νήσων ἱεράων πᾶσιν
Τυρσηνοῖσιν ἀγακλειτοῖσιν ἄνασσον.

(And Circe the daughter of Helius, Hyperion's son, loved steadfast Odysseus and bore Agrius and Latinus who was faultless and strong: also she brought forth Telegonus by the will of golden Aphrodite. And they ruled over the famous Tyrsenians, very far off in a recess of the holy islands.) (trans. H. G. Evelyn-White)

Additionally, the Homeric *Hymn to Dionysus* (6–7 and 50) narrates the myth of the Tyrrhenian pirates transformed into dolphins (Bruni 2013, 764; Simon 2013, 505):

τάχα δ᾽ ἄνδρες ἐυσσέλμου ἀπὸ νηὸς ληισταὶ
προγένοντο θοῶς ἐπὶ οἴνοπα πόντον, Τυρσηνοί·
τοὺς δ᾽ ἦγε κακὸς μόρος [...] οἳ δὲ θύραζε
κακὸν μόρον ἐξαλύοντες πάντες ὁμῶς πήδησαν,
ἐπεὶ ἴδον, εἰς ἅλα δῖαν, δελφῖνες δ᾽ ἐγένοντο.

(Presently there came swiftly over the sparkling sea Tyrsenian pirates on a well-decked ship: a miserable doom led them on [...] they leapt out overboard one and all into the bright sea, escaping from a miserable fate, and were changed into dolphins.)

Remarkably, this myth is represented on a renowned Etruscan black-figure hydria of the beginning of the fifth century BCE, attributed to the workshop of the Micali Painter (Harari 1988, 34; Conticello de' Spagnolis 2004, 54–55), which reveals how deeply this symbol was rooted in Etruscan identity, although the pirates were regarded as negative figures.[1]

Other visual sources, including vase decorations and tomb paintings, confirm the special relationship between the Etruscans and the sea, with frequent references to fish and fishing, many dating to the Early Orientalizing period.[2] Notably, this includes a series of jugs produced at Tarquinia and painted by the Pittore delle Palme, which date from the early seventh century BCE and depict friezes with large fish, in some cases associated with a line of five ships with spread sails.[3] In the same period, the incised decoration of an *oinochoe* from the necropolis of Picazzano in Veii depicts a large vessel displaying a furled sail and a line of rows, while a large fish hangs

---

Recently, the Carabinieri Tutela del Patrimonio Culturale found evidence of the illegal exportation, which resulted eventually in the repatriation of the vase to Italy, where it is currently on show at the Museo Nazionale Etrusco di Villa Giulia; Pasquinucci 2019, n. 140.

2   It is not the intention of this contribution to list and comment on all the representations of ships and sailing in Etruscan art; see recently Castello and Mandolesi 2010; Arizza and others 2013; Rizzo 2016; Pommey 2017; De Cristofaro 2019. However, in the following paragraph a rapid survey of the earlier depictions of ships in relation to fish and fishing is presented in order to show the relevance of this argument for the Etruscans in the Orientalizing period.

3   Haifa, National Maritime Museum (Jucker and others 1991, 209 n. 274), Columbia University of Missouri, Museum of Art and Archaeology (inv. no. 71.114), and a jug seized in 2014 by the Italian Guardia di Finanza (Lemmo 2015, 132 no. I-36). Martelli 1987, 252–53 nos 23–24, with further bibliography; Castello and Mandolesi 2010, 17, note 4. Friezes with fish were present already in Protocorinthian pottery (see, for instance, Rizzo 2015, 82–84, nn. 48–49; and 128) and are widely attested in Etruscan productions of this period: see, e.g., the amphoras of the Painters of the Cranes (Rizzo 2015, 111–12, figs 100, h–i) and of the Civitavecchia Fish (Martelli 1987, 257 no. 30), the vases of the Workshop of Stockholm Fish (Martelli 1987, 21–22 n. 13; and 256–58 nos 28.4 and 31), a white-on-red *pythos* from Caere (Bellelli and others 2013, 125 no. 101), a white-on-red *pyxis* from Tomb 1 at the S. Paolo tumulus in Caere (Rizzo 2015, 118–22, nn. 102–03, in association with a ship amongst a frieze of animals), the amphoras of the Workshop of the Amsterdam Painter (Martelli 1987, 4 figs 11–16), and so on. See also Harrison 2013, 1096–97.

---

1   The hydria was found in Vulci in the course of illicit excavations and reached the Toledo Art Museum (Ohio) in 1982, through the international antiquities market.

hooked (or harpooned) at its stern side (Bonino 1989, fig. 4 B3 no. 11; Castello and Mandolesi 2010, 21).

A slightly later mid-seventh-century white-on-red *pyxis* at the Louvre and the famous krater of Aristonothos from Caere present sea battles, featuring warships confronting a trade vessel in a sea full of fish. In the latter case, the scene of the blinding of Polyphemus — which encompasses the signature of the artist (Hurwitt 2015, 72; Cosentino and Maras 2020, 108–21) — adds a reference to a seafaring myth involving Odysseus (Bagnasco Gianni 2007; Bellelli 2010, 31; Bonfante 2016b, 64). Another contemporary red-on-white dish from Acqua Acetosa Laurentina, was produced in Caere and depicts a fishing scene with a sea monster or whale. The ship is slender and propelled by oars as well as by a square sail, while a solitary sailor faces the enormous fish armed with a spear or a harpoon (Martelli 1987, 26 no. 39; Gianfrotta 1988, 14 pl. IV, b).

Finally, a recently discovered impasto *kantharos* from tomb 3 of the necropolis of Via D'Avack, in the hinterland of Veii, also dating to the mid-seventh century BCE, presents a rich incised decoration including two ships transporting horses, presumably for the purpose of trade (Arizza and others 2013, 83–103; De Cristofaro 2019). This artefact confirms Veii's direct participation in overseas trade routes (Bartoloni and De Santis 2019, 90–91; De Cristofaro 2019), especially as it concerns the conflict between Rome and the Etruscan city for the control of the *salinae* (salt plains) and the coastal area north of where the Tiber flows into the sea (Rathje 2019, 101–02; Tabolli 2019, 67–68).

In this context, it is reasonable to expect that fish, and especially sea-fish, were a crucial component of Etruscan alimentation and were of particular importance as sacrificial victims and in ritual practices. Yet when considering the relevance of seafaring and overseas trade in Etruria, it is striking that there is so little evidence in the literary and visual sources on the use of fish as a food source, both for consumption and rituals. This paper explores the occurrence of fish in sacred contexts through a consideration of their remains in the archaeological record and compares these with other categories of evidence (visual and textual) to shed light on the existence of possible ideological patterns and economic reasons for fish rituals.

Fish in Sacred Places

As one can expect, the cultic sites placed along the coast of Etruria are the most likely contexts to find archaeological evidence of fish, whether from remains of meals or from votive offerings. As a partial compensation of the general lack of evidence, however, it should be kept in mind that fish-bones are particularly perishable and difficult to detect in the archaeological record.[4] Despite this, the coastal sanctuaries of Tarquinia and Caere, respectively at Gravisca and Pyrgi, have provided at least some evidence for the use of fish in rituals at sacred areas.

Gravisca, the trade port of Tarquinia from at least the late seventh century BCE, was the heir of the harbour settlement of the Saline (Borzillo and Maras 2021). The earliest frequentation of the sacred area coincided with the arrival of East Greek sailors and the consequent deposition of imported vessels as votive offerings (Fiorini and Torelli 2017, 256–61). Among these, it is worth mentioning an oil flask in the shape of a seashell of the *Cardiidae* family (Fig. 5.1), found in the Gamma building and dating from *c.* 600 BCE (Tarquinia, Museo Acheologico Nazionale, inv. no. 75/17659–17661; Boldrini 1994, 46 n. 18; Simona Fortunelli, in Sgubini Moretti and Torelli 2008, 252 no. 201). Most probably, such a votive offering was considered suitable for the goddess

---

4 See, for instance, the poor evidence listed in Donati and Rafanelli 2004, 154 nos 138bis–141; see also Rask 2014, 290–91.

Figure 5.1. Gravisca, sanctuary. East Greek oil flask in the shape of a seashell, c. 580 BCE (courtesy of the Soprintendenza Archeologia, Belle Arti e Paesaggio per la provincial di Viterbo e l'Etruria Meridionale).

Figure 5.2. Pyrgi, South Area. Terracotta *mesomphalos phiale* containing a mussel and a limpet offered at the votive feature *Kappa*, beginning of the fifth century BCE (courtesy of the Soprintendenza Archeologia, Belle Arti e Paesaggio per la provincial di Viterbo e l'Etruria Meridionale).

Aphrodite with reference to her mythical birth from the sea foam, as well as to her function as protectress of sailors (Fiorini and Torelli 2017, 276–84). Later, the renovation of the *Aphrodision* in the mid-sixth century included the construction of a small *stoa*, at a corner of which a pit has been excavated containing an Attic lebes full of fragments of coral (Colivicchi 2004, 130 and 145; Simona Fortunelli, in Sgubini Moretti and Torelli 2008, 256 no. 225). Again, this ritual use of sea-life is related to the cult of Aphrodite, with special regard to her relationship with Adonis (Fiorini 2005, 71–73; Fiorini in Sgubini Moretti and Torelli 2008, 159; Fiorini and Torelli 2017, 262).

Poorly preserved and sparse remains of fish have been found occasionally at the sanctuary at Gravisca (Donati and Rafanelli 2004, 154 no. 138bis): four examples have been identified among the osteological finds, corresponding to 0.2 per cent of the total (Sorrentino 2004). It is not, however, easy to ascertain whether sea-life was an actual part of the offering or a simple reflection of food consumption at a coastal site. At times, even the identification of traces of fish in a votive deposit are not enough to acknowledge its use in ritual practices, for it might depend on the former contents of a container reused as a cultic implement (e.g. a transport vessel previously containing salted fish).[5]

Similarly, the sanctuary of the South Area at Pyrgi has revealed some remains of fish (of undetermined species) mostly found at the

---

5 As has been suggested by Lucio Fiorini and Giulia Patrizi for a specific context involving an amphora discussed at the meeting '15 anni dalla dichiarazione di valore universale: un bilancio sulla ricerca archeologica a Tarquinia' held in Tarquinia on 22 June 2019. I thank both for discussing with me the preliminary results of their ongoing research.

Figure 5.3. Perugia, Colle Arsiccio. Two small bronze eels, third century BCE (after Arbeid 2010; courtesy of the Museo Archeologico Nazionale dell'Umbria, Perugia).

Figure 5.4. Detail of side B of two Etruscan red-figured *stamnoi* of the Funnel Group dating from the second half of the fourth century BCE: a. The Hague, private collection (since 1960); b. lost (after Schneider-Herrmann 1970).

Piazzale Nord, where the tiny remains of hundreds of sacrificial victims in the form of animal bones and ritual vessels, almost ground to powder, were mixed with the gravel of the floor (Sorrentino 2005; 2013, 208–11 and 216–18). Additionally, a votive deposit dating from the beginning of the fifth century BCE and dedicated to the divine couple Śuri and Cavatha is especially relevant here (Fig. 5.2): the votive feature *Kappa* preserves the remains of ritual practices in situ including an outstanding votive offering of molluscs — a mussel and a limpet — in a terracotta *mesomphalos phiale* (Baglione 2008, 315 n. 28; Carlucci and Maneschi 2013, 53–54). In a different sacred area at Pyrgi, in two wells of the nearby area of Temple A, the remains of sacrificial victims of the third century BCE included a number of tiny fragments of the bones of unspecified fish and shells, possibly part of a closing offering, along with several other animals (Caloi and Palombo 1992, 135–36; Donati and Rafanelli 2004, 142 and 162 nos 194–95 (Simona Rafanelli); 154 nos 140–41 (Luigi Donati)).

At inland sites, fish have been documented in a sacred context at Orvieto, where a votive feature found at the sanctuary adjacent to the Cannicella necropolis revealed the remains of seashells and freshwater fish (two specimens of chub (*Leuciscus cephalus* L.) and one specimen of common rudd (*Scardinius erythrophthalmus* L.)) in association with several large animals dedicated as sacrificial victims — turtle, a number of birds, rodents, cats, canids, swine, cervids, cattle, sheep, and goats (Wilkens 2008, 589–90). Other sacred contexts including fish remains have been found at the 'monumental compound' at the Civita of Tarquinia, associated with foundation rituals (Bagnasco Gianni 2005; Chiesa 2005; Chiaramonte Treré 2017, 154–55),[6] and in the sacred area of Sant'Omobono in Rome, where the remains of gilt-head bream (*Sparus aurata*) and brown meagre (*Sciaena umbra*) have been identified (Tagliacozzo 1989). Remarkably, however, there is no clear evidence to establish the votive nature of the finding of fish at Forcello, Bagnolo San Vito (Trentacoste 2014, 146), a site that thrived in a riverine environment and yielded a number of fishing hooks (De Marinis 2007, 252 fig. 146 no. 7; see also Russ and Trentacoste forthcoming).

---

6 Further faunal remains including fish from a well at the Civita of Tarquinia are currently under study by Ornella Prato and Angela Maccarinelli; see Prato forthcoming, and the same author's communication 'Bones from the Well: Zooarchaeological Analysis of the Faunal Remains from Tarquinia', at the PzaF. Postgraduate ZooArchaeology Forum (Toruń, Nicolaus Copernicus University, 23–25 March 2017).

The relevance of fish-related offerings can also be argued on the grounds of a few bronze statuettes of the Hellenistic period depicting either fish or people offering them. In particular, a bronze statuette representing a richly dressed woman crowned with a diadem and offering a fish has been found in a votive deposit of the third century BCE at Casa al Savio, near Castelluccio di Pienza (Siena, Museo Archeologico Nazionale, inv. no. 39501; Bentz 1992, 16–17 no. A3 Abb. 6; Minetti 1994, 112–13 figs 9–11; Cagianelli 1999, 221 n. 455). Another statuette with the same subject, but of uncertain origin, is preserved at the Historisches Museum der Pfalz of Speyer (Menzel 1960, 18–19 Taf. 30 no. 25). In a votive context of the same period at Colle Arsiccio, near Perugia, two small bronze eels (Fig. 5.3) (Perugia, Museo Archeologico Nazionale, inv. no. 722/1–2; Arbeid 2010, 279–80 tav. XXX nos 6–7) were offered along with a number of other statuettes representing a sheep, a dog, and a bird (Arbeid 2010, 65–66).[7]

A particularly interesting yet rare Etruscan depiction of a ritual (presumably sacred) involving fish is found on two Etruscan red-figured *stamnoi* of the Funnel Group, dating from the second half of the fourth century BCE (Schneider-Herrmann 1970, pls 28 and 29 nos 1–2; see also Carboni 2016, 264–66). One *stamnos* (Fig. 5.4, a) preserved in a private collection in The Hague since 1960 depicts a boy holding a tray with a fish — possibly cooked — over the head of a crouching masked

female figure, dressed as an Amazon, perhaps a type of sacred performer (like those described in Maras 2018a). On the opposite side of the vessel, an impressive female figure wearing the clothing of an Amazon and interacting with a deer and a bird may be Artemis, an identification proposed by Romina Carboni who interprets the scene as relating to the cult of the goddess (Carboni 2016, 266; see also Krauskopf 1984, nn. 18–19; 1988, 191–92 fig. 14). Significantly, an almost identical *stamnos* of the same production yet of uncertain provenance and now lost, was published by G. Schneider-Herrmann (1970, pl. 29 nos 3–4), who highlighted the discrepancies between the scenes: the sitting woman on side B (Fig. 5.4, b) is not masked and the Amazon-goddess on the opposite side holds a snake and is accompanied by a hind; additionally, the fish is even less recognizable and held by the youth with his bare hands, possibly keeping its tail bent under the body (Schneider-Herrmann 1970, 53–56 and 70).[8]

The infrequent attestations of fish in sacrificial and sacred contexts, as demonstrated above, suggest that the use of fish as sacrificial victims was unusual and rarely practised by the Etruscans. However, the very presence of these exceptions suggests a particular symbolic value attached to fish-related offerings, possibly in a specific religious environment yet to be determined.

Besides the actual remains of fish-bones, the consumption of fish is indirectly documented also by a special category of vessels called fish-plates, first produced in Attic pottery and later imitated in Magna Grecia and in Etruria (McPhee and Trendall 1987; Claudia Lucchese, in Todisco 2012, II, 147). These plates had a peculiar shape, with

---

7 See also Richardson 1998 (spec. 26–27 figs 1–2): the author argues that the wiggly elongated objects held by a number of votive bronze statuettes are eels rather than snakes, because the latter would be represented as coiled around the forearms and not dangling. However, it is worth mentioning that even as eels the stance of the relevant animals would be unrealistic and in actuality the elongated objects could be interpreted as thunderbolts of the wavy type examined by Colonna 2009, 15–26, and de Grummond 2016b, 192–201. Therefore, in the absence of further evidence that fish are involved, I find it safer not to include the relevant statuettes in my study.

8 A possible mock-depiction of a fish sacrifice is seen on a Campanian bell krater dating from 350–330 BCE, preserved at the Museum National of Rio de Janeiro (inv. no. 1500): a phlyax player is sitting on an altar and devouring a small fish to the sound of the pipes played by another phlyax player and a woman; Trendall 1959, 32 n. 53; Smith 1962; Todisco 2012, II, 293 n. 5179.

a hanging rim and a small basin at the centre, possibly designed to contain gravy. Many plates like these, either black varnished or, more often, with red-figured depictions of sea-life, dating from the fourth and third centuries BCE, have been found in tombs and sanctuaries in several sites of Etruria, thus testifying to their use for eating fish.

An example from a sanctuary worth mentioning is a fragmentary Campanian red-figured plate depicting a red bream and a red mullet found in the Piazzale Nord at Pyrgi: it belongs to the 'Wavy Gills/Dotted Stripe Group' of the McPhee and Trendall (1987, 70–74) classification and dates from around 360–330 BCE (Baglione 2000, 370, fig. 44). Another fish-plate from the same context is a black varnished one dating from the first half of the third century BCE and marked with the Latin letter A scratched after firing (Colonna and Maras 2001, 413 n. 96). The letter is part of the sigla and short Latin texts that characterize the last phase of the cult at Pyrgi, when Roman colonists attended the sacred place (Maras 2013, 202–04). Remarkably, similar contemporary graffiti with a Phoenician *qoph* have been found on two identical black varnished fish-plates from a tomb of the necropolis delle Grotte of Populonia (sector C, tomb 4) (Amadasi Guzzo and Romualdi 2007). The plates have been attributed to the Atelier des Petites Estampilles and date from the mid-third century BCE (Series Morel 1124; Amadasi Guzzo and Romualdi 2007, 162–63). In this case, however, a third example presented a long neo-Punic inscription that has been recently published by Giulia Amadasi Guzzo, who notes that the reading and interpretation is not entirely clear (Fig. 5.5):

TTLT$^{(or N)}$ BTLT$^{(or N)}$ I (?) LTT$^{(or LNN)}$. ŠQLM . RʻL . ʼTN . LMʼẒ TLT$^{(or NLN)}$. TTLT$^{(or LNNT)}$. LTT

Although the sequence is unparalleled and uncertain, it is evident that there is some sort of alliteration, possibly in either a religious or magic

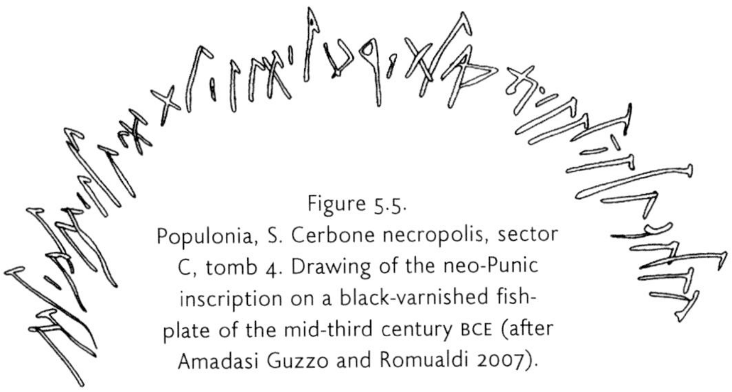

Figure 5.5. Populonia, S. Cerbone necropolis, sector C, tomb 4. Drawing of the neo-Punic inscription on a black-varnished fish-plate of the mid-third century BCE (after Amadasi Guzzo and Romualdi 2007).

context, rather than being simple wordplay. At any rate, it seems that the Punic words for 'vessel', 'to give', and, possibly, 'fish' were included, thus implying probably a funerary offering of fish (Amadasi Guzzo and Romualdi 2007, 164–68).

Foundation Rituals

In a recent contribution on Hellenistic votive deposits related to foundation rituals of public buildings and defensive walls, Adriano Maggiani (2012, 223–24) has pointed out that the evidence for such ritual practices in Etruria is paltry and infrequent, especially concerning the major centres and metropolises. A few relevant contexts, however, survive and give us a hint of the type of sacrificial rituals involved in these cases, some of which include fish offerings, even in contexts where water- and fishing-related practices are not expected.

One peculiar context has been found at the sacred-institutional compound of Civita at Tarquinia, where a votive feature has been discovered in connection with the entrance to the *Gamma* area (Bagnasco Gianni 2005; Rottoli 2005; Bonghi Jovino 2010, 14; Rask 2014, 276–77; Chiaramonte Treré 2017, 155; de Grummond 2016a, 149). The earliest deposit includes the fragments of an impasto bowl of the Villanovan period with some carbonic remains (Belelli Marchesini and Michetti 2017, 483). In the deposit a large part of an ox was covered with a tile, on which a number of *ollae* containing vegetal and animal remains had been deposited in two layers (possibly corresponding to two subsequent phases) during the sixth century BCE. Significantly, the animal victims included 'bony fish' (*Osteichthyes*) and a passerine bird in the former layer, and 'bony fish', shells, and pigs in the latter (Bagnasco Gianni 2005, 92–93).[9] Finally, the top layer includes earlier material, dating from the Orientalizing period, including a spindle-whorl and a cooking-stand (*fornello*), apparently preserved as objects of memory (*keimelia*) and later offered in the sacred context (Bagnasco Gianni 2005, 92; Belelli Marchesini and Michetti 2017, 483).

In a different context from the same site, the association of the remains of fish and pig (in this case a neonate piglet) along with vegetal offerings occurs in a votive deposit associated with the foundation of the walls of the *Alpha* area in the course of the sixth century BCE (Chiesa 2005; Chiaramonte Treré 2017, 154–55). Much later at Sovana, in central Etruria, a pit-deposit (*bothros*) of the third century BCE placed under a tufa structure — possibly in connection with the city wall — included a few fragments of pottery (belonging to a black varnished cup, an impasto lid, a flask of coarse ware, and a small container of fine ware), as well as some butchered bones of a pig (*Sus scrofa*) and three vertebrae of a fish (Maggiani 2012, 226–27). Further comparanda show that pigs were common victims for foundation rituals in Etruria (Maggiani 2012, 224–27),[10] but their association with fish in different periods and regions is particularly relevant in consideration of their similar contexts.

There is later confirmation of a similar practice in the Venetic area at the time of Romanization.

A large deposit discovered under the walls of the theatre of Asolo included some coins and a large amount of small bones (both inscribed and uninscribed), among which the remains of freshwater fish and pigs stand out, along with bovids, sheep, dogs, ducks, rabbits, and eggs (Gambacurta 2005; Maggiani 2012, 227).[11] Similarly, a votive deposit in the sacred area at Este-Maggiaro, closed between the second and first centuries BCE, included a large number of piglets and pregnant sows, as well as sheep, birds, amphibians, and fish in the closing layer (Fiore and Tagliacozzo 2002; Belelli Marchesini and Michetti 2017, 479).

While it is not easy to interpret the symbolic meaning of the different victims chosen for these rituals — whether related to the local economy or to the people involved — it is worth highlighting the recurrence of rare fish offerings in these cases. In this regard, an amazing albeit anachronistic parallel to these pre-Roman foundation deposits has been recently brought to light in the medieval town of Tusculum, south of Rome, during the excavations of the Escuela Española de Historia y Arquéologia de Roma in 2015 (Beolchini and others 2016). A rare votive deposit dating from the end of the twelfth century CE[12] has been recovered in the foundation pit of the eastern side of the defensive wall of the citadel of Tusculum. Here, a small *olla* of coarse ware contained the remains of grape, fig, and wild herbs, as well as two whole skeletons of chickens and a number of bones and scales belonging to a freshwater fish (Beolchini and others 2016, 29). Along with these offerings an illegible imperial coin

---

9 In both layers some intruded land snails were found in the *ollae*.

10 Notably, one of the deposits analysed by Maggiani shares with the earlier contexts at the Civita of Tarquinia the deposition of bones in *ollae*; Belelli Marchesini and Michetti 2017, 483 n. 71.

11 Some comparanda for this association of victims is found in the cult of Hecate; Sassù 2016, 401 n. 36.

12 On the medieval foundation deposits, see Beolchini and others 2016, 31–34 and n. 29, with further bibliography, with special regard to the deposition of coins. I have a debt of gratitude to the specialists of the Escuela and especially to my friend and colleague Valeria Beolchini for discussing this important archaeological find with me.

was preserved and a lead seal of the preceding pope, Alexander III Bandinelli, who died in 1181 (Beolchini and others 2016, 29–31). This exceptional context relates to the final years of the independence of Tusculum, when the city was under siege by the Romans and protected by an imperial garrison. We know that at the end, in 1191, the Emperor Federico Barbarossa recalled his troops, following an agreement with the Church of Rome, and as a consequence Tusculum was annihilated. Some years earlier, however, the besieged citizens still put their faith in divine protection, offering a sacrifice of food and the symbolic seal of a former pope, who had lived in the town for twenty-six months between 1170 and 1173 and one year more between 1180 and 1181 (Beolchini 2006, 55–98 and 369–85; Beolchini and others 2016, 34–36).

It is remarkable that the ritual offering included the only fish found in the whole area of the town, as confirmed by the systematic water screening of large amounts of dirt in the course of the excavations of the Escuela Española. Although it might seem unlikely, the coincidence of fish offering in connection with the consecration of city walls in ancient Etruria and in medieval Latium shares a strong symbolic value lasting centuries in the same area.[13]

Fish as Substitute Victims?

A reason why fish sacrifices were not widespread in the classical world is that most sacrifice rituals in the Mediterranean area involved bloodshed as a crucial part of the performance (Burkert 2003, 148–50; Rafanelli 2013, 571; Carboni 2016, 266–67 and 270–71). Blood was intended to pour

---

13 Presumably, while facing a terrible danger during the siege of Tusculum, the inhabitants invoked the divine protection on the walls of the citadel by resorting to a very ancient sacrificial ritual, which had possibly been preserved in the ambit of magic lore and/or superstition.

over the altar, be collected in cups, and offered separately to the gods with different forms of consumption. Fish, however, have generally little blood to be shed, with the significant exception of tuna (among the larger species) which was, perhaps for this reason, one of the favourite sacrificial victims among fish (Carboni 2016, 263–70; see in general Burkert 1997, 204–12, and Lefèvre-Novaro 2010, 37–39). Additionally, the fictional performance of sacrifice was usually based upon the assumption that a victim went willingly towards its ritual killing, a fiction that is difficult to maintain in the case of fish drawn out of their aquatic environment (Plut., *Quaest. conv.*, VIII. 8 (728C–730F); Burkert 2001, 1–21; Volpe Cacciatore 2008, 788–89; Carboni 2016, 270–71; 2017; cf. Naiden 2007, 66–67, for a different opinion). On the other hand, the very same reason why fish were considered unsuitable for the usual type of sacrificial performance allows them to be selected specifically as victims for special purposes. In this regard, it is worth mentioning an archaic ritual of early Rome, which is so described by Varro in *De lingua latina* (VI. 20): 'Volcanalia a Volcano, quod ei tum feriae et quod eo die populus pro se in ignem animalia mittit' (The *Volcanalia* take name from *Volcanus*, for there is a festival to this god and on that day people throw living beings in the fire on behalf of themselves [or possibly 'in the place of themselves']). According to this source, the festival of Volcanus (which occurred on 23 August) included offerings of living beings either as a substitute for human beings, or as votive gifts on behalf of human beings (Rose 1933, 58 and 63; Dumézil 1958; Donati and Rafanelli 2004, 154; Haudry 2013, 72–73).

A passage of Festus (238.57–62 L.) probably refers to the same ritual, although mentions a different festival in June:

Piscatori ludi vocantur qui quotannis mense Iunio trans Tiberim fieri solent a praetore urbano pro piscatoribus Tiberinis; quorum quaestus non in macellum pervenit, sed fere in aream Volkani, quod id genus pisciculorum vivorum datur ei deo pro animis humanis.

(With the name of 'Fishermen's games' are defined those that the Urban *praetor* usually organizes every year in the month of June on behalf of the fishermen of the Tiber. Their produce does not go to the marketplace, but as a rule in the (sacred) place of Volcanus, for this kind of small living fish is offered to this god in the place (or on behalf) of human souls.)

Finally, a further passage of Festus (213.37–210.2 L.) provides information on the festival: 'Piscatorii ludi vocantur, qui mense Iunio trans Tyberim fieri solent pro quaestu piscantium' ('Fishermen's games' is the name of those (games) that used to be held in the month of June on the opposite bank of the Tiber for fishermen's profit).

The discrepancy between these sources is resolved if the games so described are those held in June on behalf of the fishermen of the Tiber River while the results of their work — that is to say a quantity of small living fish — are destined to be offered to Volcanus during the *Volcanalia* in August, and presumably during the rest of the year too (Dumézil 1958, 128–29). At any rate, what is most relevant in the perspective of this study is the statement by both Varro and Festus that living fish (that is to say *animalia*) were offered as a substitute victim in the place of human beings and therefore on behalf of them.[14] This type of ritual matches with Ovid's account of the cunning of Numa Pompilius (*Fasti*, III. 339–44), who deceived Jupiter offering onions, hair, and fish in the place of human sacrifices (Capdeville 1971, 289–91):

'Caede caput' dixit; cui rex 'parebimus' inquit; | 'caedenda est hortis eruta cepa meis.' | addidit hic 'hominis'; 'sumes' ait ille 'capillos.' | postulat hic animam; cui Numa 'piscis' ait. | risit, et 'his' inquit 'facito mea tela procures, | o vir conloquio non abigende deum. | Sed tibi, protulerit cum totum crastinus orbem | Cynthius, imperii pignora certa dabo'.

([Jupiter] said: 'cut off the head.' The king answered him 'we will obey;' and he added: 'the onions unearthed from my garden are to be cut off.' [Jupiter] clarified: 'human.' [Numa] said 'you will have hair.' The former asked for a life; Numa answered '[that] of a fish.' At that Jupiter laughed and said: 'See that with these things you expiate my bolts, o man who cannot be kept from conversing with the gods. But when tomorrow's Sun will have completed his orb, I will give you certain pledges of empire'.)

The same story is reported by Valerius Antias (*apud* Arnob., *nat.*, v. 1 = *hist.*, 6) with almost identical words, but an important difference, involving a particular species of fish, the *maena*:[15]

Iovem diu cunctatum 'expiabis' dixe 'capite fulgurita'; regem respondisse 'caepicio'; Iovem rursus 'humano'; rettulisse regem 'sed capillo'; deum contra 'animali'; < 'maena' > subiecisse Pompilium.

(After a long pause, Jupiter said: 'You shall expiate bolts with a head'; the king answered 'with an onion.' Jupiter replied: 'human'; and the king answered 'but (only) hair.' The god specified 'living'; and (Numa) Pompilius added 'with a fish'.)

---

14 On the phenomenon of substitute sacrificial victims, see Willerslev 2013, esp. 144–48; in regard to Etruria and the classical world, see Capdeville 1971; Grottanelli 1999, 57–66; Arbeid 2010, 311; and, specifically on fish, Scarano Ussani 2006.

15 Probably a blotched picarel (*Spicara maena* L.); Citti 1994, 155; Berrino 2003, 12–15, with reference to Plut., *Num.*, XV. 8–10, as well.

Notwithstanding the fairy-tale narrative, the relevance of this myth in Roman religion is evident, since it involves the explanation of how human sacrifices were avoided and how Rome received the *pignora imperii*, the tokens of the everlasting favour of the gods over the city and its rulers. As a by-product, Ovid's passage explains how living fish came to be used in the place of human lives in the case of expiation of thunderbolts. The parallel sacrifice of fish thrown alive into a fire in the *area Volcani* is not different. In both cases a living underwater being is used to contrast and appease a divinity of fire.

While the dialectics between fire and water in relation to these rituals have been noted already in George Dumézil's studies, it is still perhaps possible to offer other observations (Dumézil 1958, 121–28; Haudry 2013, 72–73). The efficacy of sacrifices in the classical world depends on the use of one of the four elements as means of communication with the gods: fire, in the case of burning or partially burning offerings; water, when dipping votive objects in rivers, lakes, or the sea; earth, when burying offerings or pouring liquids into holes (*bothroi*) and pierced altars; air, when using perfumes or burning incense. It was rare, however, that offering rituals used only one of these means; rather, they used two or more of them, as a sort of short-circuit that allowed contact between natural and supernatural, as in the case of pouring the blood of the victims during a burning sacrifice and when letting the smoke of the fire reach the heavens. It seems, therefore, that the special nature of fish — at once animated and inanimate (Volpe Cacciatore 2008, esp. 785–86), living under water beyond the human sphere, and mediator between mankind and the underworld — made it a favourite substitute for human beings in rituals involving higher forms of sacrifice (Scarano Ussani 2006, 360–61). The offering of living water creatures through the sacred fire was supposed to appease the gods — and presumably to prevent the risk of fire in Rome — and, at the same time, had

the symbolic meaning of a substitute sacrifice of human lives.

A further step in the way of substitute offerings is probably a ritual described briefly by Festus in relation to the federal sanctuary of Jupiter Latiaris in Latium (210.7 L.): 'Piscatorium aes vetusto more appellatur, quod in monte Albano datur pro piscibus' (According to an old tradition, it is called 'fishermen's bronze', what is offered on the mount Albanus in the place of fish). It is possible that in this Latin ritual the bronze earned by fishermen (the 'profit', *quaestus*, mentioned for Rome) was offered to Jupiter with reference to a legendary substitution of fish for human beings, in parallel to the tale of Numa.[16] If one, therefore, accepts that fish were considered a valuable substitute for human beings, it is intriguing to see how they appear in foundation rituals at least from the Archaic to the Late Hellenistic periods.

The presence of ritual killings or even human sacrifices at the Civita of Tarquinia has been acknowledged many times by scholars with reference to the unusual burials found at that site (Bonghi Jovino 2008; Bonfante 2012; de Grummond 2016a; Bonghi Jovino 2017; see further Di Fazio 2001 and 2017). Additionally, the connection of early or legendary foundation rituals with human sacrifices is also well known (Bonfante 2012, 73–74; 2016a, 163–64; Carafa 2008; D'Alessio 2013, 323–28). It is not unreasonable, therefore, to suppose that the original meaning of the use of fish in those specific sacrificial rituals was to provide substitute victims for human beings in more civilized times.

---

16 Notably, evidence for the frequentation of fishermen at the sanctuary at Mons Albanus (Monte Cavo) is provided by a stone net weight (Cecamore 1993, 37–38, cat. no. I.4), similar to those found at the Comitium in Rome (not far from the *area Volcani*; Roscini 2013, 246–47, who compares them to *oscilla*). Further evidence has been found in the hinterland of Caere, including hooks and fishing net weights at Pyrgi and Punta della Vipera (Donati and Rafanelli 2004, 154), as well as Furbara and Grottini (Gianfrotta 1988, 14 and n. 20).

Funerary Offerings

In consideration of the possible association of fish with human souls, it is worth reviewing the funerary contexts for evidence of offerings involving water creatures. Unfortunately, the evidence for this is practically non-existent, even though it is possible that the scarcity of actual findings depends on the poor preservation of the remains of fish — usually reduced to single scales or vertebrae.

Actual funerary contexts including fish offerings have been found in two eighth-century burials at Verucchio, such as the remains of a seabass (*Dicentrarchus labrax* L.) featured in tomb Lippi 89/1972 (*Tomba del Trono*), and more sea-fish, a sea urchin, and a shell, as well as freshwater fish in tomb Lippi 102/1972 (von Eles 2005, 33 tav. II nos 2–3; see also Turfa 2012, 156). Additionally, it is worth mentioning a porbeagle's tooth found in tomb 5 of the necropolis of S. Cerbone at Populonia, dating from the second half of the sixth century BCE (Donati and Rafanelli 2004, 154 no. 139; for the funerary context see Minto, in *Notizie degli Scavi di Antichità*, 1934: 351–53). However, single shark teeth used as talismans — at times mounted into pendants — are well attested in Etruria[17] and therefore should not be counted among the remains of ritual meals or offerings.

In terms of visual sources, the Tomb of Hunting and Fishing of Tarquinia, dating from around 510 BCE, has particular relevance. In this case, the symbolic value of water as a barrier separating this world from the afterlife and a frontier to be crossed as an ordeal for the deceased is expressed at its best in the case of the 'Tuffatore'

(the 'Diver'): a metaphor of the last plunge into the unknown (Cerchiai and d'Agostino 1999, 53–71; Ross Holloway 2006; see also Marcattili 2012, 74–75 fig. 5). From this perspective, fishing and consuming fish means getting in contact with the alterity of water and communicating with the underworld. As far as ritual is concerned, this form of sacred communication is depicted in a scene on the entrance wall of the Tomb of the Inscriptions (Fig. 5.6), again at Tarquinia, dating from around 520 BCE (Cousin 2009, 79–80; Colonna 2016, 135; Maras 2018b, 96 and n. 47; 2020, 34). In this scene, a young man is represented naked and wearing a long headband; he bows towards a sort of grill or small table with fire underneath. Unfortunately, the ill-preserved surface prevents us from fully understanding the nature of the object, possibly a portable altar or a grill? The youth holds a tool in his right and a fish in his left, as if putting it over the fire. It seems clear that this is meant to be an offering to the eerie figure standing opposite the youth. Depicted as an old — albeit athletic — man, the figure is naked but for a *kynodesme* (a sort of ribbon-shaped jockstrap) and a sceptre held in his left hand. In addition, the figure gestures with the right hand lifted and the left index finger pointing at the offered fish. The pale yellowish skin of the latter figure is probably alluding to his ghostly nature (that is to say an *eidolon* in Greek) — a sort of ancestor spirit (Maras 2020, 34). Over the figures a long inscription is painted, only legible today in a drawing by Carlo Ruspi (1835) (*ET* Ta 7.13; Sannibale 2019, n. 35, with bibliography): 'civesanamatvesicalesece : eurasvclesvasfesθiχvaχa'.

In the first part of the text the name *Matves*(*i*) can be identified, belonging to the family buried in the tomb (Colonna 2016, 135; Maras 2020, 34). In addition, the numeral *ci*, 'three', might be recognized at the beginning of the sequence and a verb ending -*ce* is present at the end, just before a line of three punctuation dots. The most likely word divisions and translations are the following:

---

17 See the pendants at Oxford (Pitt Rivers Museum, inv. no. 1985.50.310), Copenhagen (Thorvaldsens Museum, inv. no. H1862), and New York (Metropolitan Museum of Art, inv. no. 95.15.288, 289), as well as a fossilized shark tooth — probably belonging to a Great White Shark (*Carcharodon*) — from the sanctuary site of Poggio Colla (cat. no. 11–202; Trentacoste 2013, 85–86 and 96–97).

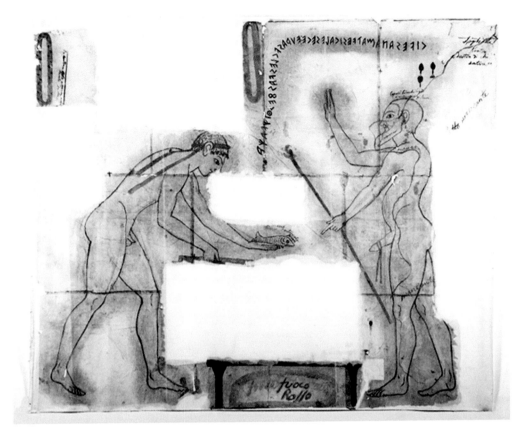

Figure 5.6. Tarquinia, Tomb of the Inscriptions (c. 520 BCE). Watercolour drawing on tracing paper by Carlo Ruspi (1835), depicting the painting on the back wall at the right of the entrance (courtesy of the Soprintendenza Archeologia, Belle Arti e Paesaggio per la provincial di Viterbo e l'Etruria Meridionale).

'ci vesana matvesi cale sece' (Cale offered (?) three *vesana* to Matve) (Colonna 2016, 135, n. 50; Maras 2018b, 96); or, less probably, 'ci ves ana matvesi calesece' (Ana offered (?) three *ves* to Matve). In both cases, the ghostly divine figure who receives the offering is labelled as *Matve*, the common ancestor of the namesake *gens* who owned the tomb. The name of the bowing youth who seems to be placing a fish onto the fire might be Ana or Cale (the 'Gaul') depending on what reading one chooses (Colonna 1990, 553 n. 25). If this interpretation can be accepted, the object of the offering is defined as *ves* or *vesana*, which might be either the name of the ritual[18] or the common name of the fish in Etruscan.

However the inscription is read, it can be gathered from this single visual source that fish were considered suitable offerings for divinized ancestors. In this regard, it is interesting that from much later sources we know that the *Etrusca Disciplina* — that is the religious tradition that survived the end of the Etruscan independence — prescribed special rituals which were meant to make the souls of the deceased divine, the so-called *di animales* (van der Meer 2011, 62–64; Maras 2016, 89–90; Krämer 2017, 517–18; Maras 2017, 285–86):

> esse quaedam sacra quibus animae humanae vertantur in deos, qui appellantur animales, quod de animis fiant.
>
> (There are some religious practices that change human souls into deities, which are called *animales*, for they derive from souls.) (Cornelius Labeo, *apud* Serv., ad Aen., III. 168)

Quod Etruria libris in Acheronticis pollicentur, certorum animalium sanguine numinibus certis dato divinas animas fieri et ab legibus mortalitatis educi.

---

18 Significantly, the word *ves* (with marked /ś/) has been found elsewhere in ritual funerary contexts; Maggiani 2011, 263; see also Maras 2014, 120.

Figure 5.7. Quinto Fiorentino, Tomb *della Montagnola*. Drawing of inscriptions and graffiti on the stone slab that closed the right chamber: on the left a stylized fish is detectable (after Pallottino 1963).

Figure 5.8. Veii, sanctuary of Portonaccio. Drawing of a terracotta painted plaque depicting a scene of ichthyomancy dating from c. 470 BCE (after *Notizie degli Scavi di Antichità*, 1953; courtesy of the Soprintendenza Archeologia, Belle Arti e Paesaggio per la provincial di Viterbo e l'Etruria Meridionale).

(For the Acherontic books in Etruria promise that souls become divine, and are freed from the law of death, if the blood of certain animals is offered to certain deities.) (Nigidius Figulus, *apud* Arnob., *nat.*, II. 62)

Some visual and literary sources allow us to hypothesize that goats were among the victims suitable for these rituals, when offered to gods such as Veiovis, Menerva, Uni, and possibly Fufluns, Hercle, and Turms (Maras 2016, 89–91; Krämer 2017, 518). However, from what we have seen, fish are further candidates to be suitable victims. A possible confirmation for the inclusion of fish in the list comes from graffiti covering the entrance wall of the funerary chamber on the right side of the *dromos* of the Tomb *della Montagnola*, at Quinto Fiorentino near Florence, dating in the second half of the seventh century BCE (Pallottino 1963). In this context, drawings of animals have been scratched around the inscribed names of a number of people who took part in a burial ritual — presumably the *sodales*, that is the comrades and friends of the high-rank deceased (Colonna 2006, 449–50; Maras 2016b, 93–94). Significantly, the animals depicted include a boar, a goat, and a fish (Fig. 5.7) and might be interpreted as an allusion to the actual victims offered in the course of the funerary ritual (Pallottino 1963, 178; Maras 2016, 94).[19]

Fish(y) Divination

A last remark on the ritual uses of fish in pre-Roman Italy relates to that of divination, one of the most important parts of the *Etrusca Disciplina* (Maras 2017, 279–81; 2019, 60–61). A painted

---

19 On offerings to the deified ancestors, see Camporeale 2009, 223–37; Bonfante 2016a, 164–65; Krämer 2017, 522–32; in particular, on the identification of goat as one of the selected victims for the *di animales*, see ibid., 519, and Rafanelli 2013, 572.

plaque (Fig. 5.8) from a series found in the sanctuary of Portonaccio in Veii, dating from around 470 BCE, depicts a crouching figure performing some sort of ritual action in front of a pool full with fish of diverse species (Claudia Carlucci, in Sgubini Moretti and Torelli 2008, 206 no. 18.2; Torelli 2011, 167–69). We can recognize a rayfish, two dark fish, and a few more small animals interpreted as dolphins and molluscs by the discoverer Enrico Stefani (*Notizie degli Scavi di Antichità*, 1953: 79–80 n. 38, fig. 54a–b). The figure's white skin colour, suitable for either a woman or a young boy, holds a sort of threefold garment or bag and a long spear-like object with a sort of grid at one end. According to Mario Torelli (2011, 169), the last scholar to study the plaque, the scene represents a ritual of ichthyomancy, that is to say divination through the observation of fish. A number of literary sources describe such a ritual with reference to two cult places of Apollo in Anatolia, respectively at Sura and at Myra. In both cases, Greek authors such as Claudius Aelianus (*Hist. anim.*, VIII. 5 and XII. 1), Plutarch (*Sollert. anim.*, 12, 976C) and Athenaeus (*Deipn.*, VIII.333d–334a) note that the meat of sacrificed animals was divided into portions on spits and put into the water of a sacred pool: a priest watched if fish ate from the offering and derived an oracular response from what species and in what order they approached the meat (Torelli 2011, 169–70). A further passage of Pliny (*Nat. hist.*, XXXI. 22) got the information mixed up, for it attributed the ritual attached to Myra to an Apollo Surius (that is of Sura); in this case, he says that the response derived from whether the fish accepted an offering of food or pushed it away with their tails. If we accept Torelli's interpretation, fish were considered by the Etruscans to be a reliable living means of communication with the gods in addition to the birds in the sky (Capdeville 2016).[20]

Conclusion

The survey of the available sources on rituals involving fish has provided evidence that the relationship between fish consumption and religion in Etruria is particularly complex and articulated. As one expects from a seafaring people such as the Etruscans, fish held symbolic value in rituals, including sacrificial offerings at coastal sanctuaries (such as at Pyrgi and Gravisca), as well as funerary or chthonic offerings in necropoleis (such as at Cannicella and Verucchio). Significantly, such dual significance is confirmed by the context of inscribed fish-plates at Pyrgi and Populonia.

Visual sources depicting rituals involving fish are attested from time to time on red-figured vessels, in a few bronze statuettes, on a painted plaque from Veii possibly alluding to fish divination, and in a unique scene depicted in the Tomb of the Inscriptions at Tarquinia. The last also provides evidence for the offering of fish to a deified ancestor, thus supporting the hypothesis that fish was included among the sacrificial victims selected in order to 'change human souls into deities' (as recorded by a passage of Arnobius).

Additionally, the use of fish in foundation rituals — attested at several places in Etruria and in contexts possibly involving human sacrifices at Tarquinia — is consistent with some Latin literary sources referring to early sacrificial rituals of fish thrown into fire either 'in the place of human beings' or 'on behalf of human souls'. The unusual nature of fish according to the ancient mentality — both animated and inanimate, living but not bleeding, and breathing under water but not in air — made them suitable to become substitute victims for human beings, as well as mediators between humankind and the gods.

---

20 On a Latin quasi-magic ritual mentioned by Ovid (*Fasti*,

II. 571–82) and involving the head of a picarel (*maena*; see above) toasted in fire and offered to Tacita Muta in order to reject slander and gossip, see Berrino 2003.

Works Cited

Amadasi Guzzo, Maria Giulia, and Antonella Romualdi. 2007. 'Cartaginesi a Populonia: l'iscrizione neopunica dalla necropoli delle Grotte', *Annali della Fondazione per il Museo C. Faina di Orvieto*, 14: 161–75

Ampolo, Carmine. 2000. 'Il mondo operico e la cultura orientalizzante mediterranea', in *Principi etruschi tra Mediterraneo ed Europa* [catalogue of the exhibition, Bologna, 1 October 2000–1 April 2001] (Venice: Marsilio), pp. 27–35

Annoscia, Giorgia Maria, Beatrice Casocavallo, and Flavia Trucco. 2019. 'Progetti di ricerca per la tutela del paesaggio antico della costa di Tarquinia', *Scienze dell'antichità*, 25.1: 227–40

Arbeid, Barbara. 2010. 'Bronzi votivi etruschi a figura animale. Problemi culturali, storico-artistici e cultuali' (unpublished doctoral thesis, University of Ferrara)

Arizza, Marco, Alessio De Cristofaro, Alessandra Piergrossi, and Daniela Rossi. 2013. 'La tomba di un aristocratico naukleros dall'agro veientano. Il kantharos con scena di navigazione di via A. d'Avack', *Archeologia classica*, 64: 51–131

Baglione, Maria Paola. 2000. 'I rinvenimenti di ceramica attica dal santuario dell'area sud', *Scienze dell'antichità*, 10: 337–82

——. 2008. 'Esame del santuario meridionale di Pyrgi', in *'Saturnia Tellus': Definizioni dello spazio consacrato in ambiente etrusco-italico; atti del convegno internazionale svoltosi a Roma dal 10 al 12 novembre 2004*, ed. by Xavier Dupré Raventos, Sergio Ribichini, and Stephane Verger (Rome: CNR Edizioni), pp. 301–18

Bagnasco Gianni, Giovanna. 2005. 'Tarquinia, il deposito reiterato: una preliminare analisi dei *comparanda*', in *Offerte dal regno vegetale e dal regno animale nelle manifestazioni del sacro: atti dell'incontro di studio, Milano 26–27 giugno 2003*, ed. by Maria Bonghi Jovino and Federica Chiesa (Rome: L'Erma di Bretschneider), pp. 91–97

——. 2007. 'Aristonothos. Il vaso', *Aristonothos: Scritti per il Mediterraneo antico*, 1: v–xvi

Bartoloni, Gilda, and Anna De Santis. 2019. 'Veii during the Seventh and Sixth Centuries BCE. Political Structure and Organization of the Territory', in *Veii*, ed. by Jacopo Tabolli (Austin: University of Texas Press), pp. 87–94

Belelli Marchesini, Barbara, and Laura Maria Michetti. 2017. 'Pozzi, bothroi, cavità. Atti rituali, tracce di sacrifici e modalità di chiusura in contesti sacri di ambito etrusco', *Scienze dell'antichità*, 23.3: 465–90

Bellelli, Vincenzo. 2010. 'L'impatto del mito greco nell'Etruria orientalizzante: la documentazione ceramica', *Bollettino d'archeologia online*, special volume: 27–40

Bellelli, Vincenzo, Rita Cosentino, Françoise Gautier, Laurent Haumesser, Alfonsina Russo Tagliente, and Paola Santoro (eds). 2013. *Gli Etruschi e il Mediterraneo: la città di Cerveteri* [catalogue of the exhibition, Lens, 5 December 2013–10 March 2014; Rome, 15 April–20 July 2014] (Paris: Somogy Editions d'Art)

Bentz, Martin. 1992. *Etruskische Votivbronzen des Hellenismus* (Florence: Olschki)

Beolchini, Valeria, and Elena Castillo Ramírez (eds). 2006. *Tusculum, II. Tuscolo: una roccaforte dinastica a controllo della Valle Latina; fonti storiche e dati archeologici*, Bibliotheca Italica. Monografías de la Escuela española de historia y arqueología en Roma, 29 (Rome: L'Erma di Bretschneider)

Beolchini, Valeria, Mandatori Gianluca Diarte-Blasco Pilar, and Peña-Chocarro Leonor Moreno-García Marta. 2016. 'Il circuito murario medievale di Tusculum: un rito di fondazione di XII secolo', *Temporis signa: Archeologia della tarda antichità e del medioevo*, 11: 21–36

Berrino, Nicoletta Francesca. 2003. 'La loquacità di Tacita Muta e la maena di Ovidio *fast*. 2, 578', *Invigilata Lucernis*, 25: 7–17

Boldrini, Sabrina. 1994. *Gravisca: Scavi nel santuario greco*, IV: *Le ceramiche ioniche* (Bari: Edipuglia)

Bonfante, Larissa. 2012. 'Human Sacrifice: Etruscan Rituals for Death and for Life', in *Interpretando l'Antico: scritti di archeologia offerti a Maria Bonghi Jovino*, I, ed. by Cristina Chiaramonte Treré, Giovanna Bagnasco Gianni, and Federica Chiesa, Quaderni di Acme, 134 (Milan: Cisalpino), pp. 67–82

——. 2016a. 'Human Sacrifices and Taboos in Antiquity: Notes on an Etruscan Funerary Urn', *Notes in the History of Art*, 35.1–2: 156–70

——. 2016b. 'Innovations: Myth, Inscriptions, and Meaning', in *Caere*, ed. by Nancy T. de Grummond and Lisa C. Pieraccini (Austin: University of Texas Press), pp. 61–72

Bonghi Jovino, Maria. 2008. 'L'ultima dimora. Sacrifici umani e rituali sacri in Etruria. Nuovi dati sulle sepolture nell'abitato di Tarquinia', in *Sepolti tra i vivi: evidenza ed interpretazione di contesti funerari in abitato; atti del convegno internazionale, Roma, 26–29 aprile 2006*, ed. by Gilda Bartoloni and Maria Gilda Benedettini, *Scienze dell'antichità*, 14.2: 771–94

——. 2010. 'Tarquinia. Types of Offerings, Etruscan Divinities and Attributes in the Archaeological Record', in *Material Aspects of Etruscan Religion: Proceedings of the International Colloquium, Leiden, 29–30 May 2008*, ed. by Lammert Bouke van der Meer (Leuven: Peeters), pp. 5–16

——. 2017. '"L'Uomo di Mare" di Taquinia. Un sacrificio umano nel contesto abitatio tra riflessione teorica e documentazione archeologica', *Tarchna*, Suppl. 5: 1–15

Bonino, Marco. 1989. 'Imbarcazioni arcaiche in Italia: il problema delle navi usate dagli Etruschi', in *Atti del Secondo congresso internazionale etrusco, Florence, 26 May – 2 June 1985*, III (Rome: Giorgio Bretschneider), pp. 1517–36

Borzillo, Giuseppe, and Daniele Federico Maras. 2021. 'La costa tarquiniese: un paesaggio in divenire tra la Preistoria e l'età contemporanea', *Spolia*, 17: 1–40

Bruni, Stefano. 2013. 'Seafaring: Ship Building, Harbors, the Issue of Piracy', in *The Etruscan World*, ed. by Jean McIntosh Turfa (London: Routledge), pp. 759–77

Burkert, Walter. 1997. *Homo necans: The Anthropology of Ancient Greek Sacrificial Ritual and Myth* (Berkeley: University of California Press)

——. 2001. *Savage Energies: Lessons of Myth and Ritual in Ancient Greece* (Chicago: University of Chicago Press)

——. 2003. *La religione greca* (Milan: Jaca)

Cagianelli, Cristina. 1999. *Bronzi a figura umana* (Vatican City: Direzione Generale dei Monumenti, Musei e Gallerie Pontificie)

Caloi, Lucia, and Maria Rita Palombo. 1992. 'La fauna', *Notizie degli Scavi di Antichità*, 1988–1989, II Suppl. (Rome: Accademia dei Lincei), pp. 131–38

Camporeale, Giovannangelo. 2009. 'The Deified Deceased in Etruscan Culture', in *New Perspectives on Etruria and Early Rome: In Honor of Richard Daniel De Puma*, ed. by Synclair Bell and Helen Nagy (Madison: University of Wisconsin Press), pp. 220–50

Capdeville, Gérard. 1971. 'Substitution de victimes dans les sacrifices d'animaux à Rome', *Mélanges de l'École française de Rome: archéologie*, 83.2: 283–323

——. 2016. 'L'uccello nella divinazione in italia centrale', in *Forms and Structures of Religion in Ancient Central Italy: Proceedings of the Congress, Perugia-Gubbio, 21–25 September 2011*, ed. by Augusto Ancillotti and Alberto Calderini (Rome: L'Erma di Bretschneider), pp. 79–153

Carafa, Paolo. 2008. 'Uccisioni rituali e sacrifici umani nella topografia di Roma', in *Sepolti tra i vivi: evidenza ed interpretazione di contesti funerari in abitato; atti del convegno internazionale, Roma, 26–29 aprile 2006*, ed. by Gilda Bartoloni and Maria Gilda Benedettini, *Scienze dell'antichità*, 14.2: 667–703

Carboni, Romina. 2016. 'Unusual Sacrificial Victims: Fish and their Value in the Context of Sacrifices', in *Animals in Greek and Roman Religion and Myth: Proceedings of the Symposium Grumentinum, Grumento Nova, 5–7 June 2013*, ed. by Patricia A. Johnston, Attilio Mastrocinque, and Sophia Papaioannou (Cambridge: Cambridge Scholars), pp. 255–80

——. 2017. 'Sacrifici non cruenti. Alcune considerazioni sulle offerte di pesci nel linguaggio religioso del mondo greco', *Scienze dell'antichità*, 23.3: 207–20

Carlucci, Claudia, and Lorella Maneschi. 2013. 'La formazione dei depositi rituali nel santuario meridionale: analisi delle tipologie e delle modalità attestate', in *Riflessioni su Pyrgi: scavi e ricerche nelle aree del santuario*, ed. by Maria Paola Baglione and Maria Donatella Gentili (Rome: L'Erma di Bretschneider), pp. 41–70

Castello, Claudio, and Alessandro Mandolesi. 2010. 'Modellini di navi tirrenico-villanoviane da Tarquinia', *Mediterranea*, 6: 9–28

Cecamore, Claudia. 1993. 'Il santuario di Iuppiter Latiaris sul Monte Cavo: spunti e materiali dei vecchi scavi', *Bullettino della Commissione archeologica comunale di Roma*, 95: 19–44

Cerchiai, Luca, and Bruno d'Agostino. 1999. *Il mare, la morte, l'amore: gli Etruschi, i Greci e l'immagine* (Rome: Donzelli)

Cherici, Armando. 2006. 'Talassocrazia: aspetti tecnici, economici, poltici, con un brevissimo cenno a Novilara, Nesazio e ai Feaci', *Annali della Fondazione per il Museo C. Faina di Orvieto*, 13: 439–82

Chiaramonte Treré, Cristina. 2017. 'Riti e offerte: testimonianze di età orientalizzante e arcaica da Tarquinia', in *ArcheoTipico: l'archeologia come strumento per la ricostruzione del paesaggio e dell'alimentazione antica; atti del Convegno (Viterbo 2015)*, ed. by Gian Maria Di Nocera, Alessandro Guidi, and Andrea Zifferero, *Rivista di storia dell'agricoltura*, 56: 141–58

Chiesa, Federica. 2005. 'Un rituale di fondazione nell'area *Alpha* di Tarquinia', in *Offerte dal regno vegetale e dal regno animale nelle manifestazioni del sacro; atti dell'incontro di studio, Milano 26–27 giugno 2003*, ed. by Maria Bonghi Jovino and Federica Chiesa (Rome: L'Erma di Bretschneider), pp. 103–09

Citti, Francesco. 1994. 'Una "*mena*" per cena, Pompon. "Atell." fr. 80 s. Ribb³', *Materiali e discussioni per l'analisi dei testi classici*, 33: 151–55

Colivicchi, Fabio. 2004. *Gravisca: scavi nel santuario greco*, XVI: *I materiali minori* (Bari: Edipuglia)

Colonna, Giovanni. 1990. 'L'iscrizione etrusca del Piombo di Linguadoca', *Scienze dell'antichità*, 2: 547–55

——. 2006. 'Cerveteri. La tomba delle iscrizioni graffite', in *Archeologia in Etruria meridionale: atti delle giornate di studio in ricordo di Mario Moretti; Civita Castellana, 14–15 novembre 2003*, ed. by Maristella Pandolfini Angeletti (Rome: L'Erma di Bretschneider), pp. 419–51

——. 2009. 'Ancora su *Śur/Śuri*. 1. L'epiteto **EISTA* ("Il DIO") 2. L'attributo del fulmine', *Studi etruschi*, 75: 9–32

——. 2016. 'La scrittura e la tomba. Il caso dell'Etruria arcaica', in *L'écriture et l'espace de la mort: épigraphie et nécropoles à l'époque préromaine*, ed. by Marie-Laurence Haack [proceedings of the seminar, Rome, 5–7 March 2009] (Rome: École française de Rome), pp. 125–37

Colonna, Giovanni, and Daniele Federico Maras. 2001. 'Pyrgi', *Studi etruschi*, 54: 369–422 nos 33–96

Conticello de' Spagnolis, Marisa. 2004. *Il mito omerico di Dionysos ed i pirati tirreni in un documento da Nuceria Alfaterna* (Rome: L'Erma di Bretschneider)

Cosentino, Rita, and Daniele Federico Maras. 2020. 'Scoperte inaspettate dal santuario del Manganello a Cerveteri: una nuova lastra dipinta e la "firma invisibile" di un artista etrusco', *Rendiconti della Pontificia Accademia Romana di Archeologia*, 92: 75–145

Cousin, Catherine. 2009. 'Origine et place des didascalies dans l'imagerie funéraire étrusque', in *Écritures, cultures, sociétés dans les nécropoles d'Italie ancienne: table-ronde des 14–15 décembre 2007 'Mouvements et trajectoires dans les nécropoles d'Italie d'époque pré-républicaine et républicaine', ENS Paris*, ed. by Marie-Laurence Haack (Bordeaux: Ausonius), pp. 63–89

Cristofani, Mauro. 1983. *Gli Etruschi del mare* (Milan: Longanesi)

De Cristofaro, Alessio. 2019. 'Il linguaggio dell'arte etrusca in contesto: ancora sul kantharos di via d'Avack, Veio e il mare', *Ostraka*, 28: 275–85

de Grummond, Nancy T. 2016a. 'Etruscan Human Sacrifice: The Case of Tarquinia', in *Diversity of Sacrifice: Form and Function of Sacrificial Practices in the Ancient World and Beyond*, ed. by Carrie Ann Murray, IEMA Proceedings, 5 (Albany: SUNY Press), pp. 145–68

——. 2016b. 'Thunder versus Lightning in Etruria', *Etruscan Studies*, 19: 183–207

De Marinis, Raffaele Carlo. 2007. 'I manufatti di metallo', in *L'abitato etrusco del Forcello di Bagnolo S. Vito (Mantova): le fasi di età arcaica*, ed. by Raffaele Carlo De Marinis and Marta Rapi (Florence: Tipografia Latini), pp. 247–61

Di Fazio, Massimiliano. 2001. 'Sacrifici umani e uccisioni rituali nel mondo etrusco', *Rendiconti dei Lincei*, 9.9: 435–505

Di Fazio, Massimiliano. 2017. 'Nuove riflessioni su sacrifici umani e omicidi religiosi nel mondo etrusco', *Scienze dell'antichità*, 23.3: 449–64

di Gennaro, Francesco. 2000. 'Paesaggi di potere: l'Etruria meridionale in età protostorica', in *Paesaggi di potere: problemi e prospettive; atti del seminario, Udine, 16–17 maggio 1996*, Quaderni di Eutopia, 2 (Rome: Quasar), pp. 95–119

Donati, Luigi, and Simona Rafanelli. 2004. 'Il sacrificio nel mondo etrusco', in *Thesaurus cultus et rituum antiquorum (ThesCRA)*, I: *Processions, Sacrifices, Libations, Fumigations, Dedications* (Los Angeles: J. Paul Getty Museum), pp. 136–82

Dumézil, George. 1958. 'Les *pisciculi* des Volcanalia', *Revue des études latines*, 36: 121–30

Eles, Patricia von. 2005. 'Verucchio. Dalla terra e dal mare: la proiezione dell'ambiente nell'ambito funerario', in *Offerte dal regno vegetale e dal regno animale nelle manifestazioni del sacro: atti dell'incontro di studio, Milano 26–27 giugno 2003*, ed. by Maria Bonghi Jovino and Federica Chiesa (Rome: L'Erma di Bretschneider), pp. 29–34

Ercolani, Andrea. 2012. 'Latino e i Tirreni (Hes. *Th.* 1011–1016): questioni di storia e di cronologia', in *Le Origini degli Etruschi: storia, archeologia, antropologia*, ed. by Vincenzo Bellelli (Rome: L'Erma di Bretschneider), pp. 383–95

Fiore, Ivana, and Antonio Tagliacozzo. 2002. 'I resti ossei faunistici', in *Este preromana: una città e i suoi santuari*, ed. by Angela Ruta Serafini (Treviso: Canova), pp. 185–97

Fiorini, Lucio. 2005. *Gravisca: scavi nel santuario greco*, I.1: *Topografia generale del santuario e scavi del santuario: analisi dei contesti e delle stratigrafie* (Bari: Edipuglia)

Fiorini, Lucio, and Mario Torelli. 2017. 'L'*emporion* arcaico di Gravisca e la sua storia', in *La città etrusca e il sacro: santuari e istituzioni politiche; atti del convegno, Bologna 21–23 gennaio 2016*, ed. by Elisabetta Govi (Bologna: Bononia University Press), pp. 255–300

Gambacurta, Giovanna. 2005. 'Il *bothros* di Asolo: na cerimonia pubblica in epoca di romanizzazione', in *Depositi votivi e culti dell'Italia antica dall'età arcaica a quella tardo repubblicana*, ed. by Annamaria Comella and Sebastiana Mele (Bari: Edipuglia), pp. 491–506

Gianfrotta, Piero Alfredo. 1988. 'Le coste, i porti, la pesca', in *Etruria Meridionale: conoscenza, conservazione, fruizione; atti del convegno, Viterbo, 29/30 novembre-1 dicembre 1985* (Rome: Quasar), pp. 11–15

Giulierini, Paolo. 2007. 'La pesca in Etruria', *Florentia*, 2: 43–99

——. 2010. 'La pesca in Etruria', in *Il mare degli Etruschi: atti del Convegno, Piombino-Orbetello, 18–20 settembre 2009* (Florence: Regione Toscana), pp. 105–35

Gras, Michel. 1985. *Trafics tyrrhéniens achaïques* (Rome: École française de Rome)

Grottanelli, Cristiano. 1999. *Il sacrificio* (Rome: Laterza)

Harari, Maurizio. 1988. 'Dioniso, i pirati, i delfini', in *Navies and Commerce of the Greeks, the Carthaginians and the Etruscans in the Tyrrhenian Sea*, ed. by Tony Hackens (Rixensart: PACT), pp. 33–45

Harrison, Adrian P. 2013. 'Animals in the Etruscan Household and Environment', in *The Etruscan World*, ed. by Jean McIntosh Turfa (London: Routledge), pp. 1086–1114

Haudry, Jean. 2013. 'Les feux de rome', *Revue d'études latines*, 90: 57–82

Hurwit, Jeffrey M. 2015. *Artists and Signatures in Ancient Greece* (Cambridge: Cambridge University Press)

Jucker, Ines (ed.). 1991. *Italy of the Etruscans* (Mainz: Von Zabern)

Krämer, Robinson Peter. 2017. 'What Is Dead May Never Die. Pratiche sacrificali per la divinizzazione del defunto in Etruria e nel Lazio nell'età orientalizzante e arcaica. Un approccio di economia politica', *Scienze dell'antichità*, 23.3: 517–38

Krauskopf, Ingrid. 1984. 'Artemis/Artumes', in *Lexicon iconographicum mythologiae classicae*, ii: *Aphrodisias - Athena* (Bern: Artemis), pp. 774–92

——. 1988. 'Artumes', *Annali della Fondazione per il Museo C. Faina di Orvieto*, 4: 171–206

Lefèvre-Novaro, Daniela. 2010. 'Les sacrifices de poissons dans les sanctuaires grecs de l'Âge du Fer', *Kernos*, 23: 37–52

Lemmo, Vincenzo. 2015. '*Oinochoe* italo-geometrica', in *Symbola: Il potere dei simboli; recuperi archeologici della Guardia di Finanza*, ed. by Daniele Leoni (Mozzecane: Dielle), pp. 132–33 nos 1–36

Maggiani, Adriano. 2011. '*Ager Clusinus. Tolle*', *Studi etruschi*, 74: 262–63 no. 24

——. 2012. 'Di tre piccoli depositi di fondazione', in *Kulte, Riten, religiöse Vorstellungen bei den Etruskern und ihr Verhältnis zu Politik und Gesellschaft; Akten der 1. Internationalen Tagung der Sektion Wien/Österreich des Istituto nazionale di studi etruschi ed italici (Wien, 4.-6. 12. 2008)*, ed. by Luciana Aigner-Foresti and Petra Amann (Vienna: Verlag der Österreichischen Akademie der Wissenschaften), pp. 223–34

Mandolesi Alessandro. 2014. 'Le Saline: un grande scalo marittimo per la Tarquinia villanoviana', in *La Riserva naturale statale 'Saline di Tarquinia'*, ed. by Lorenza Colletti (Rome: Corpo Forestale dello Stato), pp. 195–203

Maras, Daniele Federico. 1998. 'Rivista di epigrafia etrusca. Pyrgi', *Studi etruschi*, 44: 413 no. 96

——. 2013. 'Area Sud: ricerche in corso sulla documentazione epigrafica, contesti, supporti, formulari, teonimi', in *Riflessioni su Pyrgi: scavi e ricerche nelle aree del santuario*, Supplementi e monografie della rivista 'Archeologia classica', 11, n.s., 8 (Rome: L'Erma di Bretschneider), pp. 195–206

——. 2014. 'La prima stesura dell'iscrizione di *Manios* e l'uso epigrafico dell'interpunzione espuntiva', in 'La Fibula Prenestina' [proceedings of the Study Day, Rome, 6 June 2011], *Bullettino di Paletnologia Italiana*, 99: 113–22

——. 2016. 'Miti e riti di divinizzazione in Italia centrale nell'età tirannica', *Scienze dell'antichità*, 21.1: 75–99

——. 2017. 'Religion', in *Etruscology*, ed. by Alessandro Naso (Berlin: De Gruyter), pp. 277–316

——. 2018a. 'Dancing Myths: Musical Performances with Mythological Subjects from Greece to Etruria', in *The Study of Musical Performance in Antiquity*, ed. by Agnes Garcia-Ventura, Claudia Tavolieri, and Lorenzo Verderame (Cambridge: Cambridge Scholars), pp. 137–53

——. 2018b. 'Kings and Tablemates. The Political Role of Comrade Associations in Archaic Rome and Etruria', in *Beiträge zur Sozialgeschichte der Etrusker: Akten der internationalen Tagung, Wien 8.-10.6.2016*, ed. by Luciana Aigner-Foresti and Petra Amann (Vienna: Verlag der Österreichischen Akademie der Wissenschaften), pp. 91–108

——. 2019. 'Children of Truth: The Role of Apprentices in Etrusco-Roman Divination', in 'Liminalità infantili: strategie di inclusione ed esclusione', ed. by Elena Zocca and Anna Maria Gloria Capomacchia [proceedings of the congress, Rome, 29–30 May 2017], *Henoch*, 41.1: 60–67

——. 2020. 'Inter-ethnic Mobility and Integration in Pre-Roman Etruria: The Contribution of Onomastics', in *Migration, Mobility and Language Contact in the Ancient Mediterranean*, ed. by James Clackson, Katherine McDonald, and Nicholas Zair [proceedings of the Laurence Seminar, Cambridge, 27–28 May 2016] (Cambridge: Cambridge University Press), pp. 23–52

Marcattili, Francesco. 2012. 'Il coloe di Caronte e le porte dell'Ade', in *Segni e colore: dialoghi sulla pittura tardoclassica ed ellenistica; atti del convegno (Pavia, Collegio Ghislieri, 9–10 marzo 2012)*, ed. by Maurizio Harari and Silvia Paltineri (Rome: L'Erma di Bretschneider), pp. 69–78

Martelli, Marina. 1987. *Ceramica degli Etruschi* (Novara: De Agostini)

McPhee, Ian D., and Arthur Dale Trendall. 1987. *Greek Red-Figured Fish-Plates*, Beiheft zur Halbjahresschrift Antike Kunst, 14 (Basel: Vereinigung der Freunde Antiker Kunst c/o Archäologisches Seminar der Universität)

Meer, Lammert Bouke van der. 2011. *Etrusco Ritu* (Leuven: Peeters)

Menzel, Heinz. 1960. *Die römische Bronzen aus Deutschland*, 1: *Speyer* (Mainz: Von Zabern)

Michetti, Laura Maria. 2016. 'Ports. Trade, Cultural Connections, Sanctuaries, and Emporia', in *Caere*, ed. by Nancy T. de Grummond and Lisa C. Pieraccini (Austin: University of Texas Press), pp. 73–86

——. 2017. 'Harbors', in *Etruscology*, ed. by Alessandro Naso (Berlin: De Gruyter), pp. 391–405

Minetti, Annalisa. 1994. 'La stipe di Castelluccio di Pienza', *Prospettiva*, 73–74: 111–18

Minniti, Claudia. 2012. 'Offerte rituali di cibo animale in contesti funerari dell'Etruria e del Lazio nella prima età del Ferro', in *Atti del 6° Convegno nazionale di archeozoologia, Orecchiella, 21–24 May 2009*, ed. by Jacopo De Grossi Mazzorin, Daniela Saccà, and Carlo Tozzi (Lucca: Associazione italiana di archeozoologia), pp. 153–61

Naiden, Fred S. 2007. 'The Fallacy of the Willing Victim', *Journal of Hellenic Studies*, 127: 61–73

Pacciarelli, Marco. 2000. *Dal villaggio alla città: la svolta protourbana del 1000 a.C. nell'Italia tirrenica* (Florence: All'Insegna del Giglio)

Pallottino, Massimo. 1963. '*Faesulae*. Quinto Fiorentino', *Studi etruschi*, 31: 176–85 nos 1–11

Pasquinucci, Simona (ed.). 2019. *La tutela del patrimonio culturale: il modello italiano 1969–2019* (Rome: De Luca)

Pommey, Patrice. 2017. 'Ships and Shipping', in *Etruscology*, ed. by Alessandro Naso (Berlin: De Gruyter), pp. 371–89

Prato, Ornella. Forthcoming. 'I resti faunistici', in *Lo scavo del riempimento del pozzo del settore I del 'complesso monumentale'*, ed. by Giovanna Bagnasco Gianni, Tarchna, Suppl. 5 (Rome: L'Erma di Bretschneider)

Rafanelli, Simona. 2013. 'Archaeological Evidence for Etruscan Religious Rituals', in *The Etruscan World*, ed. by Jean McIntosh Turfa (London: Routledge), pp. 566–93

Rask, Katie A. 2014. 'Etruscan Animal Bones and their Implications for Sacrificial Studies', *History of Religions*, 53.3: 269–312

Rathje, Annette. 2019. 'Veii and the Near East', in *Veii*, ed. by Jacopo Tabolli (Austin: University of Texas Press), pp. 101–05

Richardson, Emeline H. 1998. 'The Eel Carriers', *Etruscan Studies*, 5: 25–36

Rizzo, Maria Antonietta. 2015. *Principi etruschi: le tombe orientalizzanti di San Paolo a Cerveteri*, Bollettino d'arte, special volume (Rome: L'Erma di Bretschneider)

——. 2016. 'Rappresentazioni di navi su due grandi pissidi *white-on-red* dalla tomba 1 di San Paolo a Cerveteri', in *Για το φίλο μας: Scritti in ricordo di Gaetano Messineo*, ed. by Elisabetta Mangani and Angelo Pellegrino (Rome: Espera), pp. 323–32

Roscini, Elena. 2013. 'Gli *oscilla* e l'*oscillatio* presso i Romani: fonti antiche e terminologia archeologica a confronto', *Scienze dell'antichità*, 19.1: 233–57

Rose, Herbert J. 1933. 'The Cult of Volkanus at Rome', *Journal of Roman Studies*, 23: 46–63

Ross Holloway, Robert. 2006. 'The Tomb of the Diver', *American Journal of Archaeology*, 110.3: 365–88

Rottoli, Mauro. 2005. 'Le analisi archeobotaniche a Tarquinia: i resti vegetali in due contesti del "Complesso Monumentale"', in *Offerte dal regno vegetale e dal regno animale nelle manifestazioni del sacro; atti dell'incontro di studio, Milano 26–27 giugno 2003*, ed. by Maria Bonghi Jovino and Federica Chiesa (Rome: L'Erma di Bretschneider), pp. 113–19

Russ, Hannah, and Angela Trentacoste. 2021. 'Wild Food in an Urban Environment: Freshwater Fish Consumption at the Archaic Town of Forcello (Northern Italy)', *Anthropozoologica*, 55.5: 71–85

Sannibale, Maurizio. 2019. 'Immagini svelate. Le copie al vero di Carlo Ruspi nel Museo Gregoriano Etrusco', *Mélanges de l'École française de Rome: Archéologie*, 131.2 <https://doi.org/10.4000/mefra.7920>

Sassù, Alessio. 2016. 'Through Impurity: A Few Remarks on the Role of the Dog in Purification Rituals of the Greek World', in *Animals in Greek and Roman Religion and Myth: Proceedings of the Symposium Grumentinum,*

Grumento Nova, 5–7 June 2013, ed. by Patricia A. Johnston, Attilio Mastrocinque, and Sophia Papaioannou (Cambridge: Cambridge Scholars), pp. 393–417

Scarano Ussani, Vincenzo. 2006. 'Numa e i pesci senza squame. Alle origini di un divieto', *Ostraka*, 15.2: 355–62

Schneider-Herrmann, Gisela. 1970. 'Das Geheimnis der Artemis in Etrurien', *Antike Kunst*, 13: 52–70

Sgubini Moretti, Anna Maria, and Mario Torelli (eds). 2008. *Etruschi: le antiche metropoli del Lazio* [catalogue of the exhibition, Rome, 21 October 2008–6 January 2009] (Milan: Electa)

Simon, Erika. 2013. 'Greek Myth in Etruscan Culture', in *The Etruscan World*, ed. by Jean McIntosh Turfa (London: Routledge), pp. 495–512

Smith, Henry R. W. 1962. 'A Phlyax Vase in Rio de Janeiro', *American Journal of Archaeology*, 66.3: 323–31

Sorrentino, Claudio. 2004. 'I reperti osteoloigici', in *Gravisca: Scavi nel santuario greco*, XVI: *I materiali minori*, ed. by Fabio Colivicchi (Bari: Edipuglia), pp. 175–235

——. 2005. 'Analisi paleozoologiche a Pyrgi', in *Offerte dal regno vegetale e dal regno animale nelle manifestazioni del sacro: atti dell'incontro di studio, Milano 26–27 giugno 2003*, ed. by Maria Bonghi Jovino and Federica Chiesa (Rome: L'Erma di Bretschneider), pp. 127–32

——. 2013. 'Pyrgi, ricerche di archeozoologia: dati preliminari', in *Riflessioni su Pyrgi: scavi e ricerche nelle aree del santuario*, ed. by Maria Paola Baglione and Maria Donatella Gentili (Rome: L'Erma di Bretschneider), pp. 207–20

Tabolli, Jacopo. 2019. 'Veii and the Others. Closest Neighbors', in *Veii*, ed. by Jacopo Tabolli (Austin: University of Texas Press), pp. 67–76

Tagliacozzo, Antonio. 1989. 'Analisi dei resti faunistici dell'area sacra di S. Omobono', in *Il vivero quotidiano in Roma arcaica: materiali dagli scavi del Tempio Arcaico nell'Area Sacra di S. Omobono* (Rome: Procom), pp. 65–69

Todisco, Luigi (ed.). 2012. *La ceramica a figure rosse della Magna Grecia e della Sicilia*, 3 vols (Rome: L'Erma di Bretschneider)

Torelli, Mario. 2011. 'Le amazzoni di Efeso e l'ittiomanzia di Sura. Appunti sulla decorazione pittorica del tempio di Portonaccio di Veio', in *Corollari: scritti di antichità etrusche e italiche in omaggio all'opera di Giovanni Colonna*, ed. by Daniele Federico Maras (Pisa: Serra), pp. 163–73

Trendall, Arthur Dale. 1959. *Phlyax Vases*, Bulletin of the Institute of Classical Studies, Suppl. 8 (London: Institute of Classical Studies)

Trentacoste, Angela. C. 2013. 'Faunal Remains from the Etruscan Sanctuary at Poggio Colla (Vicchio di Mugello)', *Etruscan and Italic Studies*, 16.1: 75–105

——. 2014. 'The Etruscans and their Animals: The Zooarchaeology of Forcello di Bagnolo San Vito (Mantova)' (unpublished doctoral thesis, University of Sheffield)

Turfa, Jean McIntosh. 2012. *Divining the Etruscan World: The Brontoscopic Calendar and Religious Practice* (Cambridge: Cambridge University Press)

Volpe Cacciatore, Paola. 2008. 'Due testi a confronto: *De Iside* 352F–353E – *Quaestio convivalis* VIII, 8 728C–730F', in *The Unity of Plutarch's Work: 'Moralia' Themes in the 'Lives', Features of the 'Lives' in the 'Moralia'*, ed. by Anastasios G. Nikolaidis (Berlin: De Gruyter), pp. 785–90

Wilkens, Barbara. 2008. 'Resti faunistici da una fossa rituale di Orvieto', in *'Saturnia Tellus': Definizioni dello spazio consacrato in ambiente etrusco-italico; atti del convegno internazionale svoltosi a Roma dal 10 al 12 novembre 2004*, ed. by Xavier Dupré Raventos, Sergio Ribichini, and Stephane Verger (Rome: CNR Edizioni), pp. 589–97

Willerslev, Rane. 2013. 'God on Trial. Human Sacrifice, Trickery, and Faith', *Hau: Journal of Ethnographic Theory*, 3.1: 140–54

ALEXANDRA A. CARPINO

6. Death — by Consumption — Interrupted

The Iconography of Vilia (Hesione)
on Etruscan Bronze Mirrors

Introduction

The visualization of food, drink, and/or its consumption remains one of the most characteristic aspects of Etruscan material culture. While the banquet on the lid of a bi-conical urn from Montescudaio is limited to a single participant, those found on the terracotta frieze plaques that decorated the archaic building on Poggio Civitate or in the mural paintings from Tarquinia, Orvieto, and Chiusi vividly document the participation of members of both sexes at public events connected to political, social, and/or funerary feasting (see further the chapters by Taylor and Pieraccini). Likewise, evidence for lavish banqueting, including 'merit and gift feasts' that helped to solidify 'existing hierarchical order and its ranks' (Kistler 2017, 200), comes from both domestic and tomb contexts, which not only include a wide range of utensils and vessels used during these events but also, in the case of the remains from Poggio Civitate (see chapter by Kansa), data about the critical roles given to elite women before, during, and after the banquet. Finally, faunal assemblages and other organic materials recovered from religious as well as funerary deposits broaden our understanding of Etruscan food culture (see further the chapters by Pieraccini and Maras).

Given this long-standing interest in consumption iconography and its visualization in all types of Etruscan art, one might expect to see a similar focus in the scenes that decorated the reverses of one of the most distinctive forms of Etruscan material culture, namely, the engraved bronze mirror. Production of these portable, handheld artefacts began in the late sixth century, a time when feasting had already become a fundamental part of the aristocratic lifestyle, and continued for another 450+ years, driven by their usage in life and association with significant life events: weddings, the birth of children, and funerals. In addition, they belong to what P. Gregory Warden (2013, 356) has termed the 'social landscape': as such, they expressed elite identity and helped advertise a family's wealth and prestige. Moreover, the engravings found on their non-reflecting sides, many of which were inspired by the broad Hellenic repertoire known to the Etruscans, not only document their strong tradition of visual narrative, but they also reveal their thoughts about 'marriage, fidelity, childbirth, reputation, and death' (Lowenstam 2008, 173). As such, the function of these mirrors was both reflection and transformation — literally and figuratively — with their enduring imagery serving to guide, uphold, and reinforce social behaviours grounded in cultural expectations (see further Carpino 2016).

On the earliest mirrors, engravers focused on genre scenes, such as couples in intimate settings,

Alexandra A. Carpino Professor of Art History, Department of Comparative Cultural Studies, Northern Arizona University (alexandra.carpino@nau.edu)

Consumption, Ritual, Art and Society: Interpretive Approaches and Recent Discoveries of Food and Drink in Etruria, ed. by Lisa Pieraccini and Laurel Taylor, NAA, 2 (Turnhout, 2023), pp. 113–125   BREPOLS ❧ PUBLISHERS   10.1484/M.NAA-EB.5.132808

musicians, athletes, and, occasionally, banqueters. Each of the latter portrays mixed gender events, focusing either on a single couple reclining on a couch attended by a naked youth or clothed girl or a three-figured composition that appears above a scene of dancing satyrs and maenads (Mayer-Prokop 1967, 79–82; Jucker 2001, no. 27). Both stylistically and iconographically, they have much in common with the representations found in early fifth-century BCE tomb paintings (see further the chapter by Pieraccini). In addition, while their various states of preservation preclude any in-depth assessments of the meals these banqueters may have been enjoying, aside from the drinking of wine, the position of their arms and fingers suggest that some of them may have originally held eggs, a food item commonly found in these artefacts' painted *comparanda*. Lisa Pieraccini (2014, 289) has suggested that

> [t]hese gestures of holding out the egg or passing it from one loved one to another belonged to aristocratic funerary ritual — one that includes ritualized food — and appear to be exclusively Etruscan. […] [The egg] could be both an icon of the afterlife and a symbol of life and rebirth.

Interestingly, two other early mirrors, one now in Berlin (Heres 1986, no. 1; Mayer-Prokop 1967, 74) and the second in Cincinnati (De Puma 1987, no. 42), show eggs in the hands of a siren, a creature the Etruscans considered to be a messenger of the afterlife (Carpino 2003, 47–48). As in contemporary and later funerary iconography, the function of this food item was not nutritional but symbolic, evoking both the cult of the dead as well as themes of fertility and rebirth, both of which speak to the mirror's ultimate function as a grave good.

By the second quarter of the fifth century, mythological figures and stories, frequently inspired by Greek myth or iconography, become more commonplace (Krauskopf 2016, 399), and it is in such imagery that additional themes related

Figure 6.1.
Uni breastfeeding Hercle in the presence of Aplu (?), Turan (?), Hebe and Tinia, Florence, Museo Archeologico Nazionale. Late fourth century BCE. Klügmann and Körte 1897, pl. 60.

to consumption appear. An overarching feature of these representations, moreover, is that the acts involving food and/or drink have nothing to do with physical sustenance — rather, what is stressed are their symbolic and/or ritual associations. For example, the engraving on a mid-fifth-century BCE mirror from Blera (Jucker 2001, 70–72 no. 34; Carpino 2009, 187–90) and the near-contemporary terracotta columen plaque from Temple A at Pyrgi (Haynes 2000, 179–81 fig. 154; Baglione 2013, 619–20) demonstrate the correlation of immortality with a drinkable substance. Each illustrates the same subject, namely, Athena witnessing her protégé, Tydeus, commit an act of cannibalism and consequently denying him the elixir that would have granted him eternal life. In the relief, the ambrosia is contained in a jug held by the recoiling goddess while on the mirror, it appears in a small bowl that rests within her right hand. A similar ritualization of drink appears in the following century in the scenes that depict either a youthful or grown Hercle suckling milk from the breast of Uni, an act signifying

Figure 6.2.
Metvia, Heasun, Menrva and Rescial, London, British Museum. Mid-fourth century BCE. Klügmann and Körte 1897, pl. 93.

both his adoption and reconciliation with the goddess as well as a uniquely Etruscan take on the concept of apotheosis. The most intricate portrayal of this ritual breastfeeding appears in the medallion of a large, late fourth-century BCE mirror (Fig. 6.1) from Volterra, now in Florence (de Grummond 2006, 83–84; Rasmussen 2013, 677), which includes an inscription underscoring the transformative power of the goddess's milk: it is capable of converting the hero from a human to 'a god worthy of the family of Tinia and Uni' (de Grummond 2006, 84). This artefact also contains a second drinking scene in its upper exergue, where a satyr both sips from and looks into a patera, possibly in search of a prophetic message, or as another evocation of the hero's impending transformation, given that wine drinking was associated with Fufluns and the belief in life after death (van der Meer 1995, 193; de Grummond 2006, 84; see further Zifferero Chapter 1 and Pieraccini Chapter 4).

6. DEATH — BY CONSUMPTION — INTERRUPTED 115

A liquid also functions as an agent of transformation on a large mid-fourth-century BCE mirror from Talamone, now in London (Fig. 6.2) (Fischer-Graf 1980, 81 n. 787; Neils 1994, 190; van der Meer 1995, 135–39). The engraving on the reverse depicts Heasun about to ingest the substance contained inside a phiale held by Metvia, which had to have originated in the pitcher held by Menrva (the goddess also helps the hero drink by resting her right hand on the back of his tilted head). Interpretations about the nature of this drink vary considerably — with proposals ranging from potions for the restoration of youth or protection against consumption by the dragon of the Golden Fleece to a recuperative tonic provided by the goddess after the hero's regurgitation (Neils 1994, 190, 192; van der Meer 1995, 135, 137). Regardless of its precise nature, the scene suggests, like the examples discussed above, that the Etruscans viewed certain liquids as transformative agents. Equally important seems to be the fact that these 'drinks' are shown being dispensed by powerful goddesses, from Uni who had the ability to bestow divinity through her breast milk to Menrva, who could either swiftly deny a hubristic warrior the chance to become immortal or aid in the healing of a protégé. With respect to the Talamone mirror, Jennifer Neils (1994, 193) has noted that 'While Medea could restore one's youth with magic, it took the power of the gods to restore life'. Van der Meer (1995, 137) concurs with this assessment, observing, as well, that the particular *interpretatio etrusca* illustrated in this mirror's medallion may have emphasized Menrva's status as a healing goddess.

In addition, during the Classical period, mirror iconography includes various depictions of Heasun's death-defying encounter with the dragon who guarded the Golden Fleece — an aspect of his story missing from the Graeco-Roman literary record — that emphasize the theme of consumption. On a mid-fourth-century BCE mirror (Freytag gen. Löringhoff 1990, no. 17; van der Meer 1995, 13), perhaps of Vulcian manufacture and the property

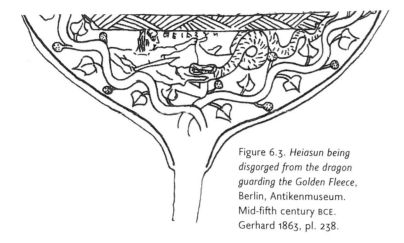

Figure 6.3. *Heiasun being disgorged from the dragon guarding the Golden Fleece*, Berlin, Antikenmuseum. Mid-fifth century BCE. Gerhard 1863, pl. 238.

of a woman named Ramtha Paithna, the hero is not present because he has already been devoured: all we see are Menrva and Artumes standing in front of a heavily bearded snake, underneath which is the frontal face and hind end of a ram signifying the fleece. That the engraver would depict the dragon in the form of a bearded snake is not unusual — this hybrid creature first appears in Etruscan art in the sixth century and by the fourth, it had been transformed into a fearsome monster with 'special underworld powers' (Pieraccini 2016, 100). On another mid-fourth-century BCE mirror (Neils 1994, 192), found in Sutri, Hiasunu attacks the dragon who has wrapped itself around the fleece, while on a third example (Fig. 6.3), created approximately a century earlier, a nearly fully disgorged and animated Heiasun appears in the lower exergue (Zimmer 1987, 21–24). Holding the prized fleece in his left hand, he uses a sword to attack the snake-shaped dragon and thereby loosen his lower limbs from the clutches of the monster's mouth. Viewers would have understood that the invincibility potion that the hero ingested prior to this encounter had rendered him suitably indigestible. In this way, the theme of consumption served to add an increased sense of drama to the story of this particular hero, providing a unique 'death — by consumption — interrupted' twist to the broader group of monster-slayer myths in Etruria. At the same time, this particular tale's emphasis on a 'devoured' hero who triumphs over death indicates a strong correlation between his victory and the theme of resurrection, the latter a topic of particular interest to the Etruscan elite and the owners of the mirrors (Neils 1994, 192; Warden 2009).

Averted consumption, along with sacrifice and exposure, also lie at the heart of the myth of Hesione, the Trojan maiden whose destiny was determined not only by the actions of her corrupt father, Laomedon, but also the hero, Herakles. After the king refused to compensate Poseidon and Apollo for building the city's walls, the latter sent a marine monster to terrorize the community while Apollo sent a pestilence. Apollo's oracle, moreover decreed that both of these plagues could only be placated by the sacrifice of Troy's virgin daughters, including, eventually, the princess herself, who was tied to a rocky outcrop to await her fate. According to the various surviving Graeco-Roman literary traditions (Fontenrose 1974, 347–48; Oakley 1987, 623; Ogden 2013, 118–23), this is when Herakles, on his way back to Greece after his successful ninth labour, the retrieval of the belt of the Amazon queen, Hippolyte, saw Hesione and made a deal with her father to rescue her in exchange for Poseidon's divine horses. In one version of the rescue, he is said to have eradicated the threat and freed the maiden by substituting himself for her, enduring ingestion, and then killing the creature from within its body over the course of three days. True to his nature, Laomedon also tricked the hero by presenting him with mortal horses. Herakles responded by returning to Troy and sacking the city. Hesione was one of the few members of her family to survive attack. Apollodorus mentions that she was given to Telamon after the sack as his reward for being the first to scale the city's walls, but other accounts record a version whereby Laomedon offered his daughter as an additional prize to whomever was successful in slaying the sea monster (Fontenrose 1974, 347–48).

In Etruria, the earliest representations of Hesione's story appear on sixth-century BCE painted pottery, both imported and locally produced, which indicate that the focus of the iconography was the role that Herakles played in thwarting her consumption. On a Corinthian krater found in Cerveteri (Carpenter 1991, 126 and fig. 199; Boardman 1997, no. 10), the freed Hesione even assists the hero by throwing rocks at the sea monster, while on an Attic black-figure kylix, she watches as Herakles removes the creature's tongue (Boardman 1997, no. 15; Carpenter 1991, 126). In contrast, on a Caeretan hydria (Carpenter 1991, 126 and fig. 159; Boardman 1997, no. 14; Oakley 1987, no. 43), the Trojan maiden is absent and the scene centres on a muscular and bearded Herakles, armed with both a harpe and a stone, advancing toward his fearsome adversary (the latter's large open mouth may have indicated that the scene was to be understood as showing the moment before the creature's ingestion of the hero). It wasn't until the second half of the fourth century BCE, however, a time when stories about 'damsels in distress' and the heroes or deities who saved them were introduced into the corpus of mirror iconography, that representations of this Trojan princess, known locally as Vilia or 'the daughter of Ilion' (Jucker 1986, 127: 'das Mädchen von Ilion'), became more popular. In a vein similar to Fufluns's rescue and romance with Areatha after her abandonment on Naxos or Elinai being saved from an attack by her angry husband through the intervention of Turan and Thethis (de Grummond 2006, figs VI.6 and V.27, respectively), this tale of 'death — by consumption — interrupted' would have resonated with mirror owners primarily because of its happy outcome. But equally significant is the story's connection to Hercle, a hero not only admired in Etruria for his strength and success as a monster-slayer but also as a suitor, an aspect of his character that would have been especially appealing to the brides and grooms who would have received the mirror on their wedding day.

The Iconography of Vilia on Engraved Etruscan Mirrors

Myths 'vary [considerably] according to geography and chronology, and on the basis of other factors as well, such as political, ritual or personal considerations' (de Grummond 2006, 15), and, by the fourth century BCE, 'an inherent Etruscan/Italic mode of visualization that is connected to Etruscan cultural attitudes' prevails (Warden 2013, 362). While none of the mirrors that illustrate the story of Vilia are identical, as a group they demonstrate that the Etruscans were not only most attracted to the parts that took place before and after the girl's exposure, but also that they favoured an ending wherein the Trojan maiden became the hero's bride instead of a war captive gifted to Telamon as a wife. As a result, the most terrifying aspects of the myth, especially the idea of Vilia as 'food' or the consequences of Laomedon's tricking of Herakles by presenting him with mortal rather than the promised divine horses, were eliminated in favour of an *interpretatio etrusca* (van der Meer 1995) that emphasized either harmony between the male protagonists and/or the tale's 'happily ever after' ending.

Both of these themes appear in the medallion of the only mirror (Fig. 6.4) where the figures are identified by inscriptions. Found in Capodimonte and dated to the last quarter of the fourth century BCE (Jucker 1986; van der Meer 1995, 113–15), this large and expertly engraved artefact also contains the most intricate and detailed representation of Vilia's story in mirror iconography. The composition is divided into two sections, a main field with two distinct but related scenes and a lower exergue. On the left side, Lamtu and Hercle stand and shake hands, a gesture that not only signifies the deal whereby the hero agreed to rescue the king's daughter in exchange for two divine horses, but also the *dexiosis* (Jucker 1986, 134) which, in Etruria, was especially relevant when a groom took possession of his bride on their wedding day. On the right side, Echpa, who either takes on the role of Hesione's lesser-known mother, Strymo or who represents herself, sits on a rocky outcrop and on her lap is a girlish Vilia who has her arms clasped around the matron's neck and her head tilted downward. Beneath them, in the lower exergue, the enormous head of a fearsome sea creature rises up at an angle in a sea full of large waves and some small fish. The monster's open mouth, suction cups, and jagged teeth serve as a poignant reminder of Vilia's exposure and near consumption while the girl's nudity, hunched-over posture, and age accentuate her innocence and vulnerability. Echpa raises her right hand in what is generally interpreted as 'an "eliciting" gesture' (de Grummond 2016, 198) and Ines Jucker (1986, 130) has argued that it signifies a plea for help. Because this same gesture is also used in Etruscan iconography in the context of prophecies (de Grummond 2016, 198), it suggests that the engraver meant for the twosome to be understood as clinging to each other prior to Vilia's exposure rather than as a scene that shows the girl being comforted after her rescue. By following the dictates of the Aplu's oracle, Echpa's plea is answered through the majestic figure of Hercle in the centre of the composition. In addition, the twosome of Echpa and the young Vilia, especially the latter's interlocked fingers that are clasped around the matron's neck, would have brought to the fore not only the intimate relationship between a mother and a child, but also a foreshadowing of Echpa's future grief over the sacrifice of her daughter, Polyxena, during the second sack of Troy. Interestingly, many scholars identify the subject depicted on a handle mirror (Fig. 6.5) from the early third century BCE as showing Echpa protecting her daughter and trying to prevent her from being taken away by two young men. As Jucker (1986, 132) has pointed out, there are striking similarities between the mother–daughter pair on the handle mirror and what is depicted on the Capodimonte artefact, especially the

Figure 6.4. *Lamtu, Hercle, Vilia and Echpa*, Switzerland, Collection of George Ortiz. Last quarter of the fourth century BCE. Drawing by Shawn R. Skabelund after Jucker 1986, fig. 1.

girls' age, nudity, tilted heads, and arms wrapped around an older woman's shoulders, all of which suggest that Vilia has yet to meet or transcend her fate as the monster's meal.

While some scholars have seen the Capodimonte matron's identity as Echpa as a mistake on the part of the engraver, who may have been unfamiliar with the name of Lamtu's wife, the inclusion of a character who alludes to future events was not uncommon in mirror iconography, especially on artefacts produced during the Late Classical and Early Hellenistic periods in central Etruscan workshops, where the mirror was most likely manufactured (Jucker 1986, 134). For example, on a contemporary mirror from Chiusi (de Grummond 2006, fig. VII.24), Vilia's brother, Tinthun, appears in a loving embrace with the goddess Thesan; framing them are a Lasa on the left and the offspring of their union, Memrun, on the right. The depiction of the couple's son

Figure 6.5. *Echpa, Polyxena, and two young men*, Lyon, Musée des Beaux Arts. Early third century BCE. Gerhard 1867, pl. 401.

Figure 6.6. *Lamtu, Aplu, Vilia and Hercle*, Rome, Museo Nazionale Etrusco di Villa Giulia. Late fourth century BCE. Drawing by Shawn R. Skabelund after Pacetti 2011, fig. 21a.

as grown up and mature is novel, but given both his gaze and his position in the composition, the reason for his inclusion would have been readily understood: he represents a proleptic figure, a reminder that his parent's relationship not only produced a son, and therefore a family, but also one who went on to distinguish himself on the battlefield. Thus, there is no reason to doubt the legitimacy of the Vilia-Echpa grouping on the Capodimonte mirror, especially as it adds even more layers to what is already an intricate and sophisticated composition.

Contemporary with the Capodimonte mirror is an engraved handle mirror (Fig. 6.6) of the Spiky Garland type now in Rome (Pacetti 2011, 74–77 (no. 21)). Possibly created in a workshop in the Tarquinia-Viterbo region, the medallion contains a four-figured composition which, despite the absence of the sea monster, most likely shows Vilia and Lamtu along with Hercle, who can be identified by his club, and Aplu, who can be recognized by his crown of laurel. Here, Vilia is no longer a frightened girl contemplating the terrible fate that awaits her but a partially nude young woman standing in the so-called hip-shot pose next to Hercle and looking down at him. Significantly, she also raises a portion of the mantle that falls down her back and is bunched between her thighs and lower legs, thereby evoking the gesture commonly understood, like the touching of a breast, 'as appropriate for a bride, wife, or a female who is interested in marriage' (de Grummond 2006, 17; see also figs II.10–11, V.28). Her sexual allure, along with the promise of future fecundity, is further accentuated by the jewellery she wears, especially the chains crossed over her torso which had strong erotic connotations in Etruria (Pacetti 2011, 76); these items, moreover, would also have served as reminders of Vilia's exposure and near consumption since most of the literary accounts mention that the maiden was sent to her fate wearing only her jewellery (see further Ogden 2013, 118), thereby enhancing her status as 'prestige food' (see further the chapter by Pieraccini on how this theme is manifested in

Etruscan wall paintings). The seated Hercle looks at Lamtu who holds a staff and sits, bent over, on a folding stool on the left side of the composition. Instead of showing them in the process of sealing their deal about the rescue, the engraver paired the Trojan king with Aplu, the god whose oracle determined Vilia's fate, and has him raising a hand to his head in a gesture communicating distress or 'forte preoccupazione' (Pacetti 2011, 77). Pacetti suggests that viewers would have understood the gesture as indicating Lamtu's awareness that his broken promises, both toward the gods and later with Hercle, would result in the destruction of his city. Because it is also juxtaposed with Vilia's gesture (they are the only ones on the mirror), viewers would have been reminded that her story, at least, had a happy ending. Thus, as is typical in mirrors of this type (van der Meer 1995, 231), the composition presents pairs of figures who are not only thematically related to each other but also to the iconography as a whole, from the lateral pairing of Lamtu and Hercle to the figures on the left, the right, and in the centre (Lamtu and Aplu; Vilia and Hercle; Aplu and Hesione), each of whom would have communicated specific aspects of the myth to the mirror's viewers. Equally significant is that this engraving presents the Etruscans' preferred status and iconography for Vilia — as Hercle's bride-to-be, standing as the paramount *interpretatio etrusca* with respect to the representations of this particular maiden on these artefacts.

A three-figured composition illustrating the Vilia myth appears on a second handle mirror (Fig. 6.7), once in Paris and dated to the early third century BCE (Jucker 1986, 133; Oakley 1987, no. 48). Here, the pictorial tradition used for the Trojan princess and Hercle on the Spiky Garland mirror discussed above is developed further. This time, Hercle stands in the centre of the composition with his right leg bent and resting on the tail of the defeated sea monster. He holds his club upright in his left hand while he uses his right to embrace the partially nude

Figure 6.7. *Vilia, Hercle and a Lasa (?)*, once Paris, Oppermann Collection. Early third century BCE. Gerhard 1867, pl. 341.1.

Vilia, once again bejewelled and holding up a portion of the mantle that falls down her backside with her right hand. A dolphin appears behind her, possibly in reference to the marine setting where the couple met, while behind the hero is a second partially nude figure, who appears to be encouraging their coupling with her outstretched arms. She may represent a Lasa, a common addition on contemporary mirrors in scenes related to love, adornment and/or fate (de Grummond 2006, 168–72). In contrast to the Capodimonte and Spiky Garland mirrors mentioned above, there is no doubt that this mirror presents Vilia and Hercle as a couple, with the romantic nature of their relationship communicated by what Larissa Bonfante (1999) has termed 'the conjugal embrace'. The implication is that Vilia's rescue from near consumption has transformed her from a daughter/girl into a wife/woman, thereby elevating her to the same status as other mythological wives and lovers in contemporary mirror iconography (e.g., Areatha,

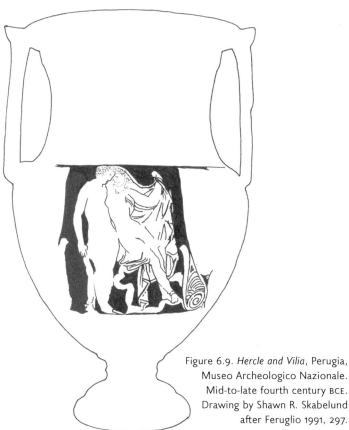

Figure 6.8. *Hercle and Vilia*, Perugia, Museo Archeologico Nazionale. Second half of the fourth century BCE. Klügmann and Körte 1897, pl. 65.

Figure 6.9. *Hercle and Vilia*, Perugia, Museo Archeologico Nazionale. Mid-to-late fourth century BCE. Drawing by Shawn R. Skabelund after Feruglio 1991, 297.

Uni, and Thesan) (see Zimmer 1995, no. 20; de Grummond 2006, figs VI.6, IV.8, and VII.24), respectively).

A nearly identical visual rhetoric appears in the fourth example of the Vilia myth in mirror iconography on an artefact now in Perugia (Fig. 6.8) that was also produced during the second half of the fourth century BCE (Oakley 1987, no. 47; Cenciaioli 1991, 302–04). As on the Capodimonte mirror, a fierce-looking, bearded, and eel-like sea monster, with an open jaw and fang-like teeth, serves as a poignant reminder of the Trojan maiden's exposure and near consumption. It glares menacingly at Vilia, who is positioned the farthest away on the right side of the composition. As in all of the previous examples, she is nude but variations include both a lean and toned body, symbolizing her healthiness (Sandhoff 2016, 28), and a sombre expression, which is conveyed by the line denoting the set of her mouth. This Vilia is also decked out in a wide range of jewellery, from a diadem and earrings to a necklace with three crescent pendants and a central bulla and an armlet also decorated with bullae. The latter type appears to have been worn by individuals, both female and male, who faced danger (Izzet 2012, 50), and it, in conjunction with the girl's expression, may have stood as references to the ordeal she had just experienced. Vilia also stares intently at Hercle, who returns her gaze. In contrast to his appearance on the other examples, this Hercle wears a cuirass, short chiton, and a cloak. As he situates a large mantle over her back and arms, the hero also shakes her right hand with his right one, a gesture, as noted above, that both recalls the deal he made with her father and denotes their forthcoming union. While the male on this artefact has sometimes been identified as Telamon, who, according to Apollodorus, received Hesione as a prize after he helped Hercle sack

Troy (Oakley 1987, 623), the examples already discussed overwhelmingly indicate that it was Hercle's romantic relationship with Vilia that was favoured in Etruria (for a discussion of this theme on a Faliscan krater, see Safran 2000). Supporting such an identification, moreover, is the mantle he uses to clothe the maiden, as it evokes the cloak Hercle was given by Athena (Fontenrose 1974, 347) and which he used to entice the sea monster to consume him instead of the girl. This feature not only adds another layer of meaning to this particular mirror's iconography but it also underscores how familiar the Etruscans were with many different aspects of the myth. Interestingly, a similar cloak appears on a mid–late fourth-century BCE Volterran red-figure column krater from the Palazzone necropolis in Perugia with the same subject matter (Feruglio 1991, 295–98), first worn by the hero on one side of the vase as a disguise as he advances into the jagged-tooth mouth of the sea monster, and then used by him to clothe the rescued Vilia, who also holds a portion aloft with her left hand, again signifying her status as his bride-to-be (Fig. 6.9).

Conclusions

When Fontenrose (1974, 349) wrote, 'It is notable that the divine horses are the great prize of victory, whereas the hero's marriage to the rescued princess has almost disappeared from the story as we have it', he was either unaware of or did not take into consideration Etruscan versions of the Hesione myth. When viewed in conjunction with each other, the images presented here indicate that the Etruscan artists and their customers were familiar enough with the different aspects of the story that they were able to select the episodes that resonated the most in the different contexts in which the artefacts that portrayed this story of exposure and near consumption by a fearsome sea monster were used. Given the association of

engraved mirrors not only with reflection and transformation, but also their frequent use as wedding gifts (see further de Grummond 2006, 11; De Puma 2013, 1056–57), it is not surprising that nuptial rather than overt consumption imagery prevailed over all other choices when the story of this young Trojan princess, known locally as Vilia, was introduced to the corpus of mirror iconography during the mid-fourth century BCE. These representations also celebrated a common theme, what might be called the 'happily ever after' motif, while downplaying the references to virgin sacrifice because of a father's impiety (the inclusion of the sea monster on most of these mirrors, nevertheless, remained a powerful reminder of the princess-as-meal motif). In addition, these characteristics placed Vilia's Etruscan iconography firmly within the larger body of contemporary mirror representations that addressed and encouraged reflection on one of the most important qualities of aristocratic female identity: marriage (see further Carpino 2016). As such, the theme of averted consumption not only represents the agent through which a social expectation is fulfilled but it also parallels the transformative roles played by other food substances in mirror imagery (e.g., Uni's breastmilk or Menrva's elixir of immortality).

The fact that Vilia's rescuer was Hercle would have only added to the myth's appeal, since he was, since his first appearance on these artefacts back in the early fifth century BCE, the embodiment of both masculine values and heroic ideals. Etruscan viewers, moreover, would not have found the union of Vilia and Hercle unbelievable, given that mirror iconography features a range of romances between their most popular of male heroes with characters who were never his paramours in Greek visual, oral, or literary traditions. For example, on a large mirror from Civita Castellana (Brommer 1981), dated to c. 300 BCE, the central part of the intricately engraved medallion includes five figures who have assembled in the aftermath of the slaying of

Thevrumines ('the Bull of Minos'; de Grummond 2006, 186). As per the Etruscan tradition, which also includes the only known representation of a baby Thevrumines sitting on the lap of his mother (Bonfante and Swaddling 2006, fig. 29), the hero responsible for the removal of the threat is Hercle, a fact that suggests that this may even have been viewed as one of his labours in Etruria (de Angelis 2015, 33). In addition to Mine, Menrva and Vile, the hero's frequent companion, are present, along with Areatha, who stands next to the hero. This royal daughter is dressed like a matron, with her mantle drawn up and over her head so as to create a veil that implies her status as a bride-to-be or wife. As with the story of Vilia, this *interpretatio etrusca* not only posits a correlation between the slaying of a monster and the winning of the hand of a king's daughter but it also emphasizes the important role that Hercle played within such narratives, particularly within the context of mirror iconography, as the suitor par excellence (de Angelis 2015, 33). For the children in elite households, such tales would have played an important role in their socialization toward adulthood, albeit with a healthy dose of fantasy thrown in, while for their parents, one of whom would most likely have received the mirror as a wedding gift, they would have represented, like the mirror itself,

constant reminders of the behaviours necessary for familial stability and continuity. Finally, for girls, more specifically, this myth would have underscored the role their fathers had not only as the heads of their families but also as the arbitrators of their destinies, especially when it came to the selection of a husband.

In sum, the iconography of Vilia on engraved bronze mirrors confirms the symbolic role that consumption narratives played, more generally, within this pictorial tradition as agents of transformation: from mortal to divinity in the case of Uni breastfeeding Hercle, from devoured to reborn in the case of Heasun, and finally, in the only example connected to a female protagonist, from a monster's meal to the wife of a hero. Unlike the destiny of the transgressive Ataiun, the hunter transformed into a stag and then killed and consumed by his own dogs, Vilia not only escapes a 'devouring death' (Lacy 1994, 171; see also Warden 2009), but her story also contains none of the eschatological associations connected to rebirth, apotheosis, or the afterlife. Instead, this tale of 'death — by consumption — interrupted' makes it abundantly clear that when an innocent, obedient princess was on the menu, so to speak, a hero would be in the wings, ready to whisk her from the jaws of death, sweep her off her feet, and restore both divine and natural order.

Works Cited

Baglione, Maria P. 2013. 'The Sanctuary of Pyrgi', in *The Etruscan World*, ed. by Jean Macintosh Turfa (London: Routledge), pp. 613–31

Boardman, John. 1997. 'Ketos', in *Lexicon iconographicum mythologiae classicae*, VIII (Bern: Artemis), pp. 731–36

Bonfante, Larissa. 1999. 'Marriage Scenes, Sacred and Otherwise: The Conjugal Embrace', *Problemi: Art Studies Quarterly*, 4: 20–25

Bonfante, Larissa, and Judith Swaddling. 2006. *Etruscan Myths* (Austin: University of Texas Press)

Brommer, Frank. 1981. 'Theseus und Minotauros in der etruskischen Kunst', *Romische Mitteilungen*, 88: 1–12

Carpenter, Thomas H. 1991. *Art and Myth in Ancient Greece: A Handbook* (London: Thames and Hudson)

Carpino, Alexandra A. 2003. *Discs of Splendor: The Relief Mirrors of the Etruscans* (Madison: University of Wisconsin Press)

——. 2009. 'Dueling Warriors on Two Etruscan Bronze Mirrors from the Fifth Century B.C.E.', in *New Perspectives on Etruria and Early Rome*, ed. by Sinclair Bell and Helen Nagy (Madison: University of Wisconsin Press), pp. 182–97

——. 2016. 'Marriage and Parenthood on Classical Period Bronze Mirrors: The Case of Latva and Tuntle', *Journal of Ancient Egyptian Interconnections*, 10: 31–38

Cenciaioli, Luana. 1991. '7.4. Specchio', in *Antichità dall'Umbria a New York (New York, Grey Art Gallery, 9 settembre – 2 novembre 1991)*, ed. by Benedetta Adembri and Francesco Roncalli (Perugia: Electa), pp. 302–04

de Angelis, Francesco. 2015. *Miti greci in tombe etrusche: le urne cinerarie di Chiusi* (Rome: Giorgio Bretschneider)

de Grummond, Nancy T. 2006. *Etruscan Myth, Sacred History, and Legend* (Philadelphia: University of Pennsylvania Museum of Archaeology and Anthropology)

——. 2016. 'Thunder versus Lightning in Etruria', *Etruscan Studies*, 19.2: 183–207

De Puma, Richard D. 1987. *Corpus speculorum Etruscorum: USA, I: Midwestern Collections* (Ames: Iowa State University Press)

——. 2013. 'Mirrors in Art and Society', in *The Etruscan World*, ed. by Jean Macintosh Turfa (London: Routledge), pp. 1041–67

Feruglio, Anna Eugenia. 1991. '7.1. Kelebe volterrana a figure rosse', in *Antichità dall'Umbria a New York (New York, Grey Art Gallery, 9 settembre – 2 novembre 1991)*, ed. by Benedetta Adembri and Francesco Roncalli (Perugia: Electa), pp. 295–98

Fischer-Graf, Ulrike. 1980. *Spiegelwerkstätten in Vulci*, Archäologische Forschungen, 8 (Berlin: Mann)

Fontenrose, Joseph E. 1974. *Python: A Study of Delphic Myth and Its Origins* (New York: Biblo & Tannen)

Freytag gen. Löringhoff, Bettina. 1990. *Corpus speculorum Etruscorum: Bundesrepublik Deutschland, III: Stuttgart - Tübingen, Privatsammlungen Esslingen - Stuttgart* (Munich: Hirmer)

Gerhard, Eduard. 1843–1867. *Etruskische Spiegel*, 4 vols (Berlin: Reimer)

Haynes, Sybille. 2000. *Etruscan Civilization: A Cultural History* (Los Angeles: J. Paul Getty Museum)

Heres, Gerald. 1986. *Corpus speculorum Etruscorum: Deutsche Demokratische Republik, I: East Berlin 1* (Berlin: Akademie-Verlag)

Izzet, Vedia. 2012. 'Reflections of Greek Myth in Etruria', in *Making Sense of Greek Art*, ed. by Viccy Coltman (Exeter: University of Exeter Press), pp. 39–52

Jucker, Ines. 1986. 'Hercle bei Lamtu: Ein neuer etruskischer Spiegel', *Antike Kunst*, 29: 126–36

——. 2001. *Corpus speculorum Etruscorum: Schweiz, I: Basel-Schaffhausen-Bern-Lausanne* (Bern: Stämpfli)

Kistler, Erich. 2017. 'Feasts, Wine and Society, Eighth-Sixth Centuries BCE', in *Etruscology*, ed. by Alessandro Naso, 2 vols (Berlin: De Gruyter), I, pp. 195–206

Klügmann, Adolf, and Gustav Körte. 1897. *Etruskische Spiegel*, V (Berlin: Reimer)

Krauskopf, Ingrid. 2016. 'Myth in Etruria', in *A Companion to the Etruscans*, ed. by Sinclair Bell and Alexandra A. Carpino (Malden: Wiley), pp. 388–409

Lacy, Lamar R. 1994. 'The Flight of Ataiun. A Black-Figure Amphora of the Orvieto Group and the Running Aktaion', in *Murlo and the Etruscans: Art and Society in Ancient Etruria*, ed. by Richard Daniel De Puma and Jocelyn Penny Small (Madison: University of Wisconsin Press), pp. 165–79

Lowenstam, Steven. 2008. *As Witnessed by Images: The Trojan War Tradition in Greek and Etruscan Art* (Baltimore: Johns Hopkins University Press)

Mayer-Prokop, Ilse. 1967. *Die gravierten etruskischen Griffspiegel archaischen Stils* (Heidelberg: Kerle)

Meer, L. Bouke van der. 1995. *Interpretatio Etrusca: Greek Myths on Etruscan Mirrors* (Amsterdam: Gieben)

Neils, Jennifer. 1994. 'Reflections of Immortality. The Myth of Jason on Etruscan Mirrors', in *Murlo and the Etruscans: Art and Society in Ancient Etruria*, ed. by Richard Daniel De Puma and Jocelyn Penny Small (Madison: University of Wisconsin Press), pp. 190–95

Oakley, John H. 1987. 'Hesione', in *Lexicon iconographicum mythologiae classicae*, VIII (Bern: Artemis), pp. 623–29

Ogden, Daniel. 2013. *Drakōn: Dragon Myth and Serpent Cult in the Greek and Roman Worlds* (Oxford: Oxford University Press)

Pacetti, Maria Stella. 2011. *Corpus speculorum Etruscorum Italia*, VI: *Roma – Museo nazionale etrusco di Villa Giulia*, fasc. 3, *Antiquarium: la collezione del Museo Kircheriano* (Rome: L'Erma di Bretschneider)

Pieraccini, Lisa C. 2014. 'The Ever Elusive Etruscan Egg', *Etruscan Studies*, 17.2: 267–92

——. 2016. 'Sacred Serpent Symbols: The Bearded Snakes of Etruria', *Journal of Ancient Egyptian Interconnections*, 10: 31–38

Rasmussen, Tom B. 2013. 'The Imagery of Tomb Objects (Local and Imported) and its Funerary Relevance', in *The Etruscan World*, ed. by Jean Macintosh Turfa (London: Routledge), pp. 672–80

Safran, Linda. 2000. 'Hercle in Washington, DC: A Faliscan Vase at the Catholic University of America', *Etruscan Studies*, 7: 51–79

Sandhoff, Bridget. 2016. 'Mirror, Mirror on the Wall: Reflections on Etruscan Bronze Mirrors', in *More than Mere Playthings: The Minor Arts of Italy*, ed. by Julia C. Fischer (Newcastle upon Tyne: Cambridge Scholars), pp. 9–37

Warden, P. Gregory. 2009. 'The Blood of Animals: Predation and Transformation in Etruscan Funerary Representation', in *New Perspectives on Etruria and Early Rome*, ed. by Sinclair Bell and Helen Nagy (Madison: University of Wisconsin Press), pp. 198–219

——. 2013. 'The Importance of Being Elite: The Archaeology of Identity in Etruria (500–200)', in *A Companion to the Archaeology of the Roman Republic*, ed. by Jane D. Evans (Chichester: Blackwell), pp. 354–68

Zimmer, Gerhard. 1987. *Spiegel im Antikenmuseum* (Berlin: Mann)

——. 1995. *Corpus speculorum Etruscorum Bundesrepublik Deutschland*, IV: *Staatliche Museen zu Berlin, Antikensammlung 2* (Munich: Hirmer)

Index

afterlife/life after death/resurrection/underworld: 42, 58, 61, 80, 82, 85, 86, 101, 102, 114, 115, 116, 123

age: 11, 102, 118

agency: 11, 12, 66, 79, 83

agriculture: 11, 20, 25, 29, 31

animals *see also* fish

  amphibians: 98

  badgers: 46

  bears: 46, 67

  beavers: 46

  birds: 46, 47, 82, 95, 96, 98, 98

  birds, ducks: 82, 98

  birds, passerines: 98

  boars: 46, 67, 104

  cats: 46, 95

  cattle, wild: 46

  cattle/oxen: 42, 46, 47, 48, 49, 52, 67, 82, 83, 95, 97, 98

  chickens: 42, 82, 98

  deer: 42, 46, 52, 67, 95, 96

  dogs: 42, 46, 95, 96, 98, 123

  dolphins: 92, 105, 120

  eels: 95, 96

  equids: 45, 46

  foxes: 42, 46

  goats, wild: 46 *see also* sheep and goats

  hares: 46

  molluscs: 95, 105

  pigs and piglets: 42, 46, 47, 48, 49, 50, 51, 52, 82, 95, 98

  rabbits: 81, 82, 98

  rodents: 46, 95

  sea urchins: 102

  sharks: 102

  sheep and goats: 41, 42, 46, 47, 48, 49, 50, 51, 52, 82, 95, 96, 98, 104, 116

  snakes: 96, 116

  tortoises: 42, 46

  turtles: 95

  wolves: 46, 67, 95

archaeobotany: 12, 19, 23, 24, 31

architectural context: 13, 45, 51, 57, 58, 59, 63, 67–70, 78, 85, 104, 113

banqueting: 11, 12, 13, 17, 45, 51–54, 57–64, 66, 67, 69, 70, 77, 79, 81, 85, 113

braziers: 66, 85

breastfeeding: 14, 114, 115, 122, 123

butchery: 14, 41, 43, 48, 52, 53, 82, 83

cannibalism: 114

characters of myth *see also* gods/goddesses/deities and myth

  Aplu/Apollo: 41, 105, 114, 116, 118, 119, 120

  Artumes/Artemis: 96, 116

  Ataiun: 14, 123

  Dragon of the Golden Fleece: 14, 115, 116

  Fufluns: 104, 115, 117

  Heasun/Heiasun: 14, 115, 116, 117, 123

  Hercle/Herakles: 14, 66, 104, 114, 116, 117, 118, 119, 120, 121, 122, 123

  Jupiter: 100, 101

  Menrva/Menerva/Athena: 14, 104, 115, 116, 122, 123

  Tydeus: 14, 114

  Uni: 14, 104, 114, 115, 121, 122, 123

  Vilia (Hesione): 14, 113, 116, 117, 119–23

  sea monster: 93, 116, 117, 118, 120, 121, 122, 123

cheese graters: 82

communication/mediation: 13, 14, 53, 70, 77, 79, 80, 85, 87, 101, 102, 105, 120

consumption: 11, 12–14, 17, 19, 20, 33, 43, 52, 57, 64, 66, 67, 70, 78, 82, 83, 93, 94, 102, 113–23

cooking implements: 45, 82, 98, 102, 113 *see also* braziers, cheese graters, and fish-plates

depictions

  banquet/feast: 12, 13, 18, 51, 52, 57–67, 70, 77–81, 84–87, 113, 114

  drinking: 17, 18, 57–61, 64, 65, 66, 70, 80, 85, 114, 115

  eating: 13, 18, 51, 57, 58, 60, 61, 67, 85, 114

  eating (by nonhumans): 14, 105, 116, 117, 118, 122, 123

  food: 13, 57, 58, 59, 60, 61, 63, 66, 67, 70, 77–87, 97, 113

Dietler, Michael: 57, 58, 59, 70

diet: 11, 52, 67

domestication: 12, 21, 22, 22, 23, 24, 25, 26, 28, 33

drink: 14, 17, 18, 19, 59, 61, 65, 66, 113, 114, 115

---

* The editors would like to thank Susanna Faas-Bush for compiling the index.

economy: 13, 82, 93, 98
eggs: 60, 61, 63, 65, 67, 78, 83, 84, 85, 98, 114

fish: 13, 14, 46, 81, 82, 91–105
    bony fish: 98
    bream: 95, 97
    maena: 100
    mullet: 97
    rayfish: 105
    seabass: 102
    tuna: 99
fish-plates: 96, 97, 105
fishing: 13, 14, 91, 92, 93, 96, 97, 102
food *see also* animals, fish, meat, eggs, and grapes
    food display: 11, 12, 41, 51, 52, 59, 85
    food distribution: 41, 42, 43, 45, 46, 50, 51, 52, 53, 93
    food performance: 11, 13, 57, 61, 62, 62, 79, 83
    food preparation: 12, 43, 48, 82, 83, 85, 87
    food production: 11, 12, 14, 82
    food ritualization: 11, 12, 13, 41, 43, 51, 52, 53, 54, 57, 58, 70, 83, 86, 114
    bread: 61, 63, 66, 79, 80, 81, 82, 83
    cake: 66, 79, 80, 81
    cheese: 17, 82
    figs: 79, 82, 98
    fruit: 21, 61, 63, 64, 66, 79, 80, 81
    grain: 80
    hazelnuts: 80, 81
    laurel: 81, 82, 119
    milk: 14, 47, 114, 115, 122 *see also* breastfeeding
    nuts: 80, 81, 82
    olives: 80, 81, 82
    onions: 100
    plums: 79
    pomegranates: 61, 79, 80, 82, 83
    quince: 79
    salt: 91, 93
    wild herbs: 98
funerary practice: 11, 12, 13, 17, 42, 57, 59, 61, 67, 77–87, 97, 102, 103, 104, 105, 114

gastropolitics: 13, 77, 78, 87
gender: 11, 14, 48, 52, 61, 65, 66, 70, 82, 113, 118–23
gods/goddesses/deities: 14, 42, 93, 94, 96, 99, 100, 101, 104, 114, 115, 116, 117, 118, 120
grapes: 20–28, 79, 80, 81, 82, 83, 98
    Lambrusco (grape variety): 32, 33
    Marzemino (black grape vine variety): 26, 27
    Perusinia (grape variety): 28, 33

hierarchy/differentiation: 13, 30, 52, 57, 58, 64, 65, 67, 69, 70, 78, 113
hunting: 45, 47, 52, 53

iconography: 13, 14, 54, 57, 59, 113, 114, 117, 118, 120, 122
identity: 11, 12, 13, 98, 114

material culture: 11, 12, 17, 19, 20, 25, 45, 51, 58, 62–64, 70, 79–82, 85, 92, 93, 94, 96, 97, 98, 113–23
meat: 41, 42, 43, 48, 51, 52, 53, 81, 82, 105
memory: 13, 78, 79, 83, 85, 86, 87, 98
myth: 14, 26, 28, 42, 92, 93, 100, 101, 114–23

Phoenician-Cypriot connections: 17, 19, 20, 27, 97

religion: 13, 14, 41, 42, 53, 54, 93, 95, 96, 97, 98, 99, 100, 101, 103, 104, 105, 114, 115, 118
remains, faunal: 41, 42, 43, 45–54, 67, 81, 82, 86, 87, 93, 94, 95, 98, 102, 113 *see also* seashells
remains, non-faunal food: 78, 79, 80, 81, 82, 85, 86, 87, 98, 113
ritual: 11, 12, 13, 14, 17, 41–43, 52–54, 57, 58, 83, 86, 93–105, 114, 115, 117
ritual, foundation: 95, 97–99, 101, 105

sacrifice: 13, 14, 41, 42, 54, 82, 93, 95–102, 104, 105, 116, 118, 122
salt-works: 91
sanctuaries: 14, 41–42, 93, 94, 95, 97, 105
sea: 13, 14, 92, 93, 94, 102, 105
seashells: 93, 94, 95, 98, 102
sites
    Acquarossa: 59, 62, 63, 66, 67, 69
    Blera: 114
    Calabria: 24, 25, 26
    Cannicella: 95, 105
    Capodimonte: 117, 118
    Casa al Savio near Castelluccio di Pienza: 96
    Cerveteri/Caere: 20, 25, 29, 59, 79, 80, 81, 82, 85, 91, 93, 117
    Chiusi: 59, 61, 113, 118
    Civita of Tarquinia: 95, 97, 101
    Colle Arsiccio near Perugia: 95, 96
    Este: 27, 98
    Felsina: 28, 29
    Ficana: 17
    Forcello, Bagnolo San Vito: 33, 45, 95
    Ghiaccio Forte: 21, 22, 24
    Giglio shipwreck: 81
    Gravisca: 14, 91, 93, 94, 105

Magna Graecia: 23, 24, 25

Orvieto: 59, 80, 82, 83, 95, 113

Perugia: 28

Po Valley: 27, 28, 30, 33

Poggio Civitate, Murlo: 12, 13, 18, 41–54, 62–69, 113

Populonia: 17, 97, 102, 105

Portonaccio sanctuary at Veii: 104, 105

Pyrgi: 14, 93, 94, 95, 97, 105, 114

Rome: 62, 65, 95, 99–101

Saline: 91, 93

Sarteano: 59

Satricum: 17

Sicily: 23, 24, 25

Sovana, central Etruria: 98

Spina: 27

Tarquinia: 13, 59, 60, 61, 79–84, 91, 92, 93, 95, 97, 101, 102, 103, 105, 113

Theatre of Asolo, Venetic area: 98

Tolle necropolis at Chiancino Terme: 85

Tuscania: 62, 66

Tusculum: 98, 99

Val Padana: 28, 29, 30

Veii: 62, 65, 92, 93, 104, 105

Veio: 29

Velletri: 62, 65

Verucchio: 102, 105

Vulci: 20, 21, 24, 25, 29, 91

sites, tomb

Bartoccini tomb: 59

Golini tomb: 61, 80, 82, 83

Maroi Tomb III: 85

Querciola Tomb I: 79, 82

Tomb 5513: 79

Tomb G (Casale Marittimo): 80

Tomb della Montagnola: 104

Tomb of Hunting and Fishing: 13, 14, 60, 79, 102

Tomb of the Augurs: 79

Tomb of the Chariots: 79, 83, 84

Tomb of the Diver: 102

Tomb of the Funerary Bed: 79

Tomb of the Inscriptions: 82, 102, 103, 105

Tomb of the Leopards: 79, 81, 83, 84

Tomb of the Lionesses: 59, 60, 79, 83

Tomb of the Maiden: 83

Tomb of the Olives: 81

Tomb of the Reliefs: 82

Tomb of the Shields: 59, 79, 80, 81, 82, 83

Tomb of the Ship: 79

Tomb of the Triclinium: 60, 61, 79, 81, 82

Tomb of the Warrior: 80

status: 11, 12, 13, 14, 17, 20, 33, 41–44, 47, 48, 51–54, 57–64, 66, 67, 69, 70, 78–80, 82, 83, 85, 96, 113, 114, 120, 122–23

symbolism: 11, 13, 14, 42, 52–54, 57, 58, 61, 62, 65, 70, 77, 78, 80, 83, 85–87, 96, 98, 99, 101, 102, 113, 114, 117

trade networks: 12, 18, 19, 20, 23, 24, 25, 26, 27, 33, 91

transformation: 11, 14, 79, 85, 92, 103–04, 113–15, 120, 122, 123

vessels, ceramic: 13, 14, 17, 19, 23, 24, 25, 33, 45, 57, 59, 61, 64–66, 79, 80, 81, 85, 92, 93, 96, 97, 98, 113

vessels, drinking: 13, 17, 18, 19, 23, 45, 57, 58, 59, 61, 63, 64, 65, 66, 67, 70, 79, 80, 81, 85, 92, 113, 114, 115

Ionian drinking cup: 64, 70

cauldron: 63, 64, 66, 82

hydria: 92, 117

kantharos: 93

krater: 59, 93, 117, 122

kyathos: 17

kylix: 59, 65, 66, 117

oinochoe: 59, 92

oinotron: 26

olla: 97, 98

rhyton: 65

skyphos: 64, 65

stamnos: 95, 96

visual evidence: 12, 13, 14, 51, 57–64, 66, 67, 70, 77–87, 92, 93, 96, 102, 103, 104, 105, 113–23

mirrors: 13, 14, 57, 80, 113–23

plaques: 13, 51, 52, 57, 59, 62–67, 70, 104, 105, 113, 114

reliefs: 13, 57, 82

tombs: 13, 14, 17, 57, 59, 60, 61, 77, 78, 79, 80, 81, 82, 83, 84, 85, 86, 87, 92, 97, 102, 103, 104, 113

wall/mural paintings: 13, 77–87, 113, 114

visual studies: 14, 57, 58, 86, 113, 117

viticulture: 11, 12, 19–26, 28, 30, 31, 32, 33

ArcheoVino: 12, 24, 33

VINUM: 12, 24, 33

arbustum: 20, 30

piantata: 30, 31, 32, 33

vines: 21, 22, 23, 24, 25, 26, 27, 28, 30, 31, 32, 33

vinum: 18, 19

votive offerings: 63, 82, 85, 93–105

wine: 12, 13, 14, 17–20, 24, 28, 57, 59, 63–66, 70, 79, 80, 81, 85, 98, 114, 115

kykeon: 17

marzeah: 17

wine production: 12, 14, 19–28, 33

workshops/production: 12, 45–53, 91, 118

zooarchaeology: 12, 14, 41, 42, 43, 45, 46, 47, 48, 49, 50, 51, 52, 53, 67, 82

NEW APPROACHES IN ARCHAEOLOGY

All volumes in this series are evaluated by an Editorial Board, strictly on academic grounds, based on reports prepared by referees who have been commissioned by virtue of their specialism in the appropriate field. The Board ensures that the screening is done independently and without conflicts of interest. The definitive texts supplied by authors are also subject to review by the Board before being approved for publication. Further, the volumes are copyedited to conform to the publisher's stylebook and to the best international academic standards in the field.

Titles in Series

Animals and Animated Objects in the Early Middle Ages, ed. by Leszek Gardeła and Kamil Kajkowski (2023)